STAR W...
X-WING
ROGUE SQUADRON
MANDATORY RETIREMENT

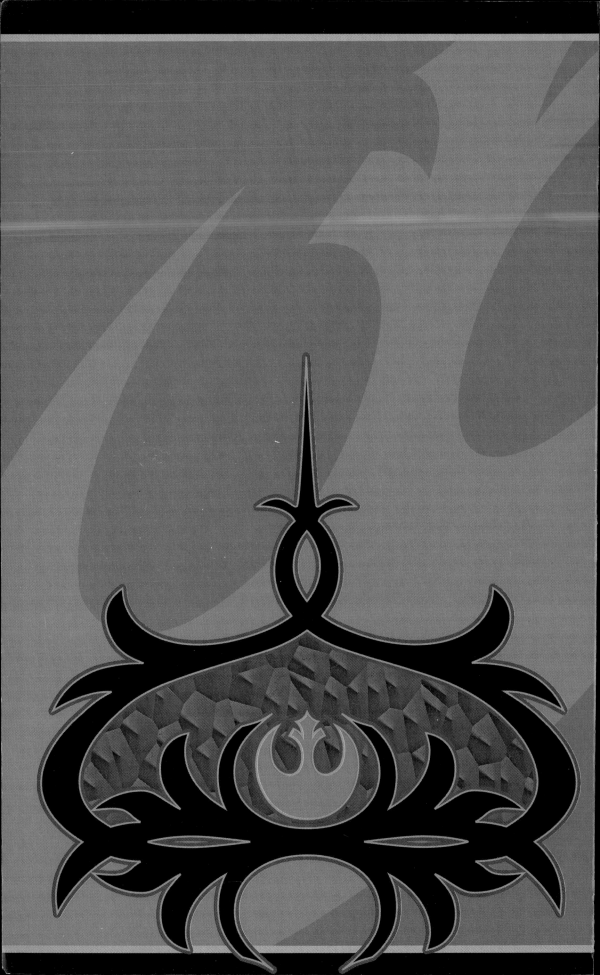

STAR WARS®
X-WING
ROGUE SQUADRON
MANDATORY RETIREMENT

Michael A. Stackpole
story

Steve Crespo and **John Nadeau**
pencils

Chip Wallace and **Jordi Ensign**
inks

Dave Nestelle
colors

Vickie Williams
lettering

Terese Nielsen
cover art

DARK HORSE COMICS®

Mike Richardson
publisher

Peet Janes
series editor

Chris Warner
collection editor

Lia Ribacchi
collection designer

Mark Cox
art director

Special thanks to Allan Kausch and
Lucy Autrey Wilson at Lucas Licensing.

This book collects issues thirty-two through
thirty-five of the Dark Horse comic-book series
Star Wars: X-Wing Rogue Squadron.

Published by
Dark Horse Comics, Inc.
10956 SE Main Street
Milwaukie, OR 97222

www.darkhorse.com

To find a comics shop in your area,
call the Comic Shop Locator Service
toll free at 1-888-266-4226

First edition: December 2000
ISBN: 1-56971-492-4

1 3 5 7 9 10 8 6 4 2

Printed in Canada

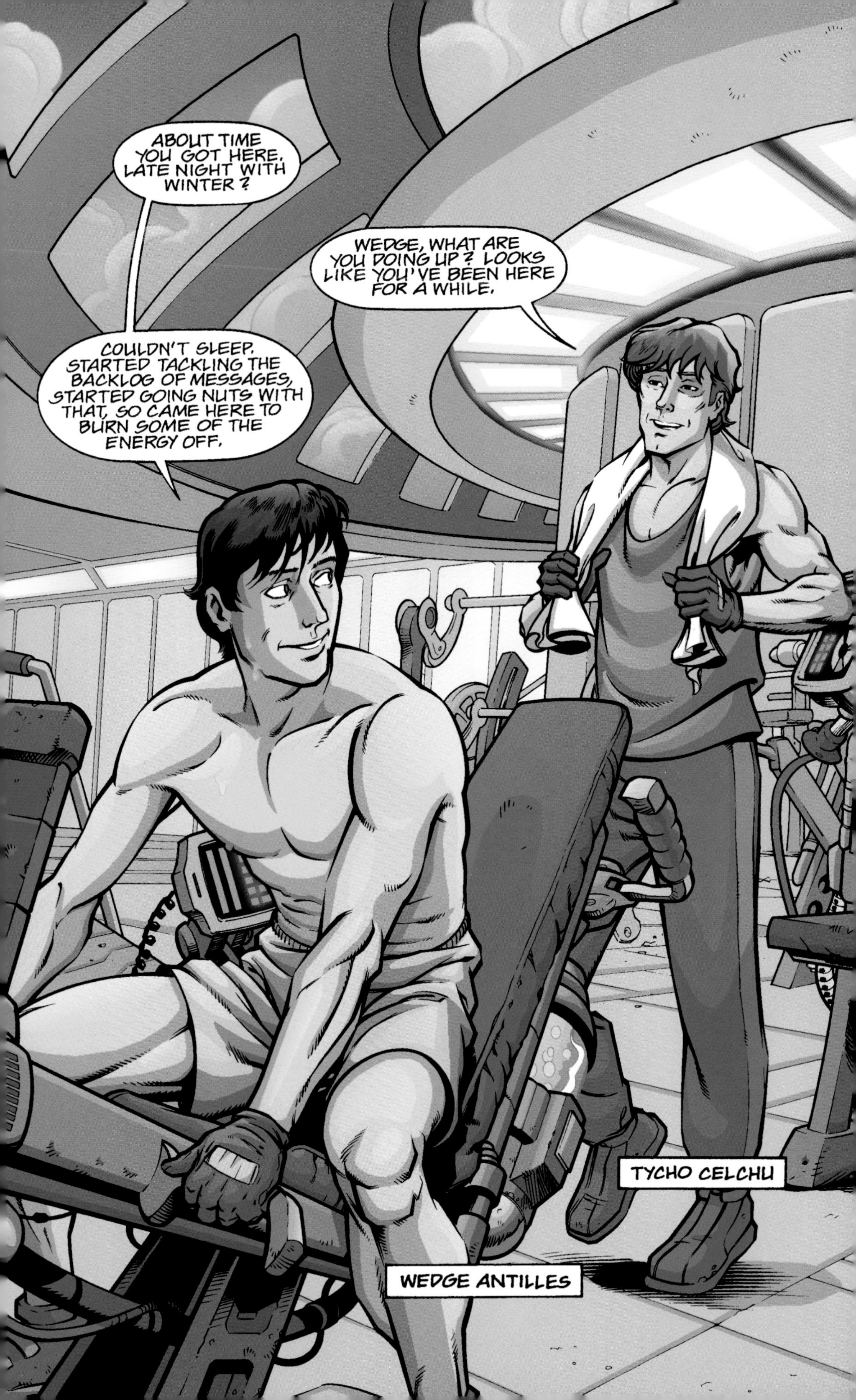
ABOUT TIME YOU GOT HERE. LATE NIGHT WITH WINTER?
WEDGE, WHAT ARE YOU DOING UP? LOOKS LIKE YOU'VE BEEN HERE FOR A WHILE.
COULDN'T SLEEP. STARTED TACKLING THE BACKLOG OF MESSAGES, STARTED GOING NUTS WITH THAT, SO CAME HERE TO BURN SOME OF THE ENERGY OFF.
TYCHO CELCHU
WEDGE ANTILLES

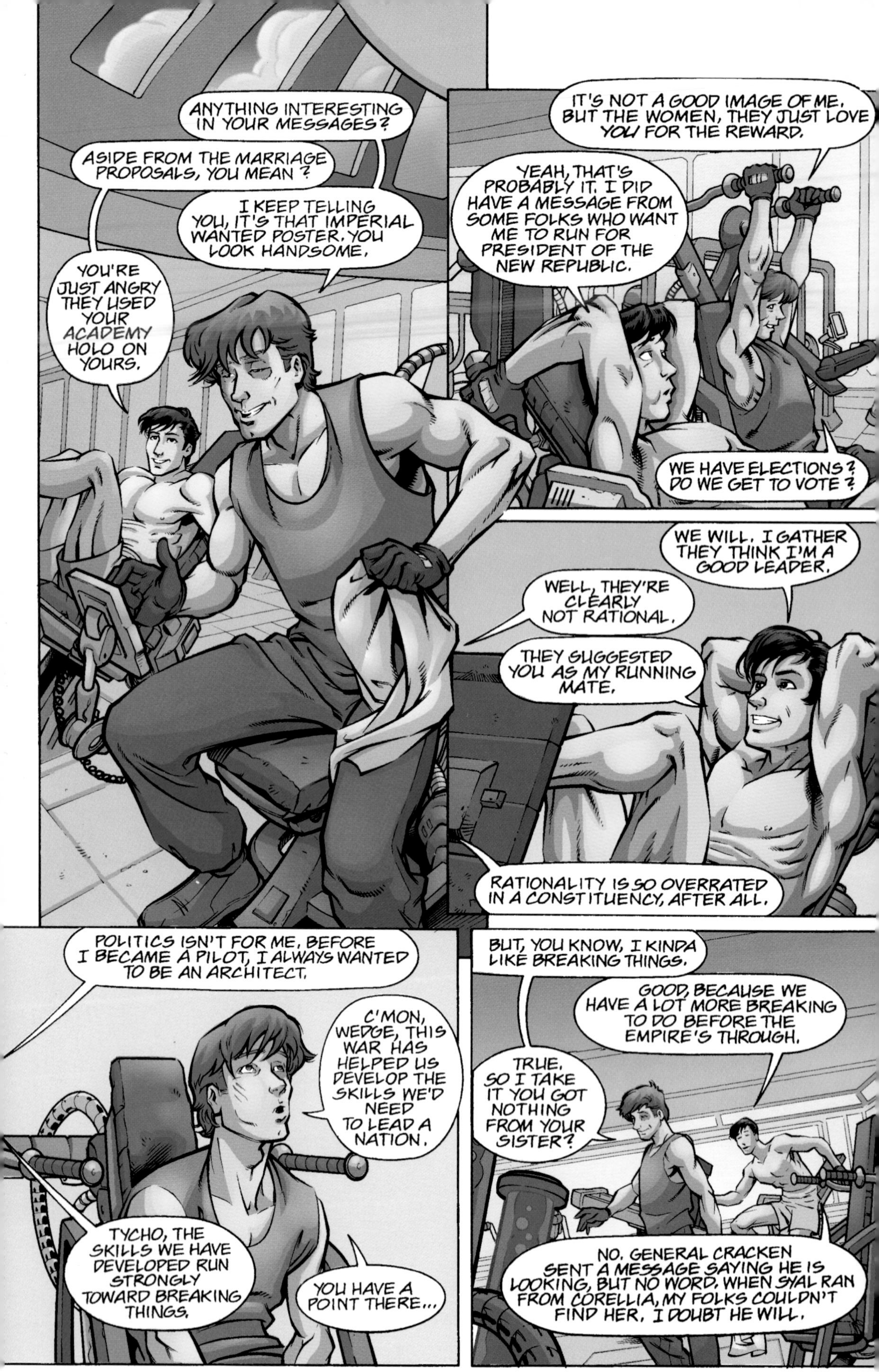
ANYTHING INTERESTING IN YOUR MESSAGES?
ASIDE FROM THE MARRIAGE PROPOSALS, YOU MEAN?
I KEEP TELLING YOU, IT'S THAT IMPERIAL WANTED POSTER. YOU LOOK HANDSOME.
YOU'RE JUST ANGRY THEY USED YOUR ACADEMY HOLO ON YOURS.
IT'S NOT A GOOD IMAGE OF ME, BUT THE WOMEN, THEY JUST LOVE YOU FOR THE REWARD.
YEAH, THAT'S PROBABLY IT. I DID HAVE A MESSAGE FROM SOME FOLKS WHO WANT ME TO RUN FOR PRESIDENT OF THE NEW REPUBLIC.
WE HAVE ELECTIONS? DO WE GET TO VOTE?
WE WILL. I GATHER THEY THINK I'M A GOOD LEADER.
WELL, THEY'RE CLEARLY NOT RATIONAL.
THEY SUGGESTED YOU AS MY RUNNING MATE.
RATIONALITY IS SO OVERRATED IN A CONSTITUENCY, AFTER ALL.
POLITICS ISN'T FOR ME. BEFORE I BECAME A PILOT, I ALWAYS WANTED TO BE AN ARCHITECT.
C'MON, WEDGE, THIS WAR HAS HELPED US DEVELOP THE SKILLS WE'D NEED TO LEAD A NATION.
TYCHO, THE SKILLS WE HAVE DEVELOPED RUN STRONGLY TOWARD BREAKING THINGS.
YOU HAVE A POINT THERE...
BUT, YOU KNOW, I KINDA LIKE BREAKING THINGS.
GOOD, BECAUSE WE HAVE A LOT MORE BREAKING TO DO BEFORE THE EMPIRE'S THROUGH.
TRUE. SO I TAKE IT YOU GOT NOTHING FROM YOUR SISTER?
NO. GENERAL CRACKEN SENT A MESSAGE SAYING HE IS LOOKING, BUT NO WORD. WHEN SYAL RAN FROM CORELLIA, MY FOLKS COULDN'T FIND HER. I DOUBT HE WILL.

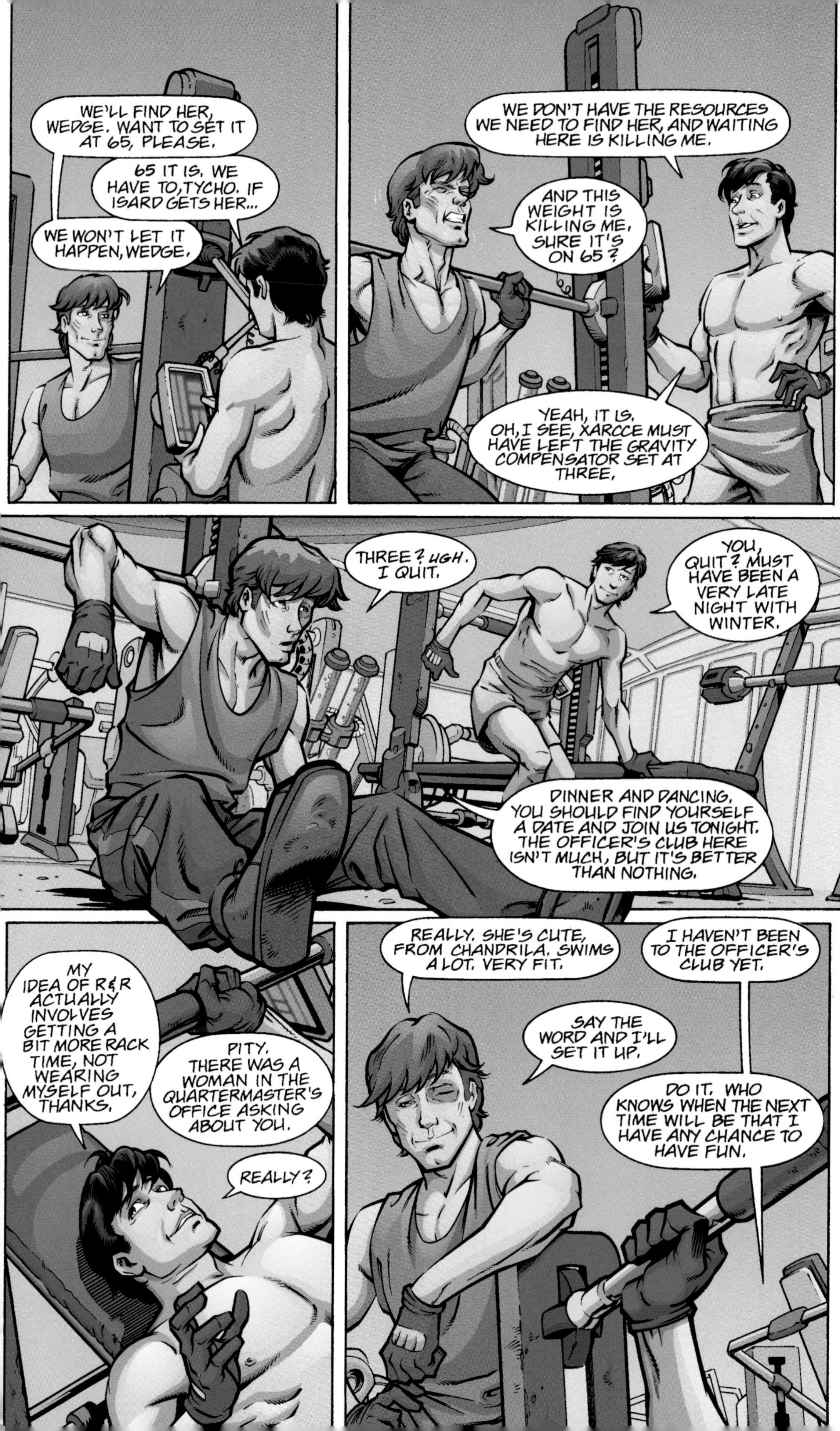

WE'LL FIND HER, WEDGE. WANT TO SET IT AT 65, PLEASE.
65 IT IS. WE HAVE TO, TYCHO. IF ISARD GETS HER...
WE WON'T LET IT HAPPEN, WEDGE.
WE DON'T HAVE THE RESOURCES WE NEED TO FIND HER, AND WAITING HERE IS KILLING ME.
AND THIS WEIGHT IS KILLING ME, SURE IT'S ON 65?
YEAH, IT IS. OH, I SEE, XARCCE MUST HAVE LEFT THE GRAVITY COMPENSATOR SET AT THREE.
THREE? UGH. I QUIT.
YOU, QUIT? MUST HAVE BEEN A VERY LATE NIGHT WITH WINTER.
DINNER AND DANCING. YOU SHOULD FIND YOURSELF A DATE AND JOIN US TONIGHT. THE OFFICER'S CLUB HERE ISN'T MUCH, BUT IT'S BETTER THAN NOTHING.
MY IDEA OF R&R ACTUALLY INVOLVES GETTING A BIT MORE RACK TIME, NOT WEARING MYSELF OUT, THANKS.
PITY. THERE WAS A WOMAN IN THE QUARTERMASTER'S OFFICE ASKING ABOUT YOU.
REALLY?
REALLY. SHE'S CUTE, FROM CHANDRILA. SWIMS A LOT. VERY FIT.
I HAVEN'T BEEN TO THE OFFICER'S CLUB YET.
SAY THE WORD AND I'LL SET IT UP.
DO IT. WHO KNOWS WHEN THE NEXT TIME WILL BE THAT I HAVE ANY CHANCE TO HAVE FUN.

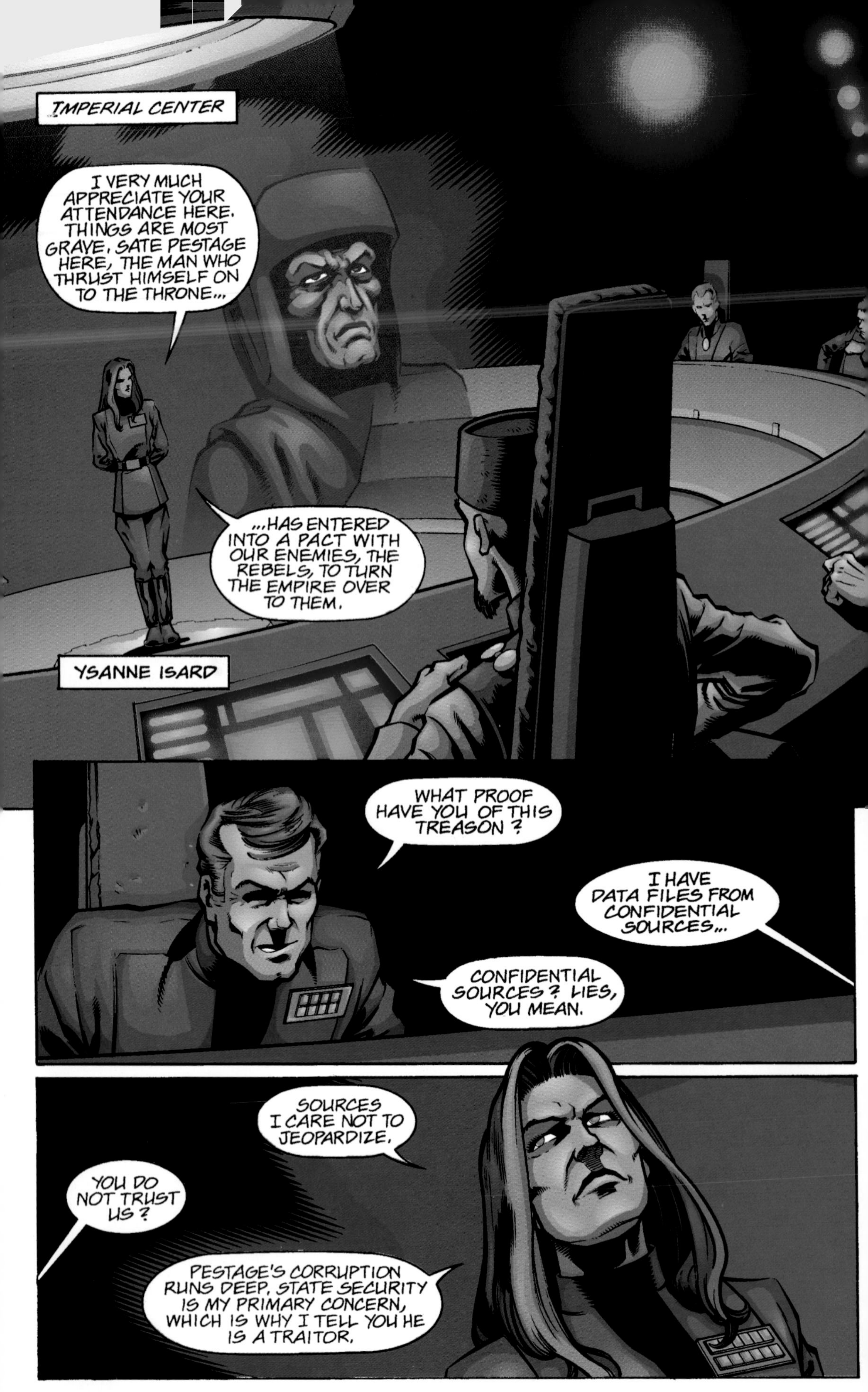
IMPERIAL CENTER
I VERY MUCH APPRECIATE YOUR ATTENDANCE HERE. THINGS ARE MOST GRAVE. SATE PESTAGE HERE, THE MAN WHO THRUST HIMSELF ON TO THE THRONE...
...HAS ENTERED INTO A PACT WITH OUR ENEMIES, THE REBELS, TO TURN THE EMPIRE OVER TO THEM.
YSANNE ISARD
WHAT PROOF HAVE YOU OF THIS TREASON?
I HAVE DATA FILES FROM CONFIDENTIAL SOURCES...
CONFIDENTIAL SOURCES? LIES, YOU MEAN.
SOURCES I CARE NOT TO JEOPARDIZE.
YOU DO NOT TRUST US?
PESTAGE'S CORRUPTION RUNS DEEP. STATE SECURITY IS MY PRIMARY CONCERN, WHICH IS WHY I TELL YOU HE IS A TRAITOR.

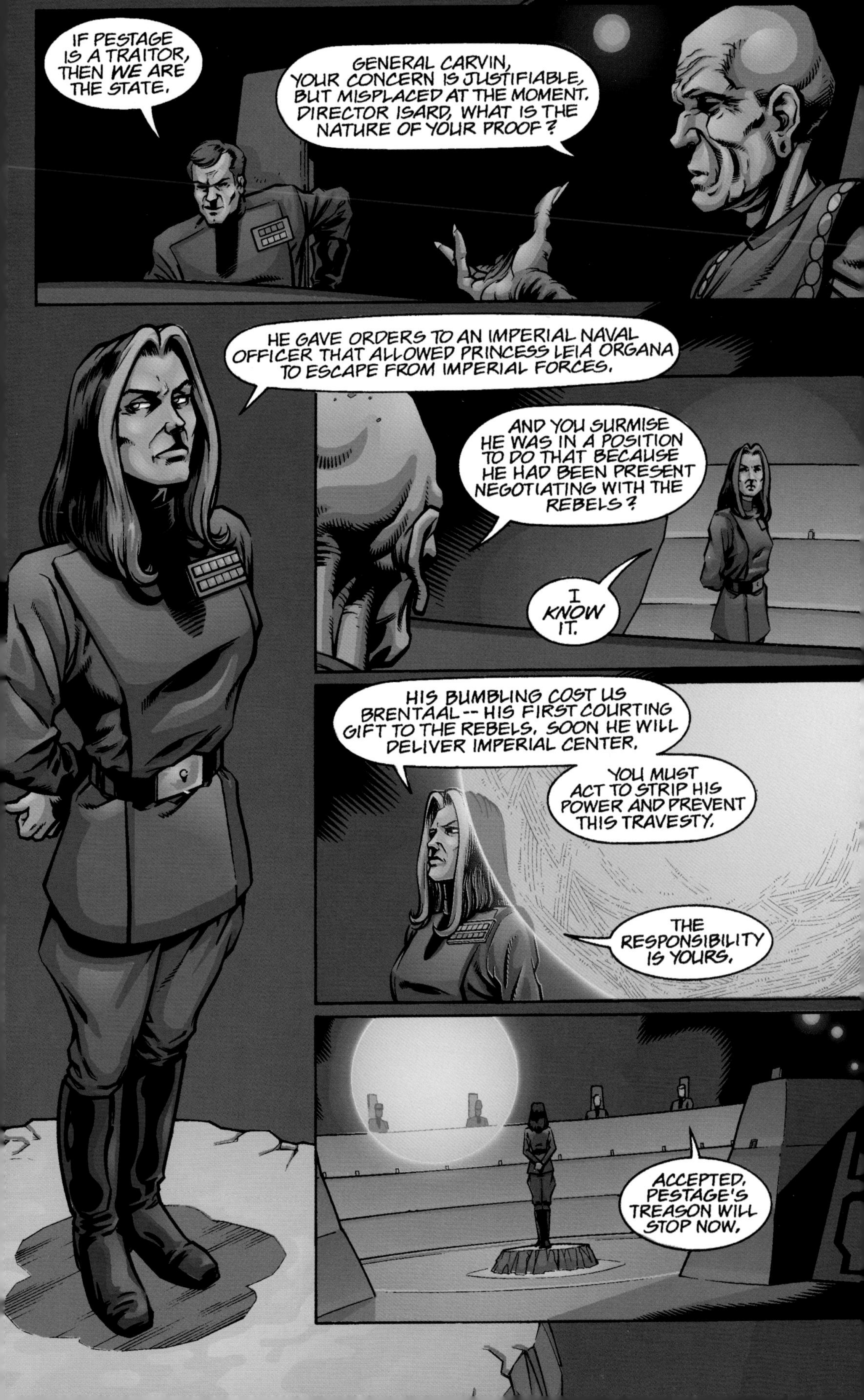

IF PESTAGE IS A TRAITOR, THEN WE ARE THE STATE.
GENERAL CARVIN, YOUR CONCERN IS JUSTIFIABLE, BUT MISPLACED AT THE MOMENT. DIRECTOR ISARD, WHAT IS THE NATURE OF YOUR PROOF?
HE GAVE ORDERS TO AN IMPERIAL NAVAL OFFICER THAT ALLOWED PRINCESS LEIA ORGANA TO ESCAPE FROM IMPERIAL FORCES.
AND YOU SURMISE HE WAS IN A POSITION TO DO THAT BECAUSE HE HAD BEEN PRESENT NEGOTIATING WITH THE REBELS?
I KNOW IT.
HIS BUMBLING COST US BRENTAAL -- HIS FIRST COURTING GIFT TO THE REBELS. SOON HE WILL DELIVER IMPERIAL CENTER.
YOU MUST ACT TO STRIP HIS POWER AND PREVENT THIS TRAVESTY.
THE RESPONSIBILITY IS YOURS.
ACCEPTED. PESTAGE'S TREASON WILL STOP NOW.

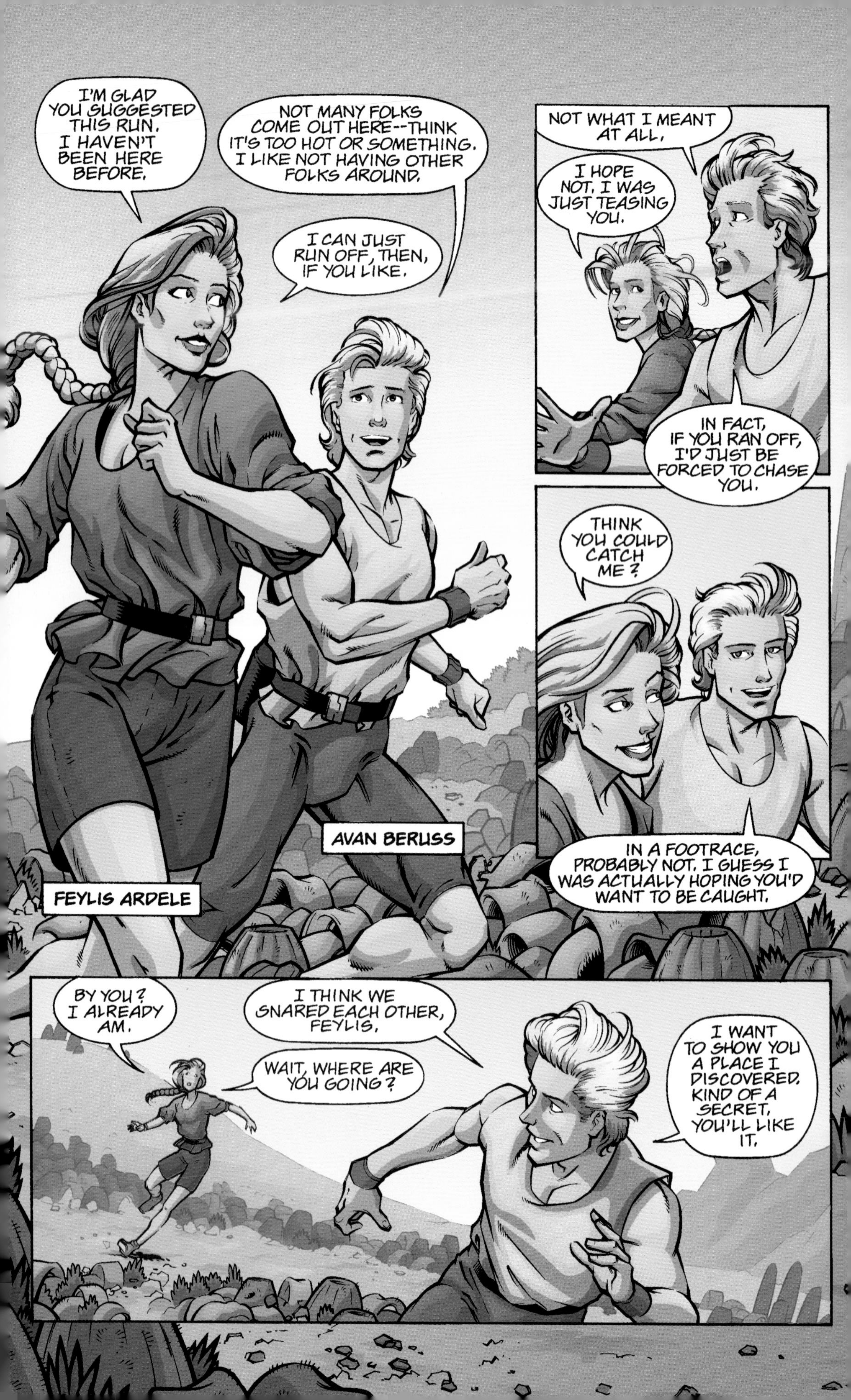
I'M GLAD YOU SUGGESTED THIS RUN. I HAVEN'T BEEN HERE BEFORE.
NOT MANY FOLKS COME OUT HERE--THINK IT'S TOO HOT OR SOMETHING. I LIKE NOT HAVING OTHER FOLKS AROUND.
I CAN JUST RUN OFF, THEN, IF YOU LIKE.
AVAN BERUSS
FEYLIS ARDELE
NOT WHAT I MEANT AT ALL.
I HOPE NOT. I WAS JUST TEASING YOU.
IN FACT, IF YOU RAN OFF, I'D JUST BE FORCED TO CHASE YOU.
THINK YOU COULD CATCH ME?
IN A FOOTRACE, PROBABLY NOT. I GUESS I WAS ACTUALLY HOPING YOU'D WANT TO BE CAUGHT.
BY YOU? I ALREADY AM.
I THINK WE SNARED EACH OTHER, FEYLIS.
WAIT, WHERE ARE YOU GOING?
I WANT TO SHOW YOU A PLACE I DISCOVERED. KIND OF A SECRET. YOU'LL LIKE IT.

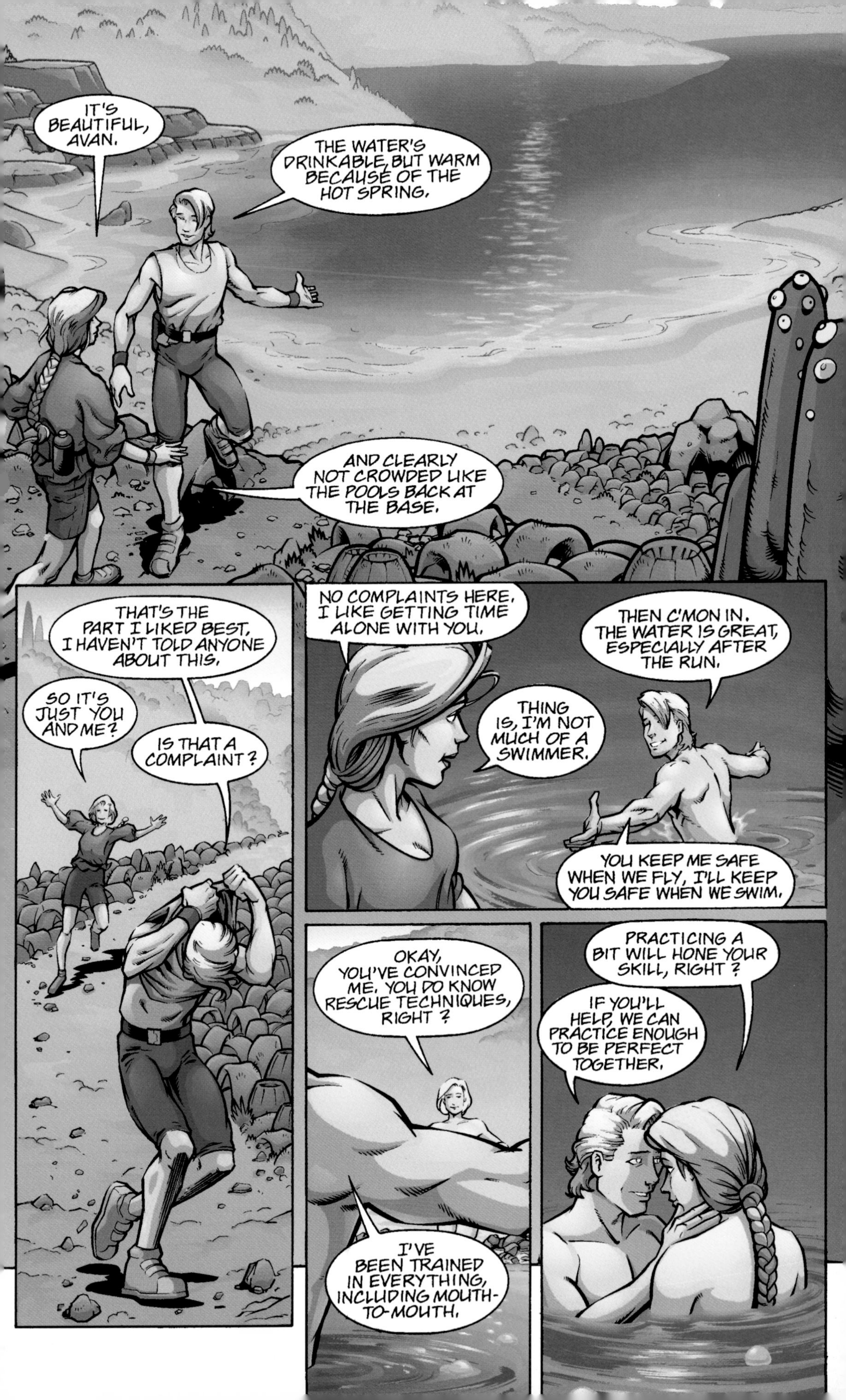
IT'S BEAUTIFUL, AVAN.
THE WATER'S DRINKABLE, BUT WARM BECAUSE OF THE HOT SPRING.
AND CLEARLY NOT CROWDED LIKE THE POOLS BACK AT THE BASE.
THAT'S THE PART I LIKED BEST. I HAVEN'T TOLD ANYONE ABOUT THIS.
SO IT'S JUST YOU AND ME?
IS THAT A COMPLAINT?
NO COMPLAINTS HERE. I LIKE GETTING TIME ALONE WITH YOU.
THEN C'MON IN. THE WATER IS GREAT, ESPECIALLY AFTER THE RUN.
THING IS, I'M NOT MUCH OF A SWIMMER.
YOU KEEP ME SAFE WHEN WE FLY, I'LL KEEP YOU SAFE WHEN WE SWIM.
OKAY, YOU'VE CONVINCED ME. YOU DO KNOW RESCUE TECHNIQUES, RIGHT?
I'VE BEEN TRAINED IN EVERYTHING, INCLUDING MOUTH-TO-MOUTH.
PRACTICING A BIT WILL HONE YOUR SKILL, RIGHT?
IF YOU'LL HELP, WE CAN PRACTICE ENOUGH TO BE PERFECT TOGETHER.

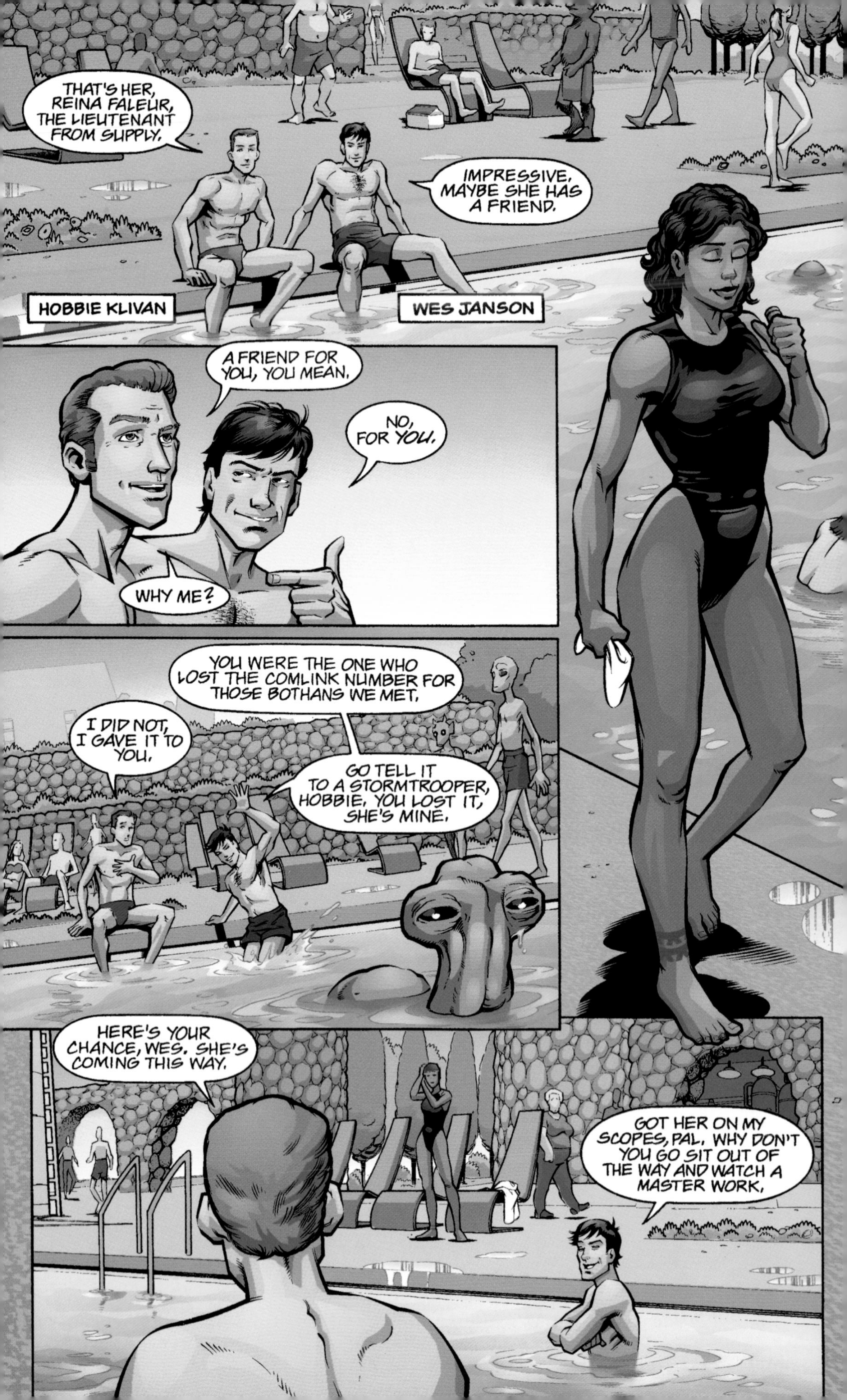
THAT'S HER, REINA FALEUR, THE LIEUTENANT FROM SUPPLY.
IMPRESSIVE. MAYBE SHE HAS A FRIEND.
HOBBIE KLIVAN
WES JANSON
A FRIEND FOR YOU, YOU MEAN.
NO, FOR YOU.
WHY ME?
YOU WERE THE ONE WHO LOST THE COMLINK NUMBER FOR THOSE BOTHANS WE MET.
I DID NOT. I GAVE IT TO YOU.
GO TELL IT TO A STORMTROOPER, HOBBIE. YOU LOST IT. SHE'S MINE.
HERE'S YOUR CHANCE, WES. SHE'S COMING THIS WAY.
GOT HER ON MY SCOPES, PAL. WHY DON'T YOU GO SIT OUT OF THE WAY AND WATCH A MASTER WORK.

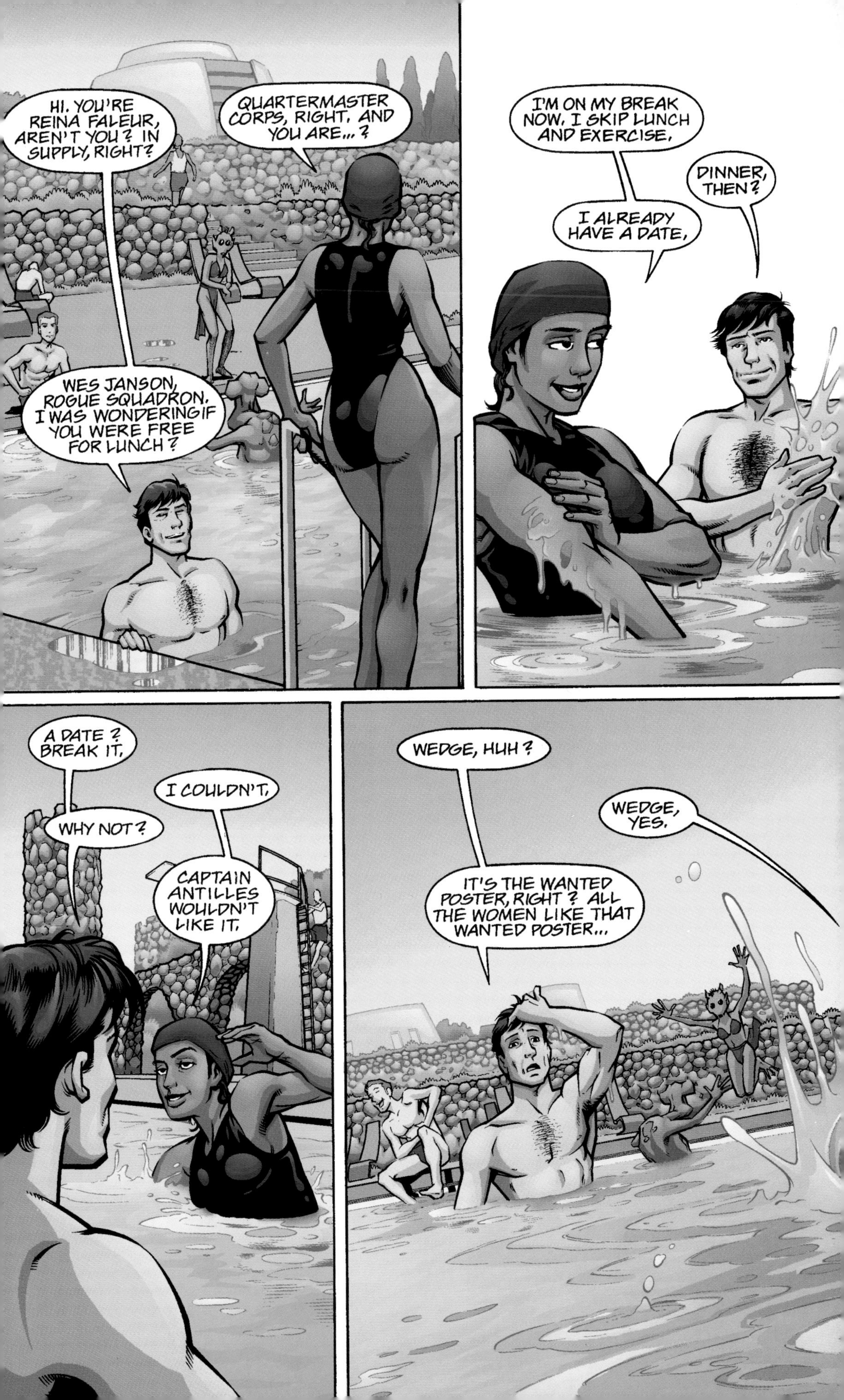
HI. YOU'RE REINA FALEUR, AREN'T YOU? IN SUPPLY, RIGHT?
QUARTERMASTER CORPS, RIGHT. AND YOU ARE...?
WES JANSON, ROGUE SQUADRON. I WAS WONDERING IF YOU WERE FREE FOR LUNCH?
I'M ON MY BREAK NOW. I SKIP LUNCH AND EXERCISE.
DINNER, THEN?
I ALREADY HAVE A DATE.
A DATE? BREAK IT.
I COULDN'T.
WHY NOT?
CAPTAIN ANTILLES WOULDN'T LIKE IT.
WEDGE, HUH?
WEDGE, YES.
IT'S THE WANTED POSTER, RIGHT? ALL THE WOMEN LIKE THAT WANTED POSTER...

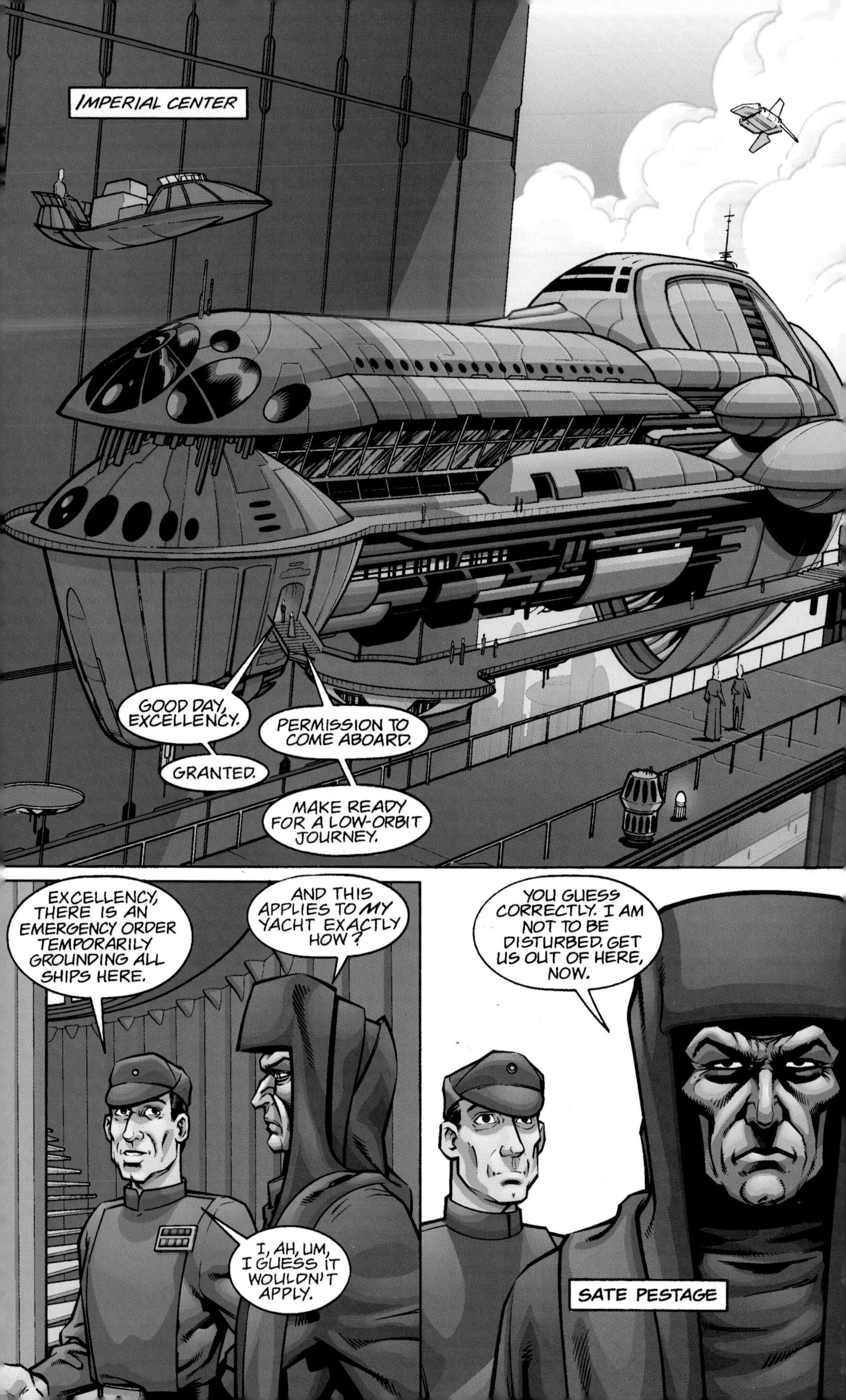
IMPERIAL CENTER
GOOD DAY, EXCELLENCY.
PERMISSION TO COME ABOARD.
GRANTED.
MAKE READY FOR A LOW-ORBIT JOURNEY.
EXCELLENCY, THERE IS AN EMERGENCY ORDER TEMPORARILY GROUNDING ALL SHIPS HERE.
AND THIS APPLIES TO MY YACHT EXACTLY HOW?
I, AH, UM, I GUESS IT WOULDN'T APPLY.
YOU GUESS CORRECTLY. I AM NOT TO BE DISTURBED. GET US OUT OF HERE, NOW.
SATE PESTAGE

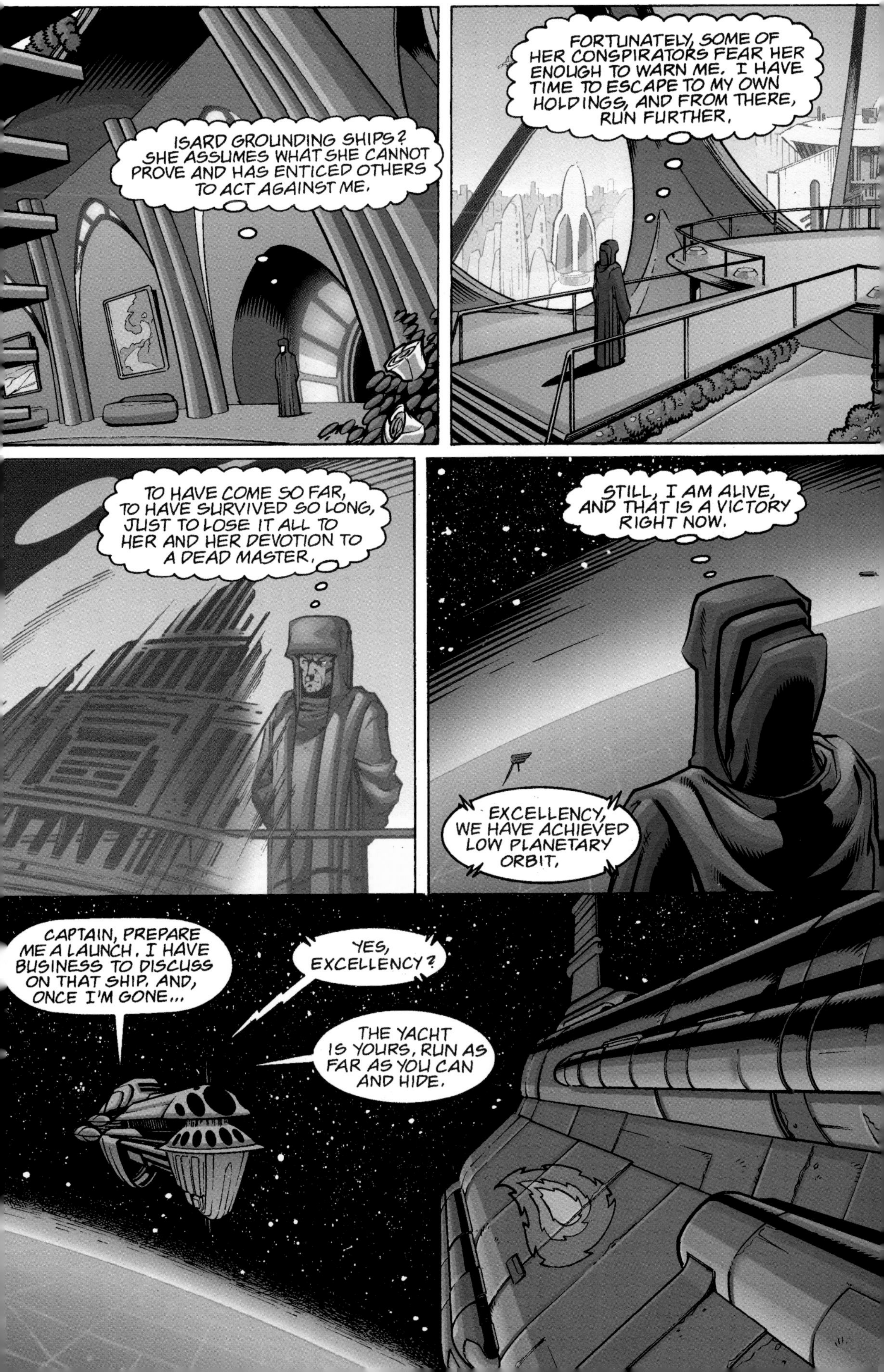
ISARD GROUNDING SHIPS? SHE ASSUMES WHAT SHE CANNOT PROVE AND HAS ENTICED OTHERS TO ACT AGAINST ME.
FORTUNATELY, SOME OF HER CONSPIRATORS FEAR HER ENOUGH TO WARN ME. I HAVE TIME TO ESCAPE TO MY OWN HOLDINGS, AND FROM THERE, RUN FURTHER.
TO HAVE COME SO FAR, TO HAVE SURVIVED SO LONG, JUST TO LOSE IT ALL TO HER AND HER DEVOTION TO A DEAD MASTER.
STILL, I AM ALIVE, AND THAT IS A VICTORY RIGHT NOW.
EXCELLENCY, WE HAVE ACHIEVED LOW PLANETARY ORBIT.
CAPTAIN, PREPARE ME A LAUNCH. I HAVE BUSINESS TO DISCUSS ON THAT SHIP. AND, ONCE I'M GONE...
YES, EXCELLENCY?
THE YACHT IS YOURS. RUN AS FAR AS YOU CAN AND HIDE.

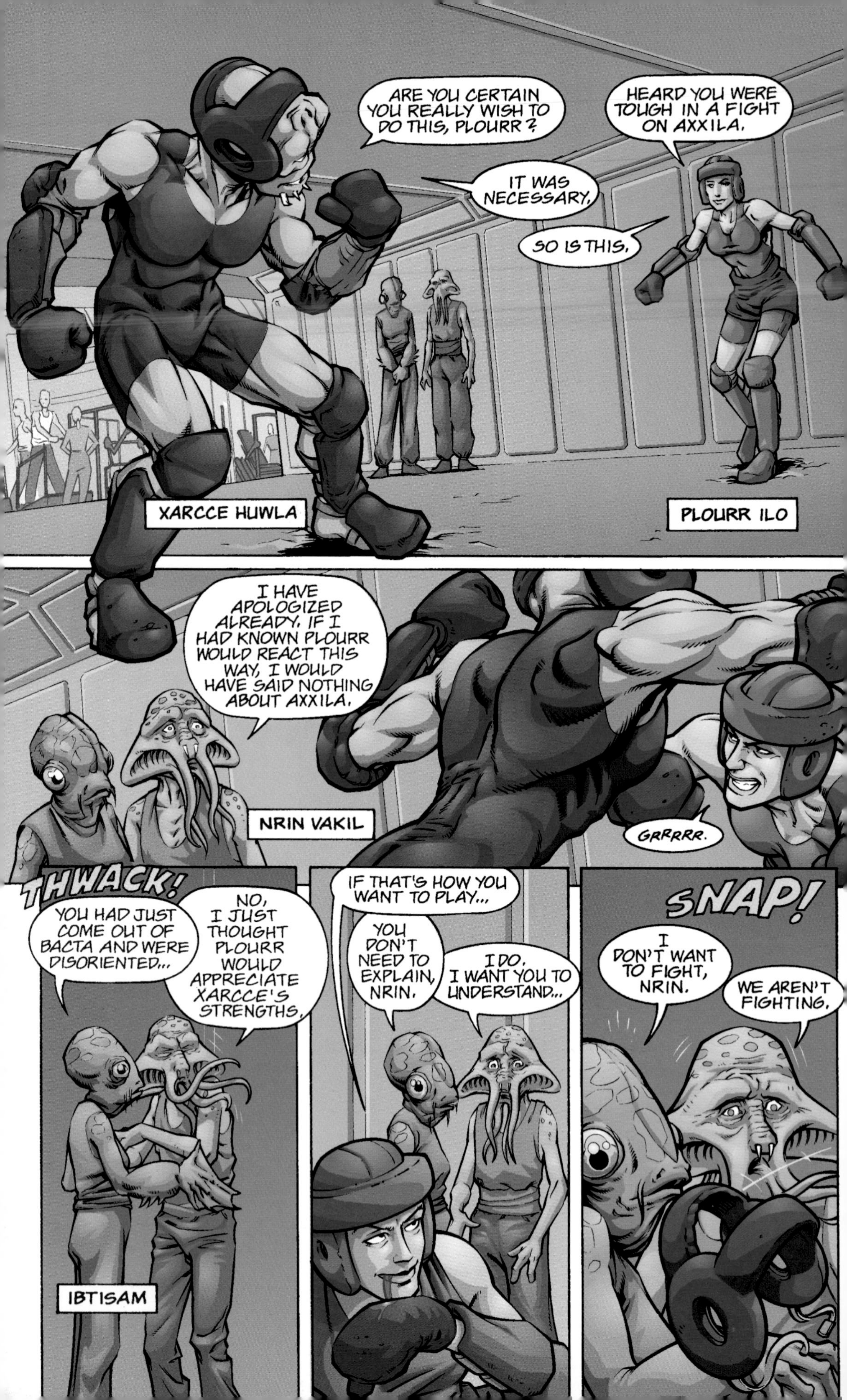
ARE YOU CERTAIN YOU REALLY WISH TO DO THIS, PLOURR?
HEARD YOU WERE TOUGH IN A FIGHT ON AXXILA.
IT WAS NECESSARY.
SO IS THIS.
XARCCE HUWLA
PLOURR ILO
I HAVE APOLOGIZED ALREADY. IF I HAD KNOWN PLOURR WOULD REACT THIS WAY, I WOULD HAVE SAID NOTHING ABOUT AXXILA.
NRIN VAKIL
GRRRRR.
THWACK!
YOU HAD JUST COME OUT OF BACTA AND WERE DISORIENTED...
NO, I JUST THOUGHT PLOURR WOULD APPRECIATE XARCCE'S STRENGTHS.
IBTISAM
IF THAT'S HOW YOU WANT TO PLAY...
YOU DON'T NEED TO EXPLAIN, NRIN.
I DO. I WANT YOU TO UNDERSTAND...
SNAP!
I DON'T WANT TO FIGHT, NRIN.
WE AREN'T FIGHTING.

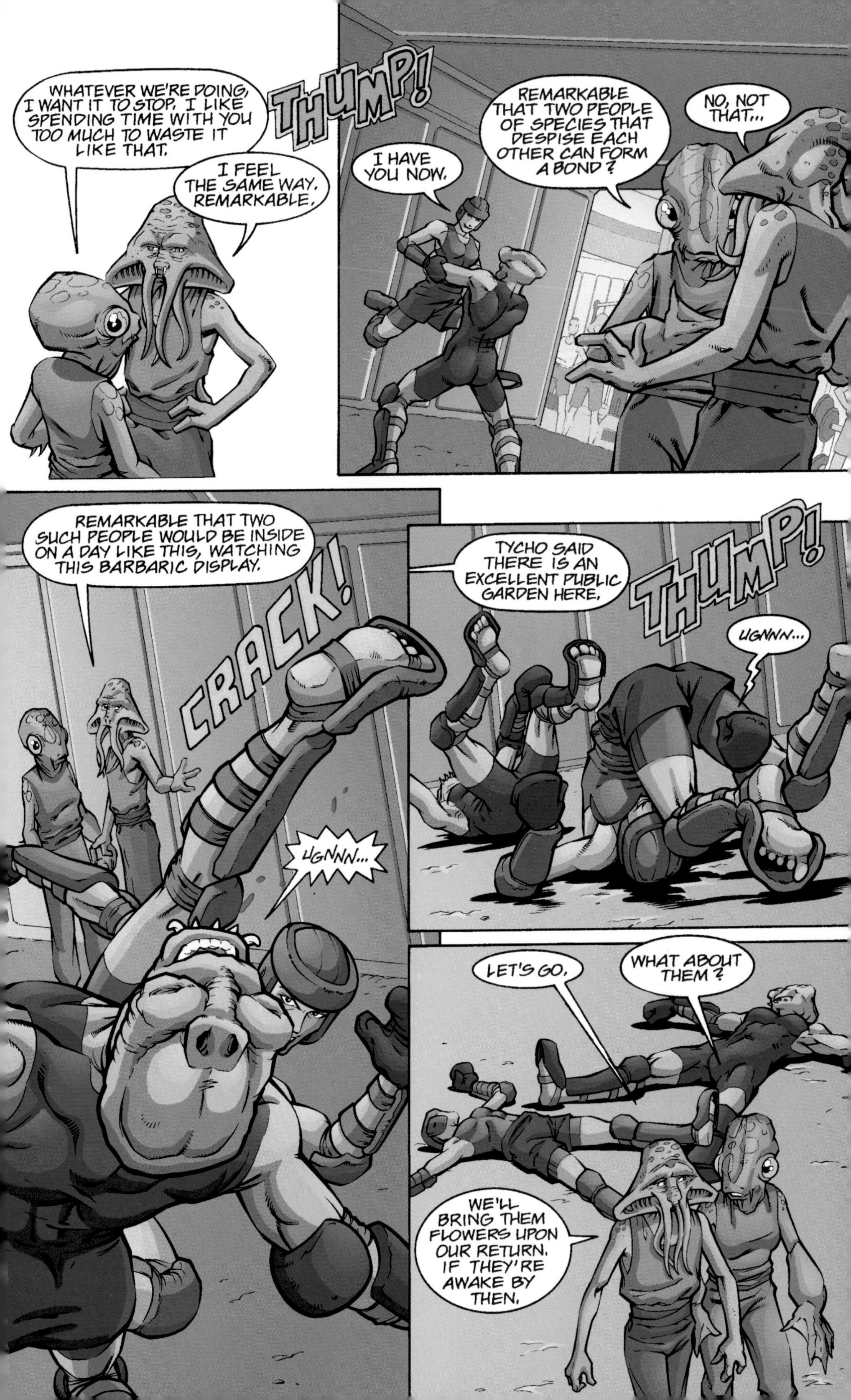
WHATEVER WE'RE DOING, I WANT IT TO STOP. I LIKE SPENDING TIME WITH YOU TOO MUCH TO WASTE IT LIKE THAT.
I FEEL THE SAME WAY. REMARKABLE.
THUMP!
I HAVE YOU NOW.
REMARKABLE THAT TWO PEOPLE OF SPECIES THAT DESPISE EACH OTHER CAN FORM A BOND?
NO, NOT THAT...
REMARKABLE THAT TWO SUCH PEOPLE WOULD BE INSIDE ON A DAY LIKE THIS, WATCHING THIS BARBARIC DISPLAY.
CRACK!
UGNNN...
TYCHO SAID THERE IS AN EXCELLENT PUBLIC GARDEN HERE.
THUMP!
UGNNN...
LET'S GO.
WHAT ABOUT THEM?
WE'LL BRING THEM FLOWERS UPON OUR RETURN. IF THEY'RE AWAKE BY THEN.

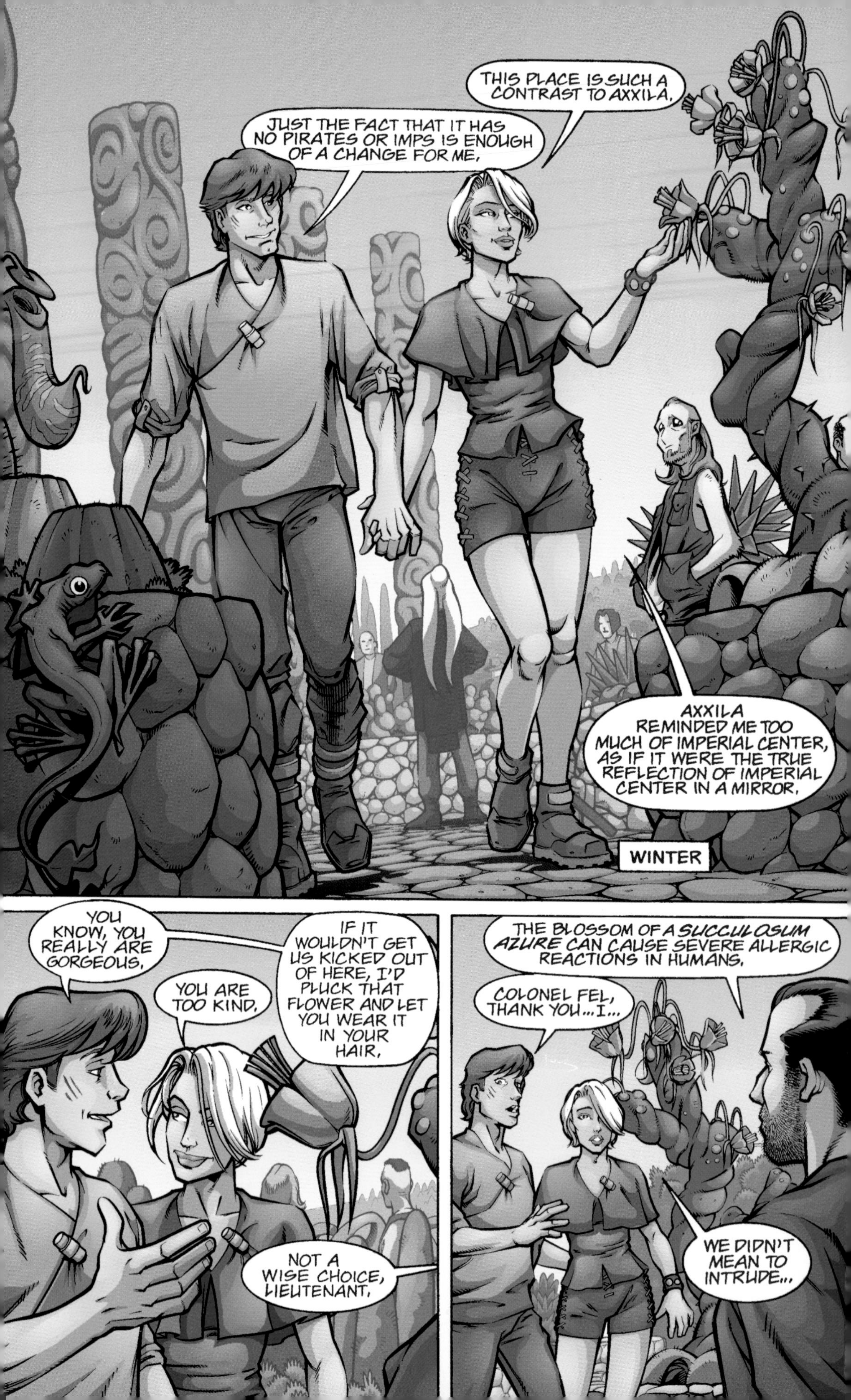

JUST THE FACT THAT IT HAS NO PIRATES OR IMPS IS ENOUGH OF A CHANGE FOR ME.
THIS PLACE IS SUCH A CONTRAST TO AXXILA.
AXXILA REMINDED ME TOO MUCH OF IMPERIAL CENTER, AS IF IT WERE THE TRUE REFLECTION OF IMPERIAL CENTER IN A MIRROR.
WINTER
YOU KNOW, YOU REALLY ARE GORGEOUS.
YOU ARE TOO KIND.
IF IT WOULDN'T GET US KICKED OUT OF HERE, I'D PLUCK THAT FLOWER AND LET YOU WEAR IT IN YOUR HAIR.
NOT A WISE CHOICE, LIEUTENANT.
THE BLOSSOM OF A *SUCCULOSUM AZURE* CAN CAUSE SEVERE ALLERGIC REACTIONS IN HUMANS.
COLONEL FEL, THANK YOU... I...
WE DIDN'T MEAN TO INTRUDE...

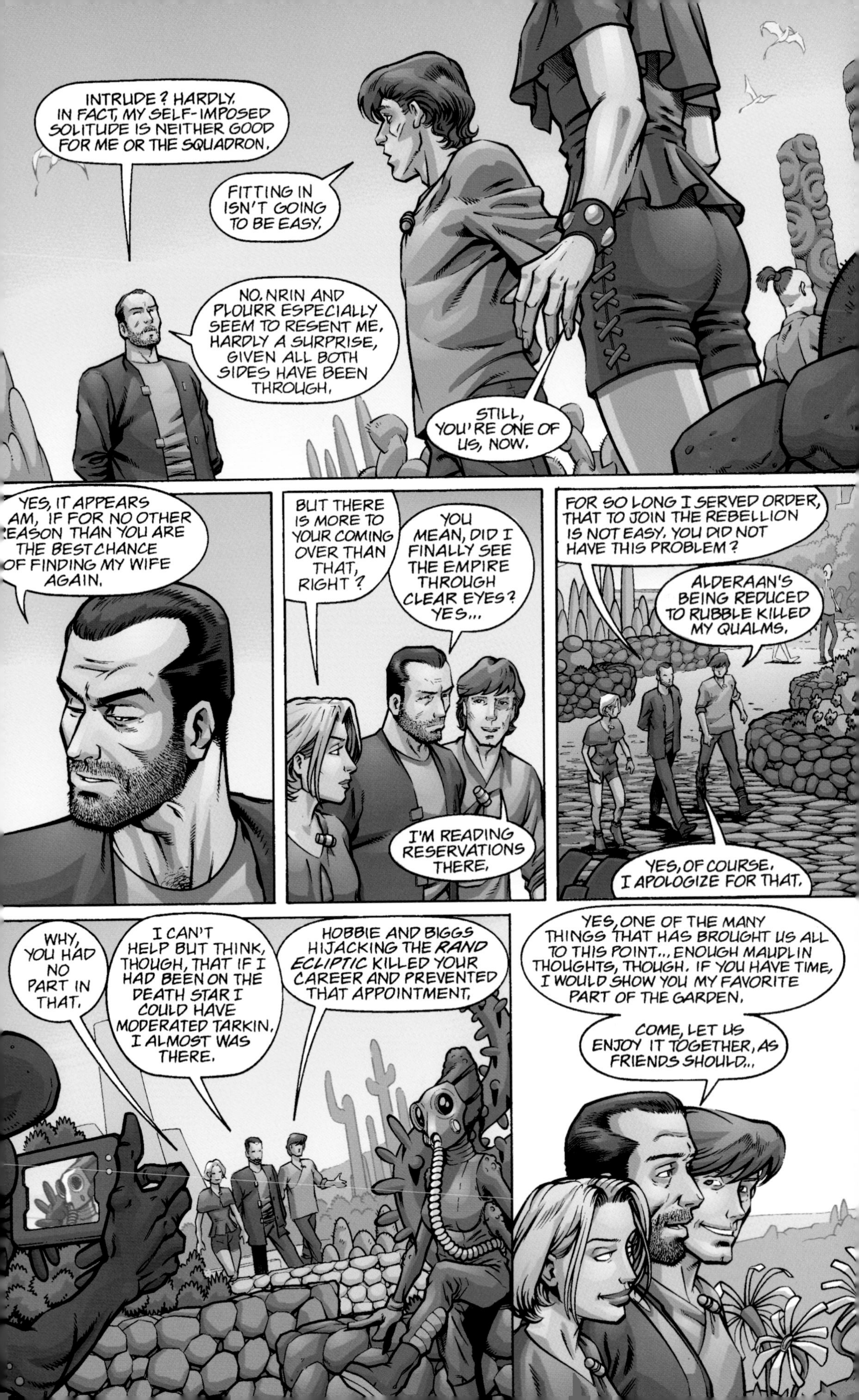
INTRUDE? HARDLY. IN FACT, MY SELF-IMPOSED SOLITUDE IS NEITHER GOOD FOR ME OR THE SQUADRON.
FITTING IN ISN'T GOING TO BE EASY.
NO, NRIN AND PLOURR ESPECIALLY SEEM TO RESENT ME, HARDLY A SURPRISE, GIVEN ALL BOTH SIDES HAVE BEEN THROUGH.
STILL, YOU'RE ONE OF US, NOW.
YES, IT APPEARS AM, IF FOR NO OTHER EASON THAN YOU ARE THE BEST CHANCE OF FINDING MY WIFE AGAIN.
BUT THERE IS MORE TO YOUR COMING OVER THAN THAT, RIGHT?
YOU MEAN, DID I FINALLY SEE THE EMPIRE THROUGH CLEAR EYES? YES...
I'M READING RESERVATIONS THERE.
FOR SO LONG I SERVED ORDER, THAT TO JOIN THE REBELLION IS NOT EASY. YOU DID NOT HAVE THIS PROBLEM?
ALDERAAN'S BEING REDUCED TO RUBBLE KILLED MY QUALMS.
YES, OF COURSE. I APOLOGIZE FOR THAT.
WHY, YOU HAD NO PART IN THAT.
I CAN'T HELP BUT THINK, THOUGH, THAT IF I HAD BEEN ON THE DEATH STAR I COULD HAVE MODERATED TARKIN. I ALMOST WAS THERE.
HOBBIE AND BIGGS HIJACKING THE *RAND ECLIPTIC* KILLED YOUR CAREER AND PREVENTED THAT APPOINTMENT.
YES, ONE OF THE MANY THINGS THAT HAS BROUGHT US ALL TO THIS POINT... ENOUGH MAUDLIN THOUGHTS, THOUGH. IF YOU HAVE TIME, I WOULD SHOW YOU MY FAVORITE PART OF THE GARDEN.
COME, LET US ENJOY IT TOGETHER, AS FRIENDS SHOULD...

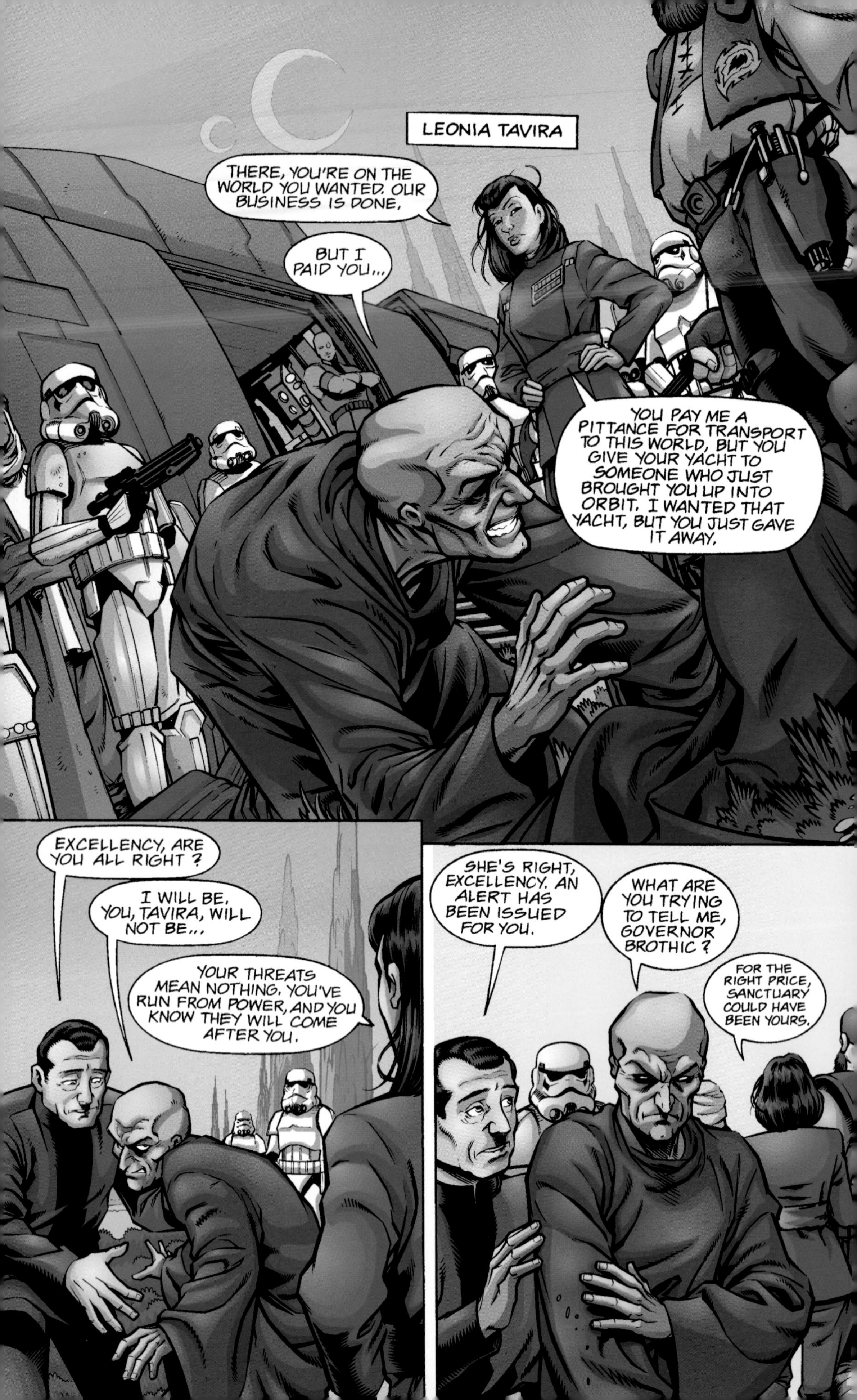
LEONIA TAVIRA
THERE, YOU'RE ON THE WORLD YOU WANTED. OUR BUSINESS IS DONE,
BUT I PAID YOU...
YOU PAY ME A PITTANCE FOR TRANSPORT TO THIS WORLD, BUT YOU GIVE YOUR YACHT TO SOMEONE WHO JUST BROUGHT YOU UP INTO ORBIT. I WANTED THAT YACHT, BUT YOU JUST GAVE IT AWAY.
EXCELLENCY, ARE YOU ALL RIGHT ?
I WILL BE. YOU, TAVIRA, WILL NOT BE...
YOUR THREATS MEAN NOTHING. YOU'VE RUN FROM POWER, AND YOU KNOW THEY WILL COME AFTER YOU.
SHE'S RIGHT, EXCELLENCY. AN ALERT HAS BEEN ISSUED FOR YOU.
WHAT ARE YOU TRYING TO TELL ME, GOVERNOR BROTHIC ?
FOR THE RIGHT PRICE, SANCTUARY COULD HAVE BEEN YOURS.

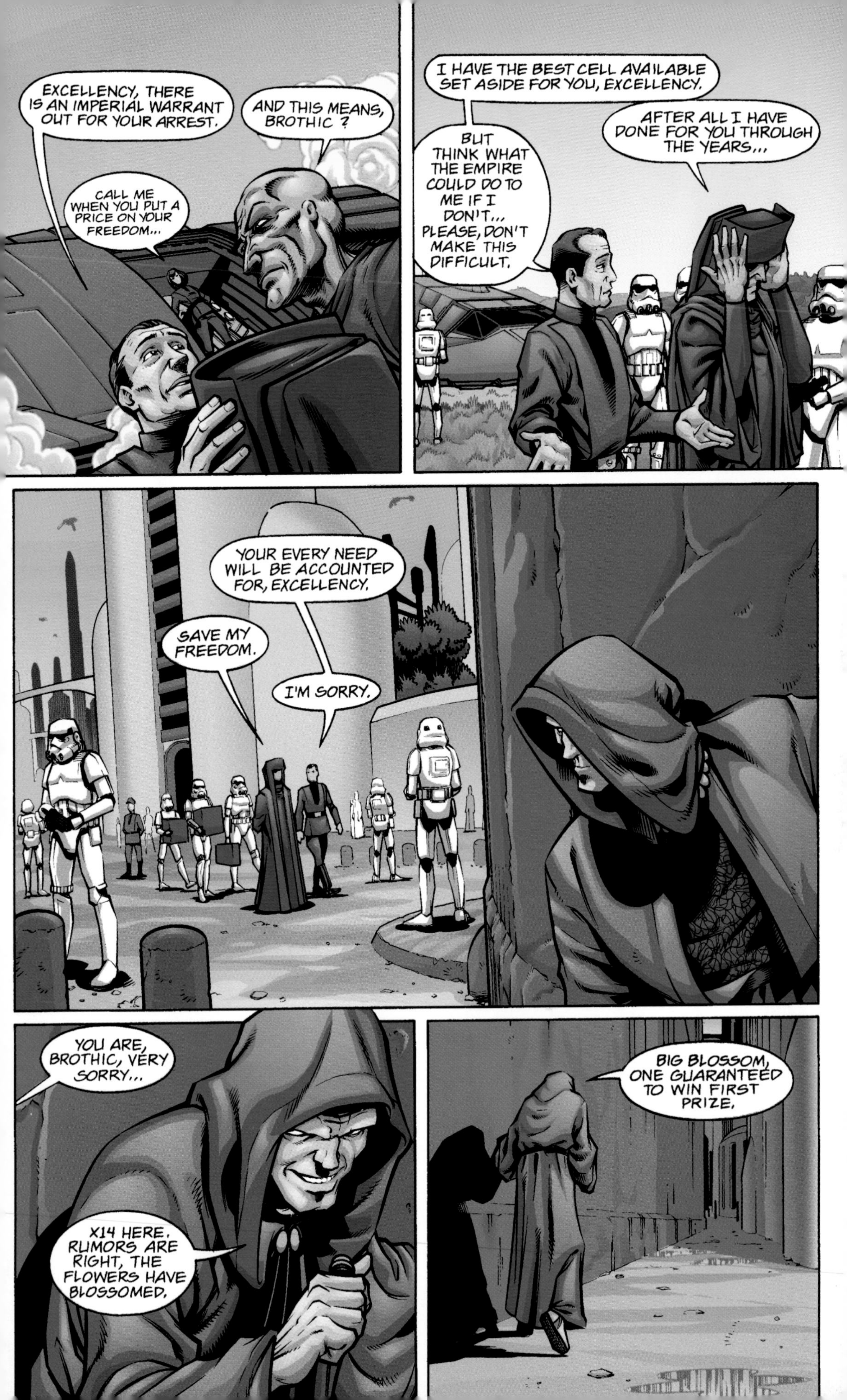
EXCELLENCY, THERE IS AN IMPERIAL WARRANT OUT FOR YOUR ARREST.
AND THIS MEANS, BROTHIC ?
CALL ME WHEN YOU PUT A PRICE ON YOUR FREEDOM...
I HAVE THE BEST CELL AVAILABLE SET ASIDE FOR YOU, EXCELLENCY.
BUT THINK WHAT THE EMPIRE COULD DO TO ME IF I DON'T... PLEASE, DON'T MAKE THIS DIFFICULT.
AFTER ALL I HAVE DONE FOR YOU THROUGH THE YEARS...
YOUR EVERY NEED WILL BE ACCOUNTED FOR, EXCELLENCY.
SAVE MY FREEDOM.
I'M SORRY.
YOU ARE, BROTHIC, VERY SORRY...
X14 HERE. RUMORS ARE RIGHT, THE FLOWERS HAVE BLOSSOMED.
BIG BLOSSOM, ONE GUARANTEED TO WIN FIRST PRIZE.

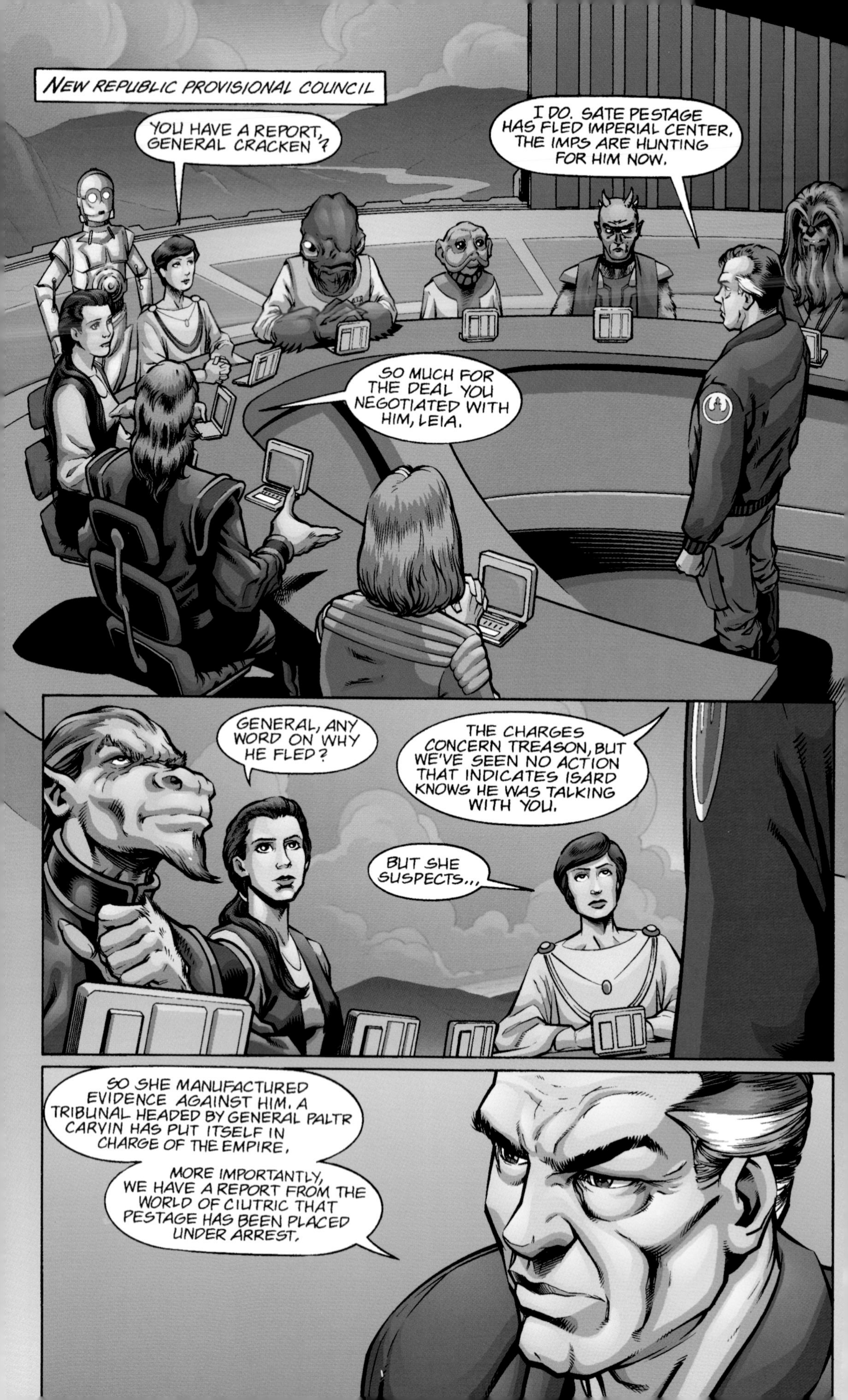
NEW REPUBLIC PROVISIONAL COUNCIL
YOU HAVE A REPORT, GENERAL CRACKEN ?
I DO. SATE PESTAGE HAS FLED IMPERIAL CENTER. THE IMPS ARE HUNTING FOR HIM NOW.
SO MUCH FOR THE DEAL YOU NEGOTIATED WITH HIM, LEIA.
GENERAL, ANY WORD ON WHY HE FLED?
THE CHARGES CONCERN TREASON, BUT WE'VE SEEN NO ACTION THAT INDICATES ISARD KNOWS HE WAS TALKING WITH YOU.
BUT SHE SUSPECTS...
SO SHE MANUFACTURED EVIDENCE AGAINST HIM. A TRIBUNAL HEADED BY GENERAL PALTR CARVIN HAS PUT ITSELF IN CHARGE OF THE EMPIRE.
MORE IMPORTANTLY, WE HAVE A REPORT FROM THE WORLD OF CIUTRIC THAT PESTAGE HAS BEEN PLACED UNDER ARREST.

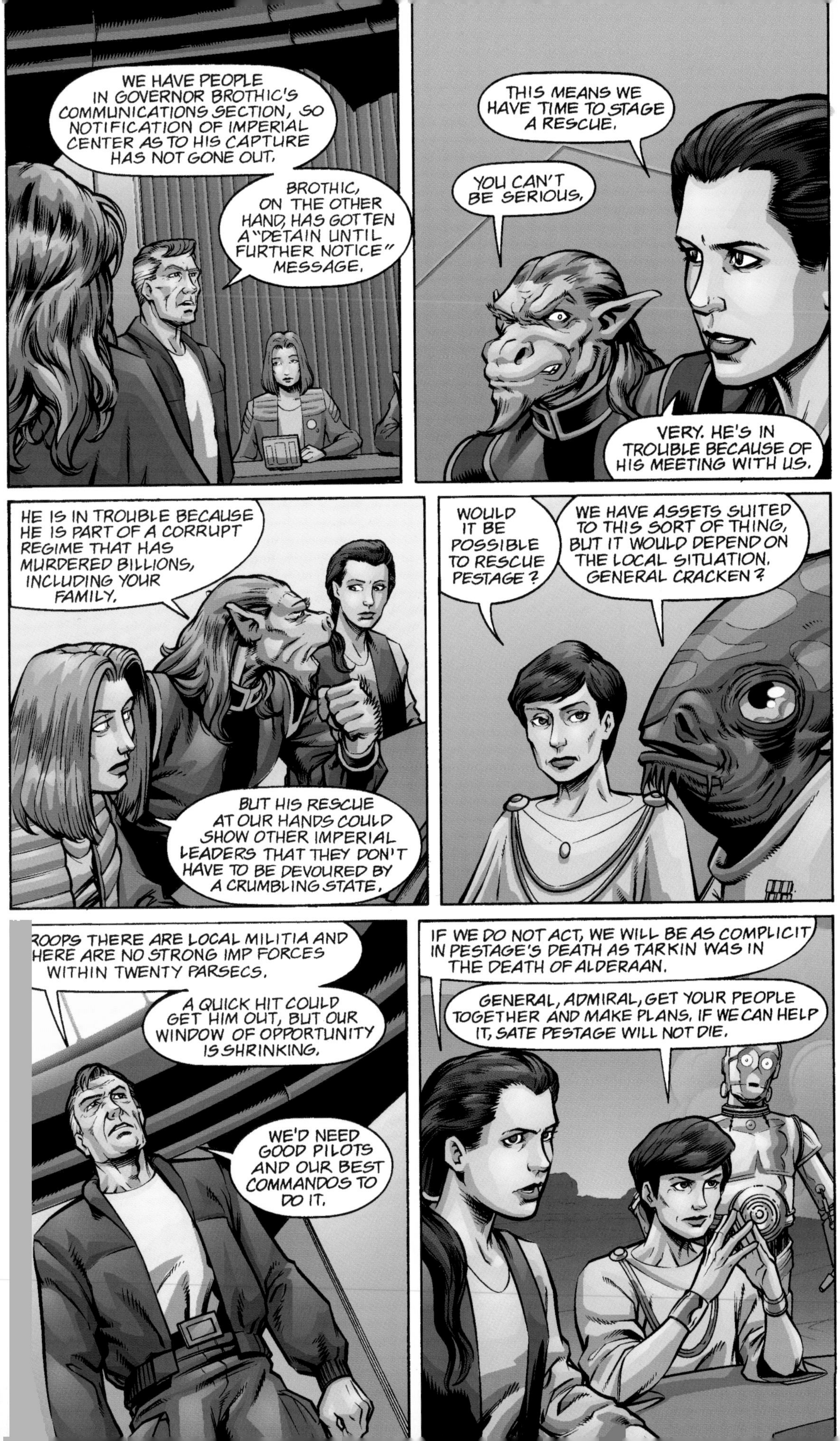
WE HAVE PEOPLE IN GOVERNOR BROTHIC'S COMMUNICATIONS SECTION, SO NOTIFICATION OF IMPERIAL CENTER AS TO HIS CAPTURE HAS NOT GONE OUT.
BROTHIC, ON THE OTHER HAND, HAS GOTTEN A "DETAIN UNTIL FURTHER NOTICE" MESSAGE.
THIS MEANS WE HAVE TIME TO STAGE A RESCUE.
YOU CAN'T BE SERIOUS.
VERY. HE'S IN TROUBLE BECAUSE OF HIS MEETING WITH US.
HE IS IN TROUBLE BECAUSE HE IS PART OF A CORRUPT REGIME THAT HAS MURDERED BILLIONS, INCLUDING YOUR FAMILY.
BUT HIS RESCUE AT OUR HANDS COULD SHOW OTHER IMPERIAL LEADERS THAT THEY DON'T HAVE TO BE DEVOURED BY A CRUMBLING STATE.
WOULD IT BE POSSIBLE TO RESCUE PESTAGE?
WE HAVE ASSETS SUITED TO THIS SORT OF THING, BUT IT WOULD DEPEND ON THE LOCAL SITUATION. GENERAL CRACKEN?
ROOPS THERE ARE LOCAL MILITIA AND HERE ARE NO STRONG IMP FORCES WITHIN TWENTY PARSECS.
A QUICK HIT COULD GET HIM OUT, BUT OUR WINDOW OF OPPORTUNITY IS SHRINKING.
WE'D NEED GOOD PILOTS AND OUR BEST COMMANDOS TO DO IT.
IF WE DO NOT ACT, WE WILL BE AS COMPLICIT IN PESTAGE'S DEATH AS TARKIN WAS IN THE DEATH OF ALDERAAN.
GENERAL, ADMIRAL, GET YOUR PEOPLE TOGETHER AND MAKE PLANS. IF WE CAN HELP IT, SATE PESTAGE WILL NOT DIE.

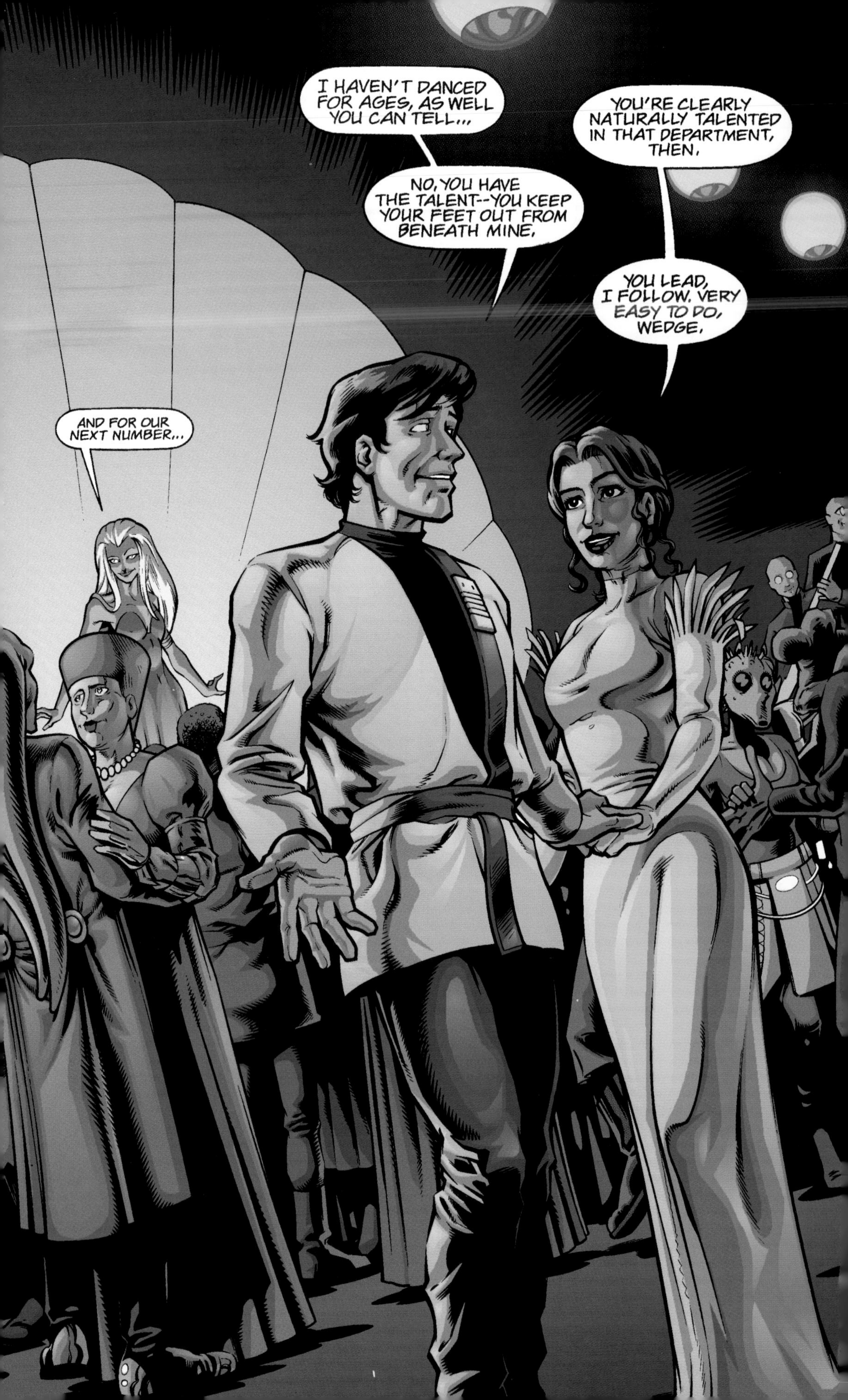
I HAVEN'T DANCED FOR AGES, AS WELL YOU CAN TELL...
NO, YOU HAVE THE TALENT--YOU KEEP YOUR FEET OUT FROM BENEATH MINE.
YOU'RE CLEARLY NATURALLY TALENTED IN THAT DEPARTMENT, THEN.
YOU LEAD, I FOLLOW. VERY EASY TO DO, WEDGE.
AND FOR OUR NEXT NUMBER...

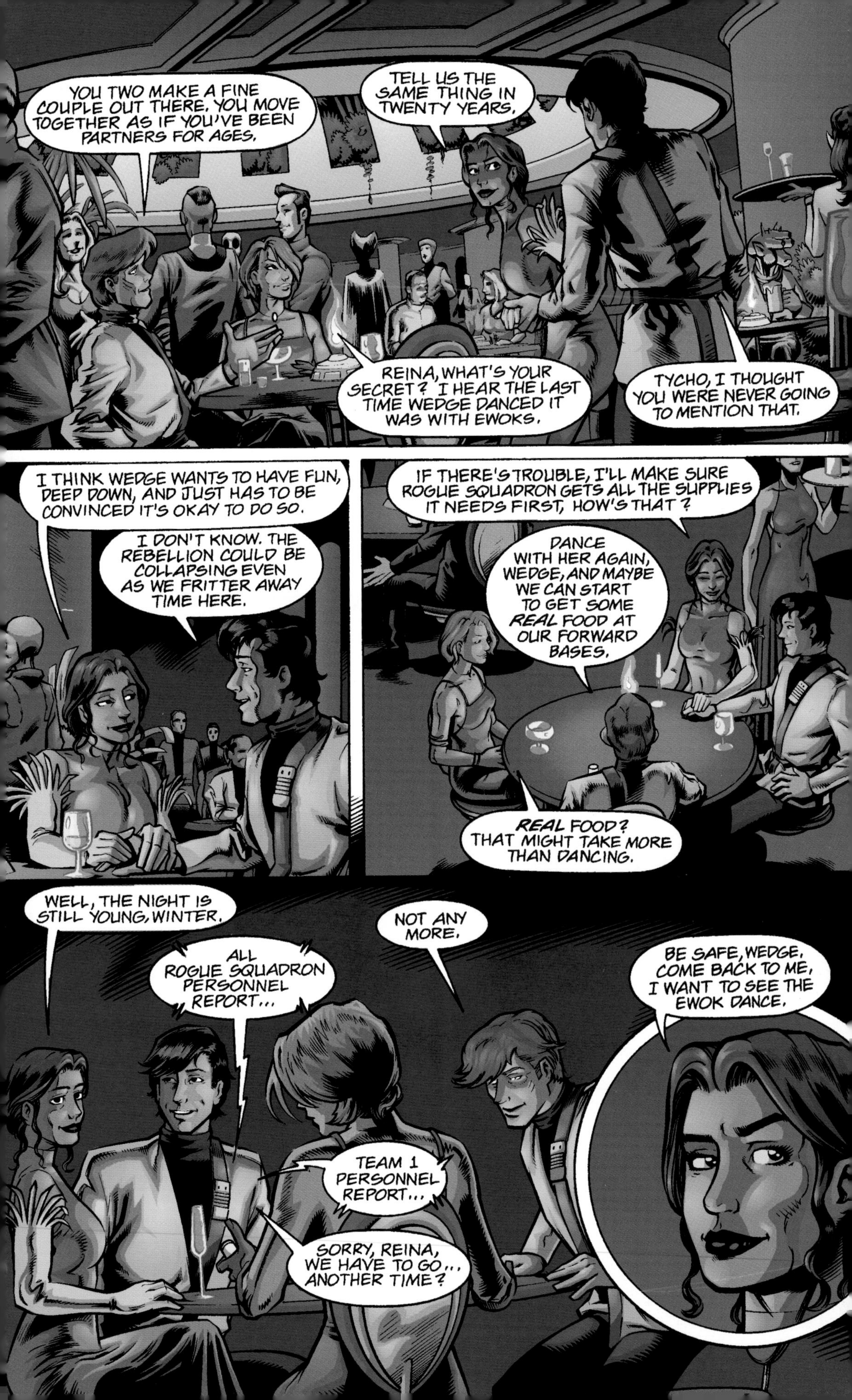
YOU TWO MAKE A FINE COUPLE OUT THERE. YOU MOVE TOGETHER AS IF YOU'VE BEEN PARTNERS FOR AGES.
TELL US THE SAME THING IN TWENTY YEARS.
REINA, WHAT'S YOUR SECRET? I HEAR THE LAST TIME WEDGE DANCED IT WAS WITH EWOKS.
TYCHO, I THOUGHT YOU WERE NEVER GOING TO MENTION THAT.
I THINK WEDGE WANTS TO HAVE FUN, DEEP DOWN, AND JUST HAS TO BE CONVINCED IT'S OKAY TO DO SO.
I DON'T KNOW. THE REBELLION COULD BE COLLAPSING EVEN AS WE FRITTER AWAY TIME HERE.
IF THERE'S TROUBLE, I'LL MAKE SURE ROGUE SQUADRON GETS ALL THE SUPPLIES IT NEEDS FIRST, HOW'S THAT?
DANCE WITH HER AGAIN, WEDGE, AND MAYBE WE CAN START TO GET SOME REAL FOOD AT OUR FORWARD BASES.
REAL FOOD? THAT MIGHT TAKE MORE THAN DANCING.
WELL, THE NIGHT IS STILL YOUNG, WINTER.
ALL ROGUE SQUADRON PERSONNEL REPORT...
NOT ANY MORE.
TEAM 1 PERSONNEL REPORT...
SORRY, REINA, WE HAVE TO GO... ANOTHER TIME?
BE SAFE, WEDGE. COME BACK TO ME. I WANT TO SEE THE EWOK DANCE.

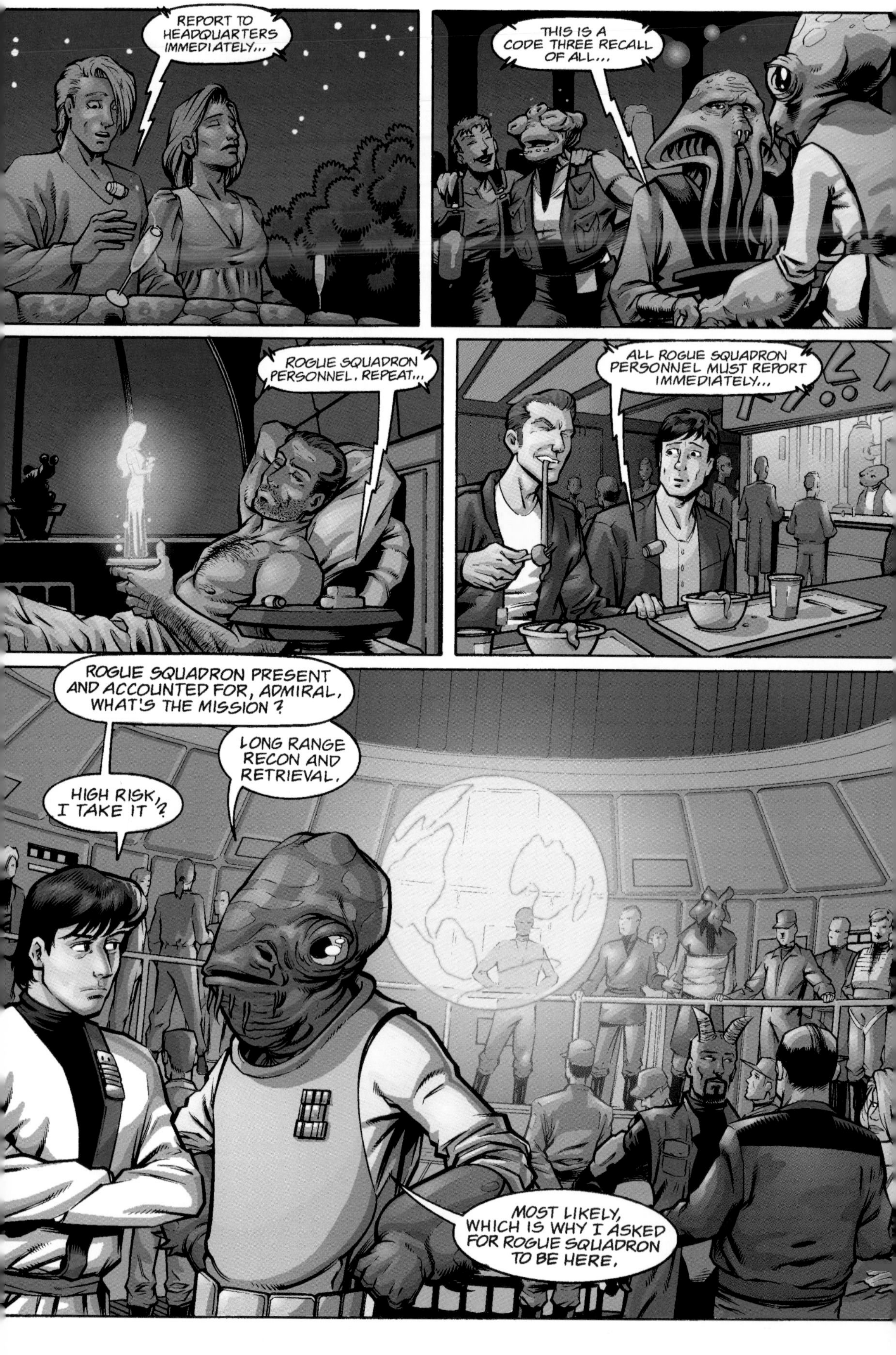
REPORT TO HEADQUARTERS IMMEDIATELY...
THIS IS A CODE THREE RECALL OF ALL...
ROGUE SQUADRON PERSONNEL. REPEAT...
ALL ROGUE SQUADRON PERSONNEL MUST REPORT IMMEDIATELY...
ROGUE SQUADRON PRESENT AND ACCOUNTED FOR, ADMIRAL. WHAT'S THE MISSION?
LONG RANGE RECON AND RETRIEVAL.
HIGH RISK, I TAKE IT?
MOST LIKELY, WHICH IS WHY I ASKED FOR ROGUE SQUADRON TO BE HERE.

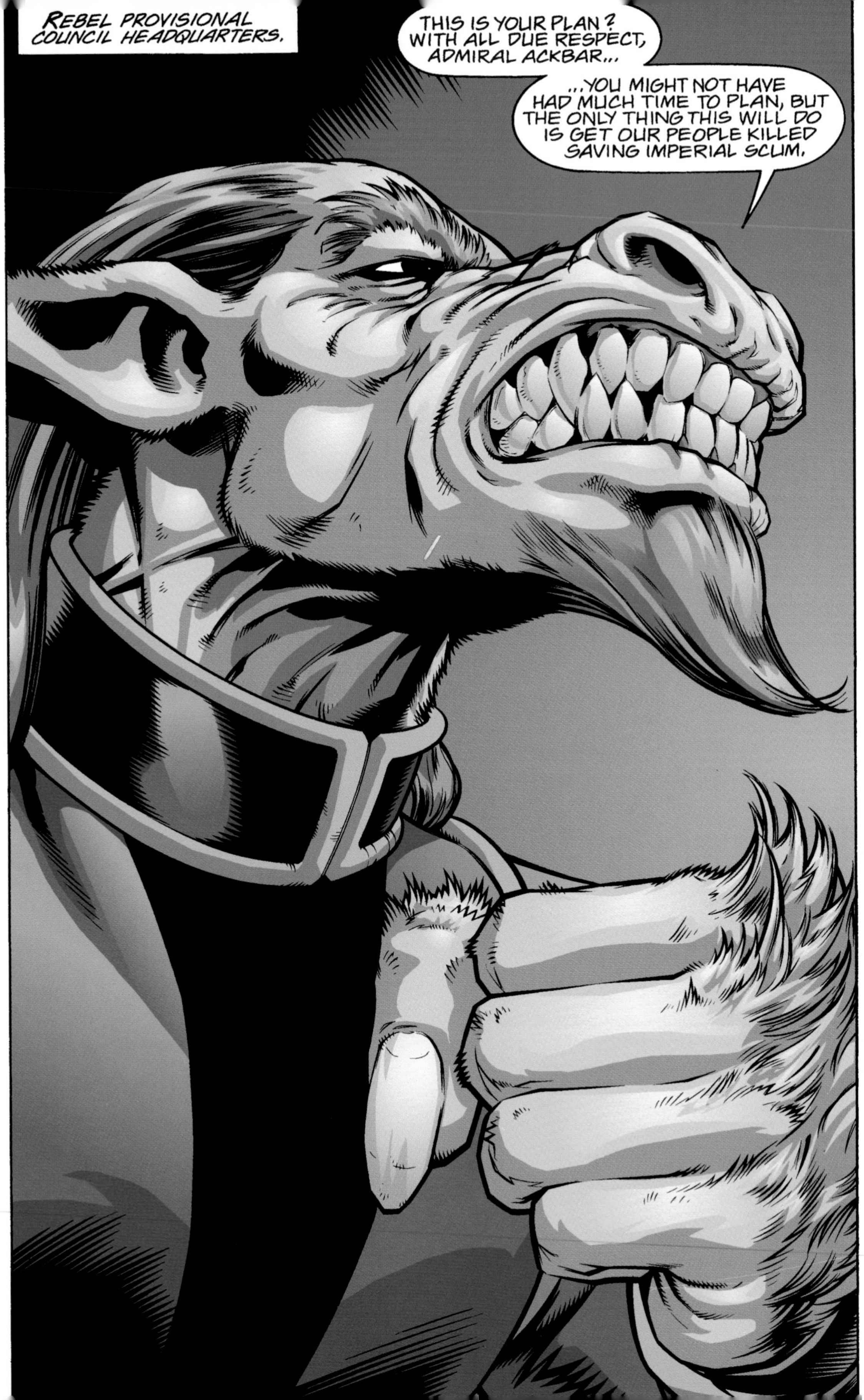
REBEL PROVISIONAL COUNCIL HEADQUARTERS.
THIS IS YOUR PLAN? WITH ALL DUE RESPECT, ADMIRAL ACKBAR...
...YOU MIGHT NOT HAVE HAD MUCH TIME TO PLAN, BUT THE ONLY THING THIS WILL DO IS GET OUR PEOPLE KILLED SAVING IMPERIAL SCUM.

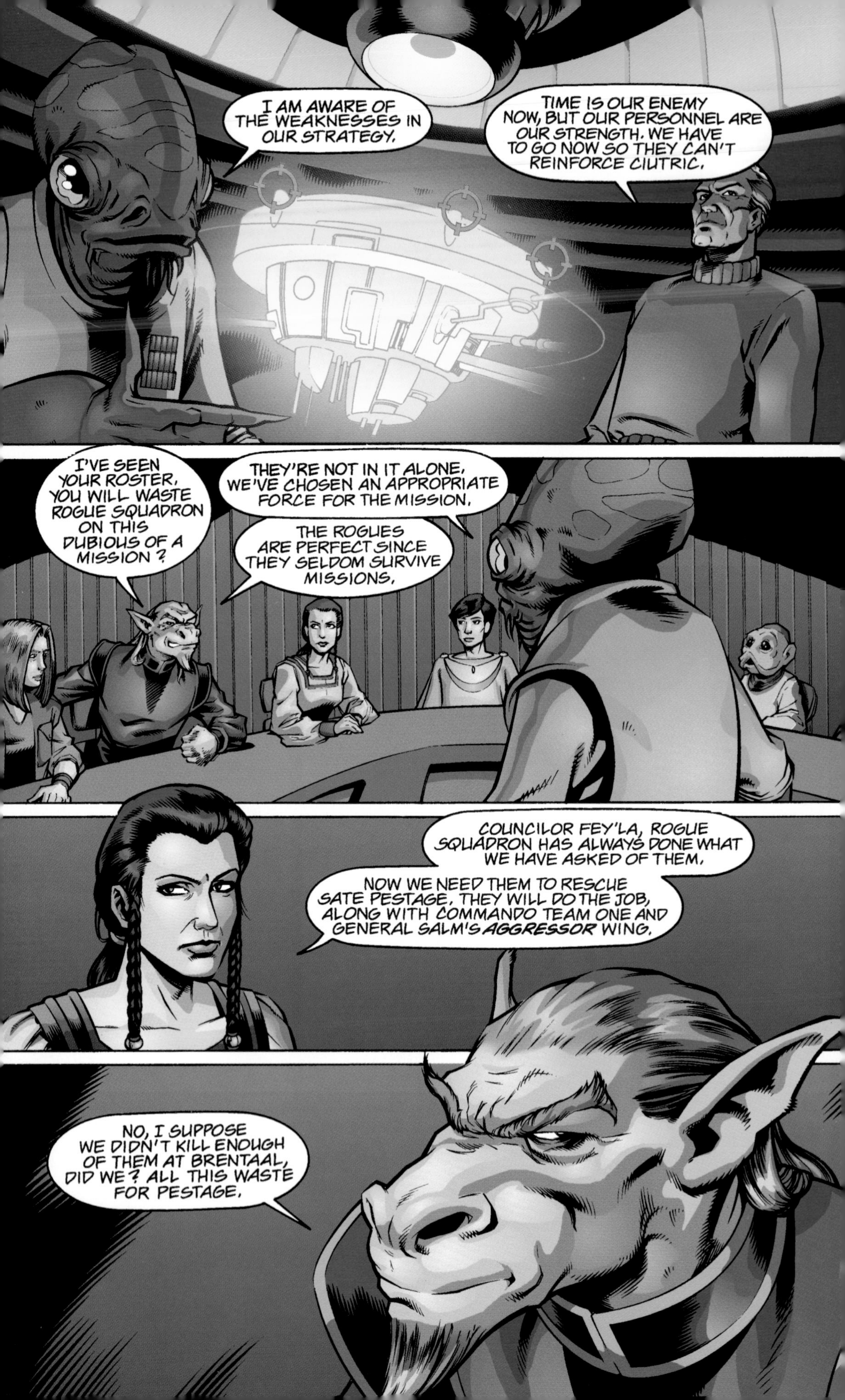
I AM AWARE OF THE WEAKNESSES IN OUR STRATEGY.
TIME IS OUR ENEMY NOW, BUT OUR PERSONNEL ARE OUR STRENGTH. WE HAVE TO GO NOW SO THEY CAN'T REINFORCE CIUTRIC.
I'VE SEEN YOUR ROSTER, YOU WILL WASTE ROGUE SQUADRON ON THIS DUBIOUS OF A MISSION?
THEY'RE NOT IN IT ALONE, WE'VE CHOSEN AN APPROPRIATE FORCE FOR THE MISSION.
THE ROGUES ARE PERFECT SINCE THEY SELDOM SURVIVE MISSIONS.
COUNCILOR FEY'LA, ROGUE SQUADRON HAS ALWAYS DONE WHAT WE HAVE ASKED OF THEM.
NOW WE NEED THEM TO RESCUE SATE PESTAGE. THEY WILL DO THE JOB, ALONG WITH COMMANDO TEAM ONE AND GENERAL SALM'S *AGGRESSOR* WING.
NO, I SUPPOSE WE DIDN'T KILL ENOUGH OF THEM AT BRENTAAL, DID WE? ALL THIS WASTE FOR PESTAGE.

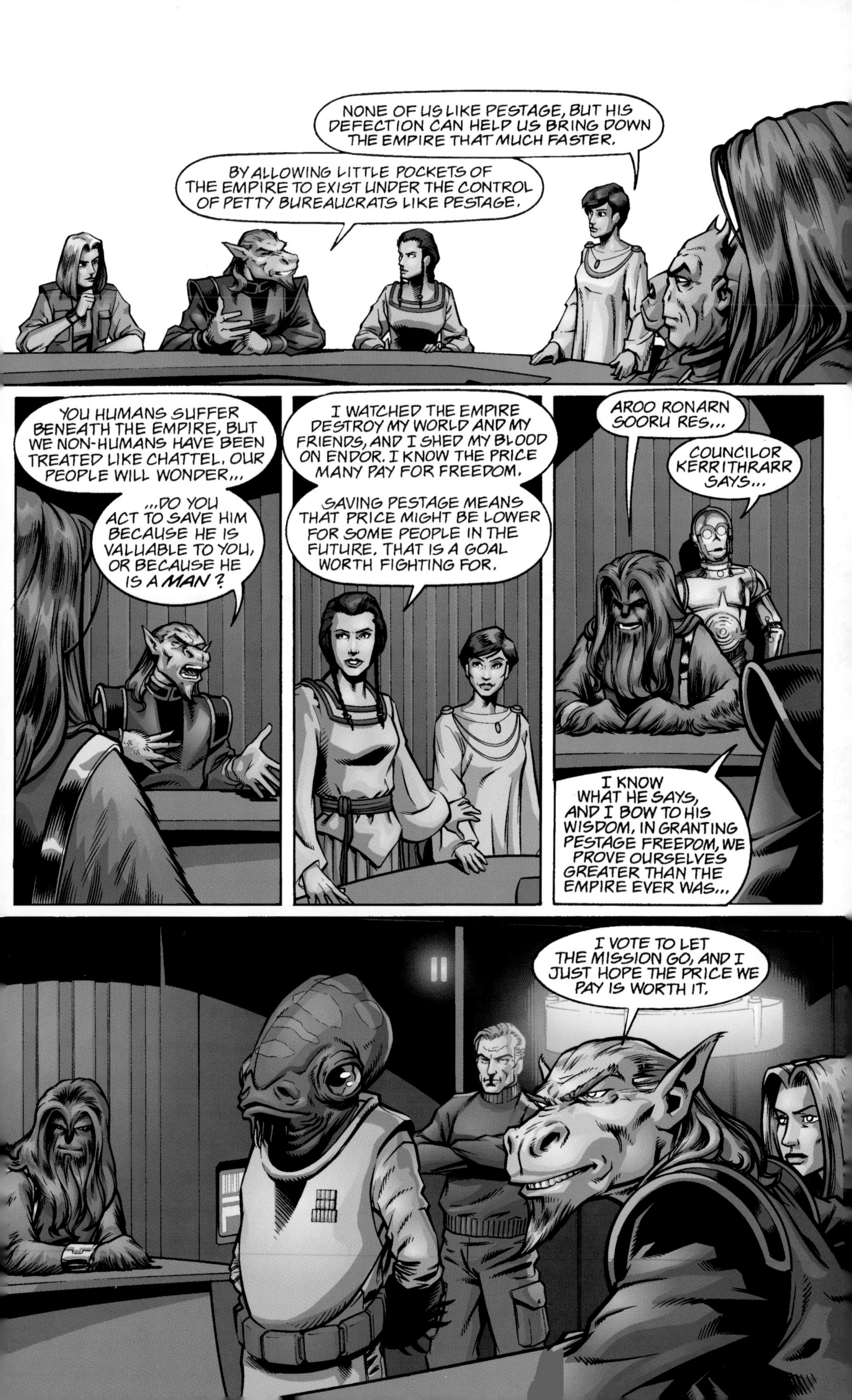
NONE OF US LIKE PESTAGE, BUT HIS DEFECTION CAN HELP US BRING DOWN THE EMPIRE THAT MUCH FASTER.
BY ALLOWING LITTLE POCKETS OF THE EMPIRE TO EXIST UNDER THE CONTROL OF PETTY BUREAUCRATS LIKE PESTAGE.
YOU HUMANS SUFFER BENEATH THE EMPIRE, BUT WE NON-HUMANS HAVE BEEN TREATED LIKE CHATTEL. OUR PEOPLE WILL WONDER...
...DO YOU ACT TO SAVE HIM BECAUSE HE IS VALUABLE TO YOU, OR BECAUSE HE IS A *MAN*?
I WATCHED THE EMPIRE DESTROY MY WORLD AND MY FRIENDS, AND I SHED MY BLOOD ON ENDOR. I KNOW THE PRICE MANY PAY FOR FREEDOM.
SAVING PESTAGE MEANS THAT PRICE MIGHT BE LOWER FOR SOME PEOPLE IN THE FUTURE. THAT IS A GOAL WORTH FIGHTING FOR.
AROO RONARN SOORU RES...
COUNCILOR KERRITHRARR SAYS...
I KNOW WHAT HE SAYS, AND I BOW TO HIS WISDOM. IN GRANTING PESTAGE FREEDOM, WE PROVE OURSELVES GREATER THAN THE EMPIRE EVER WAS...
I VOTE TO LET THE MISSION GO, AND I JUST HOPE THE PRICE WE PAY IS WORTH IT.

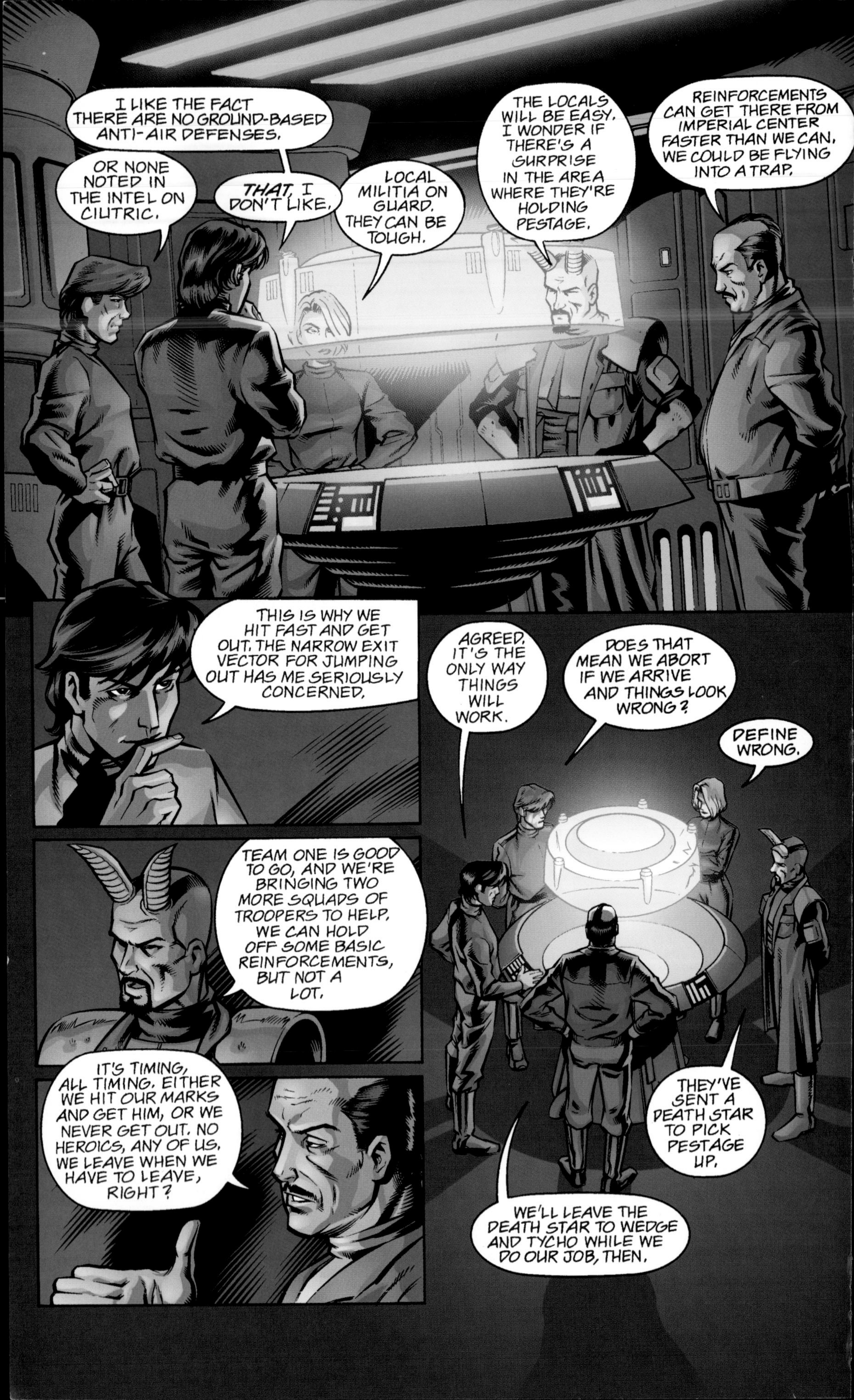
I LIKE THE FACT THERE ARE NO GROUND-BASED ANTI-AIR DEFENSES.
OR NONE NOTED IN THE INTEL ON CIUTRIC.
THAT, I DON'T LIKE.
LOCAL MILITIA ON GUARD. THEY CAN BE TOUGH.
THE LOCALS WILL BE EASY. I WONDER IF THERE'S A SURPRISE IN THE AREA WHERE THEY'RE HOLDING PESTAGE.
REINFORCEMENTS CAN GET THERE FROM IMPERIAL CENTER FASTER THAN WE CAN. WE COULD BE FLYING INTO A TRAP.
THIS IS WHY WE HIT FAST AND GET OUT. THE NARROW EXIT VECTOR FOR JUMPING OUT HAS ME SERIOUSLY CONCERNED.
TEAM ONE IS GOOD TO GO, AND WE'RE BRINGING TWO MORE SQUADS OF TROOPERS TO HELP. WE CAN HOLD OFF SOME BASIC REINFORCEMENTS, BUT NOT A LOT.
IT'S TIMING, ALL TIMING. EITHER WE HIT OUR MARKS AND GET HIM, OR WE NEVER GET OUT. NO HEROICS, ANY OF US. WE LEAVE WHEN WE HAVE TO LEAVE, RIGHT?
AGREED. IT'S THE ONLY WAY THINGS WILL WORK.
DOES THAT MEAN WE ABORT IF WE ARRIVE AND THINGS LOOK WRONG?
DEFINE WRONG.
THEY'VE SENT A DEATH STAR TO PICK PESTAGE UP.
WE'LL LEAVE THE DEATH STAR TO WEDGE AND TYCHO WHILE WE DO OUR JOB, THEN.

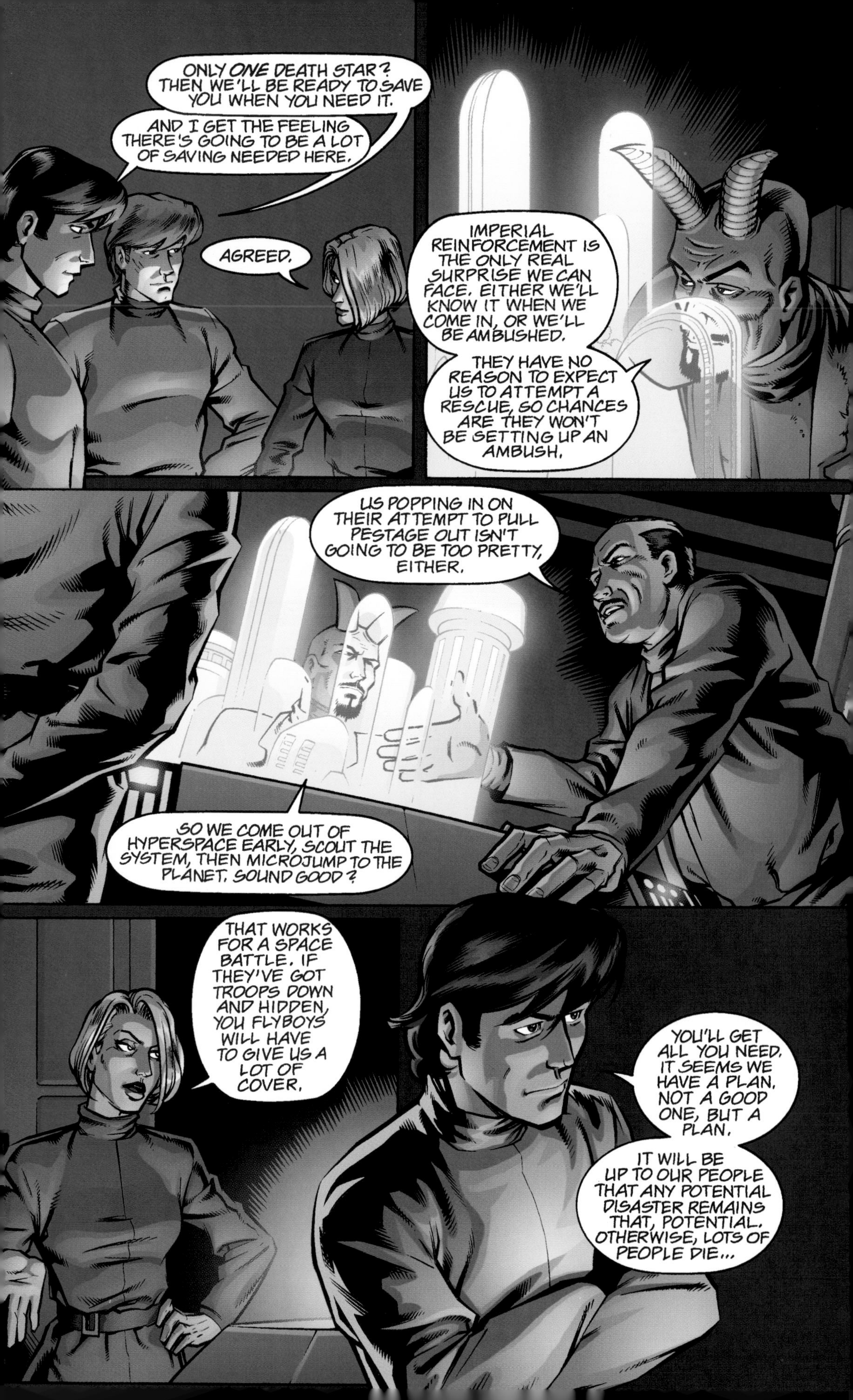
ONLY *ONE* DEATH STAR? THEN WE'LL BE READY TO SAVE YOU WHEN YOU NEED IT.
AND I GET THE FEELING THERE'S GOING TO BE A LOT OF SAVING NEEDED HERE.
AGREED.
IMPERIAL REINFORCEMENT IS THE ONLY REAL SURPRISE WE CAN FACE. EITHER WE'LL KNOW IT WHEN WE COME IN, OR WE'LL BE AMBUSHED.
THEY HAVE NO REASON TO EXPECT US TO ATTEMPT A RESCUE, SO CHANCES ARE THEY WON'T BE SETTING UP AN AMBUSH.
US POPPING IN ON THEIR ATTEMPT TO PULL PESTAGE OUT ISN'T GOING TO BE TOO PRETTY, EITHER.
SO WE COME OUT OF HYPERSPACE EARLY, SCOUT THE SYSTEM, THEN MICROJUMP TO THE PLANET. SOUND GOOD?
THAT WORKS FOR A SPACE BATTLE. IF THEY'VE GOT TROOPS DOWN AND HIDDEN, YOU FLYBOYS WILL HAVE TO GIVE US A LOT OF COVER.
YOU'LL GET ALL YOU NEED. IT SEEMS WE HAVE A PLAN. NOT A GOOD ONE, BUT A PLAN.
IT WILL BE UP TO OUR PEOPLE THAT ANY POTENTIAL DISASTER REMAINS THAT, POTENTIAL. OTHERWISE, LOTS OF PEOPLE DIE...

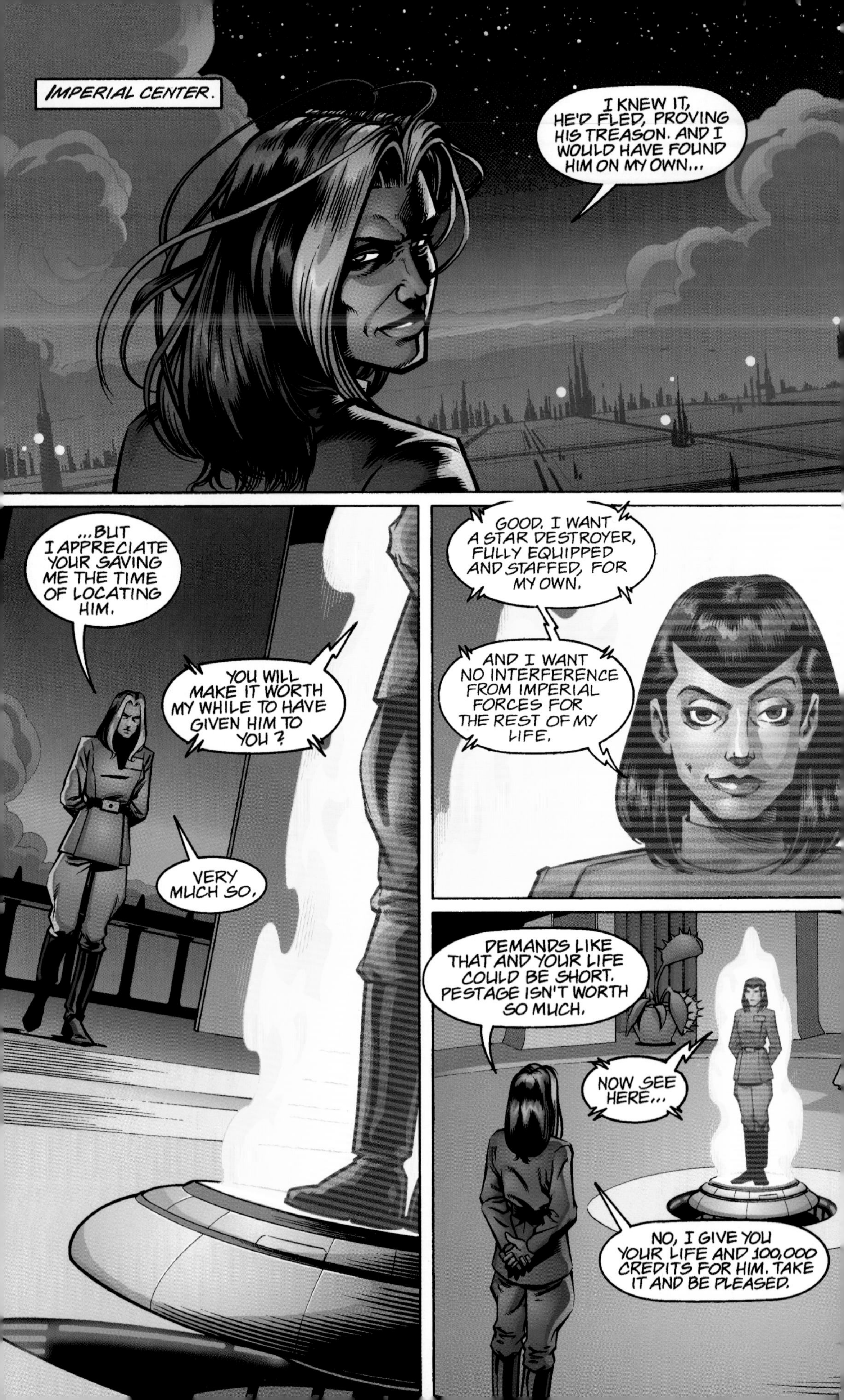
IMPERIAL CENTER.
I KNEW IT, HE'D FLED, PROVING HIS TREASON. AND I WOULD HAVE FOUND HIM ON MY OWN...
...BUT I APPRECIATE YOUR SAVING ME THE TIME OF LOCATING HIM.
YOU WILL MAKE IT WORTH MY WHILE TO HAVE GIVEN HIM TO YOU?
VERY MUCH SO.
GOOD. I WANT A STAR DESTROYER, FULLY EQUIPPED AND STAFFED, FOR MY OWN.
AND I WANT NO INTERFERENCE FROM IMPERIAL FORCES FOR THE REST OF MY LIFE.
DEMANDS LIKE THAT AND YOUR LIFE COULD BE SHORT. PESTAGE ISN'T WORTH SO MUCH.
NOW SEE HERE...
NO, I GIVE YOU YOUR LIFE AND 100,000 CREDITS FOR HIM. TAKE IT AND BE PLEASED.

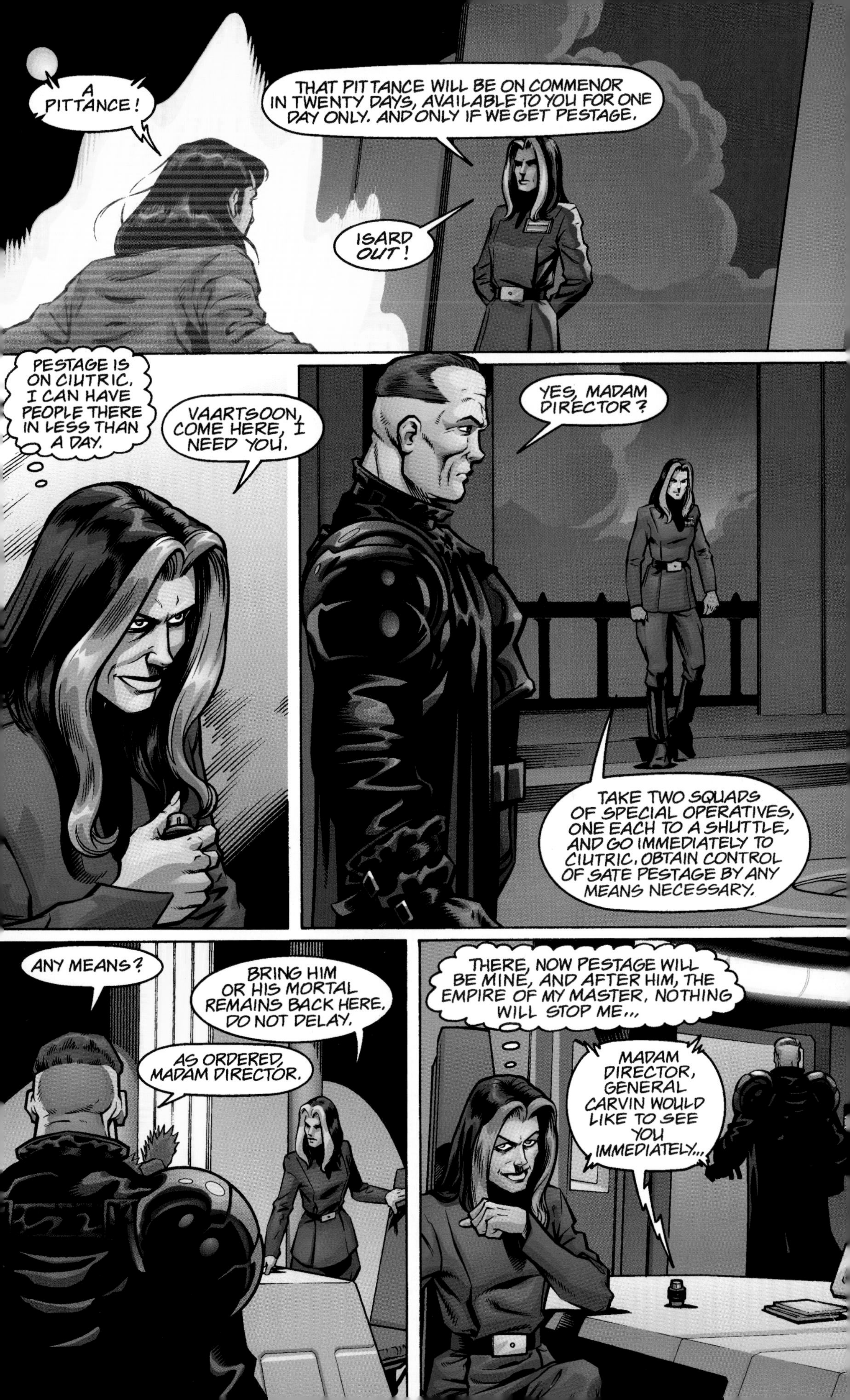
A PITTANCE!
THAT PITTANCE WILL BE ON COMMENOR IN TWENTY DAYS, AVAILABLE TO YOU FOR ONE DAY ONLY. AND ONLY IF WE GET PESTAGE.
ISARD OUT!
PESTAGE IS ON CIUTRIC, I CAN HAVE PEOPLE THERE IN LESS THAN A DAY.
VAARTSOON, COME HERE, I NEED YOU.
YES, MADAM DIRECTOR?
TAKE TWO SQUADS OF SPECIAL OPERATIVES, ONE EACH TO A SHUTTLE, AND GO IMMEDIATELY TO CIUTRIC, OBTAIN CONTROL OF SATE PESTAGE BY ANY MEANS NECESSARY.
ANY MEANS?
BRING HIM OR HIS MORTAL REMAINS BACK HERE. DO NOT DELAY.
AS ORDERED, MADAM DIRECTOR.
THERE, NOW PESTAGE WILL BE MINE, AND AFTER HIM, THE EMPIRE OF MY MASTER. NOTHING WILL STOP ME...
MADAM DIRECTOR, GENERAL CARVIN WOULD LIKE TO SEE YOU IMMEDIATELY...

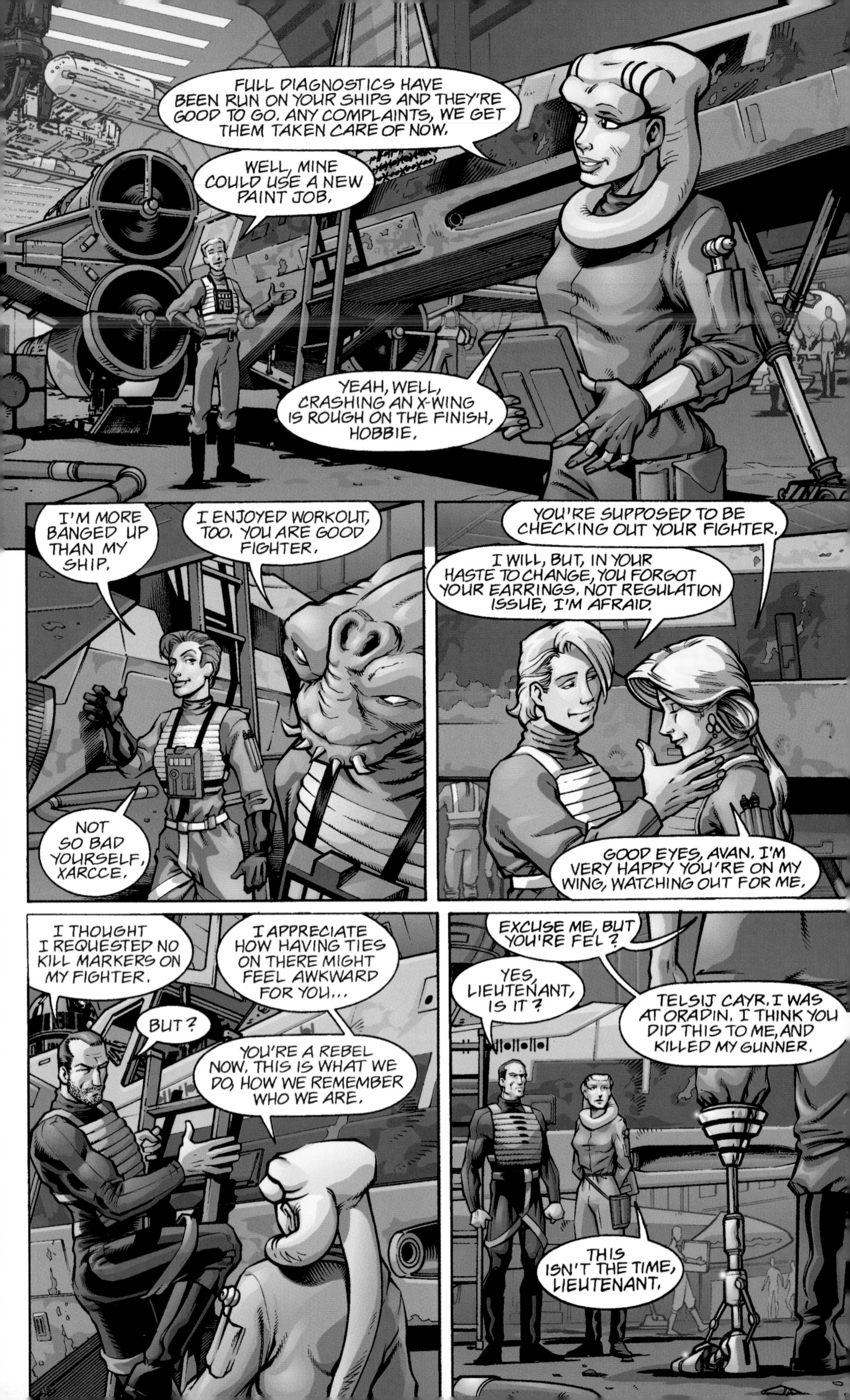
FULL DIAGNOSTICS HAVE BEEN RUN ON YOUR SHIPS AND THEY'RE GOOD TO GO. ANY COMPLAINTS, WE GET THEM TAKEN CARE OF NOW.
WELL, MINE COULD USE A NEW PAINT JOB.
YEAH, WELL, CRASHING AN X-WING IS ROUGH ON THE FINISH, HOBBIE.
I'M MORE BANGED UP THAN MY SHIP.
I ENJOYED WORKOUT, TOO. YOU ARE GOOD FIGHTER.
NOT SO BAD YOURSELF, XARCCE.
YOU'RE SUPPOSED TO BE CHECKING OUT YOUR FIGHTER.
I WILL, BUT, IN YOUR HASTE TO CHANGE, YOU FORGOT YOUR EARRINGS. NOT REGULATION ISSUE, I'M AFRAID.
GOOD EYES, AVAN. I'M VERY HAPPY YOU'RE ON MY WING, WATCHING OUT FOR ME.
I THOUGHT I REQUESTED NO KILL MARKERS ON MY FIGHTER.
I APPRECIATE HOW HAVING TIES ON THERE MIGHT FEEL AWKWARD FOR YOU...
BUT?
YOU'RE A REBEL NOW. THIS IS WHAT WE DO, HOW WE REMEMBER WHO WE ARE.
EXCUSE ME, BUT YOU'RE FEL?
YES, LIEUTENANT, IS IT?
TELSIJ CAYR. I WAS AT ORADIN. I THINK YOU DID THIS TO ME, AND KILLED MY GUNNER.
THIS ISN'T THE TIME, LIEUTENANT.

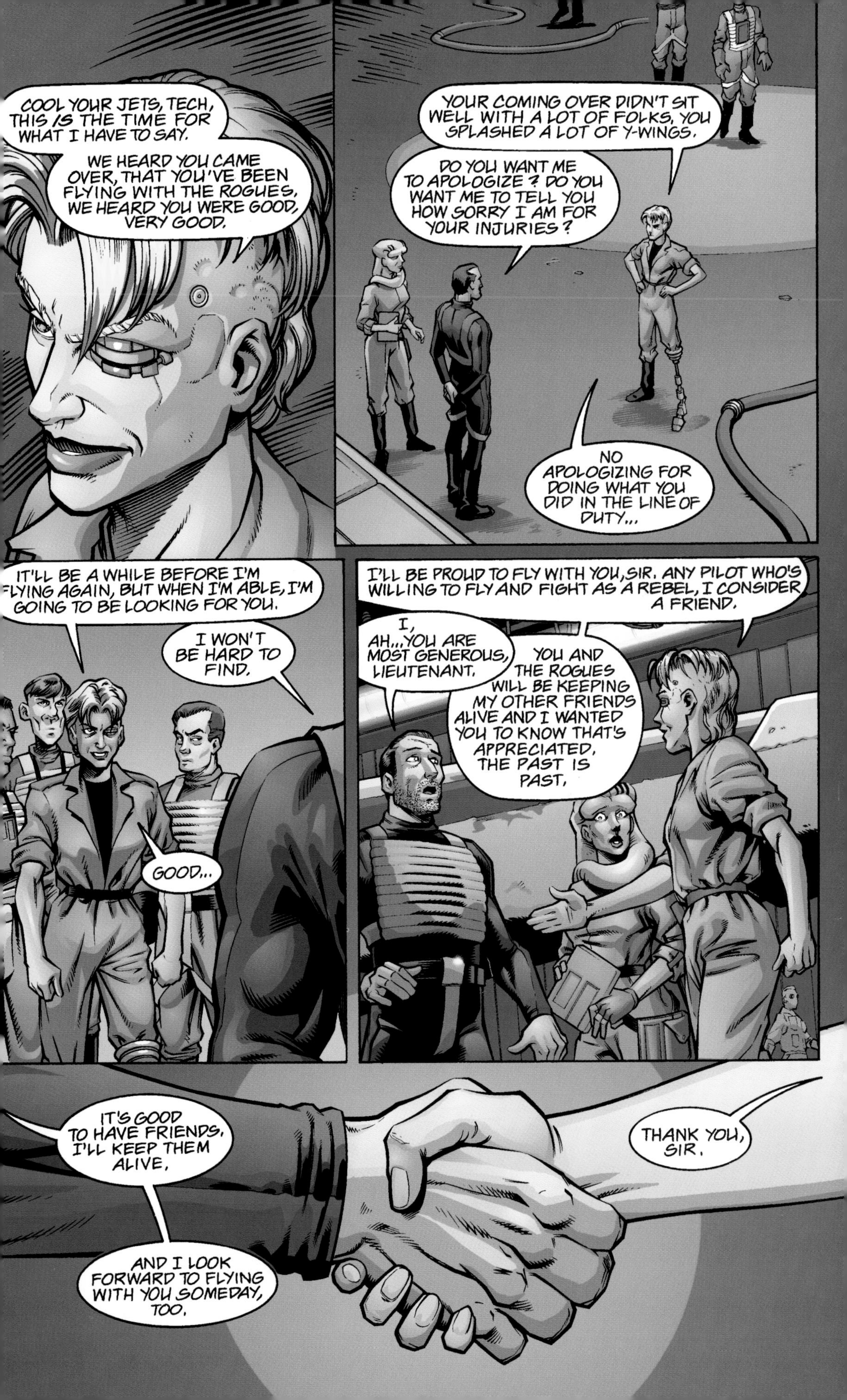
COOL YOUR JETS, TECH, THIS IS THE TIME FOR WHAT I HAVE TO SAY.
WE HEARD YOU CAME OVER, THAT YOU'VE BEEN FLYING WITH THE ROGUES. WE HEARD YOU WERE GOOD, VERY GOOD.
YOUR COMING OVER DIDN'T SIT WELL WITH A LOT OF FOLKS, YOU SPLASHED A LOT OF Y-WINGS.
DO YOU WANT ME TO APOLOGIZE? DO YOU WANT ME TO TELL YOU HOW SORRY I AM FOR YOUR INJURIES?
NO APOLOGIZING FOR DOING WHAT YOU DID IN THE LINE OF DUTY...
IT'LL BE A WHILE BEFORE I'M FLYING AGAIN, BUT WHEN I'M ABLE, I'M GOING TO BE LOOKING FOR YOU.
I WON'T BE HARD TO FIND.
GOOD...
I'LL BE PROUD TO FLY WITH YOU, SIR. ANY PILOT WHO'S WILLING TO FLY AND FIGHT AS A REBEL, I CONSIDER A FRIEND.
I, AH... YOU ARE MOST GENEROUS, LIEUTENANT.
YOU AND THE ROGUES WILL BE KEEPING MY OTHER FRIENDS ALIVE AND I WANTED YOU TO KNOW THAT'S APPRECIATED. THE PAST IS PAST.
IT'S GOOD TO HAVE FRIENDS. I'LL KEEP THEM ALIVE.
AND I LOOK FORWARD TO FLYING WITH YOU SOMEDAY, TOO.
THANK YOU, SIR.

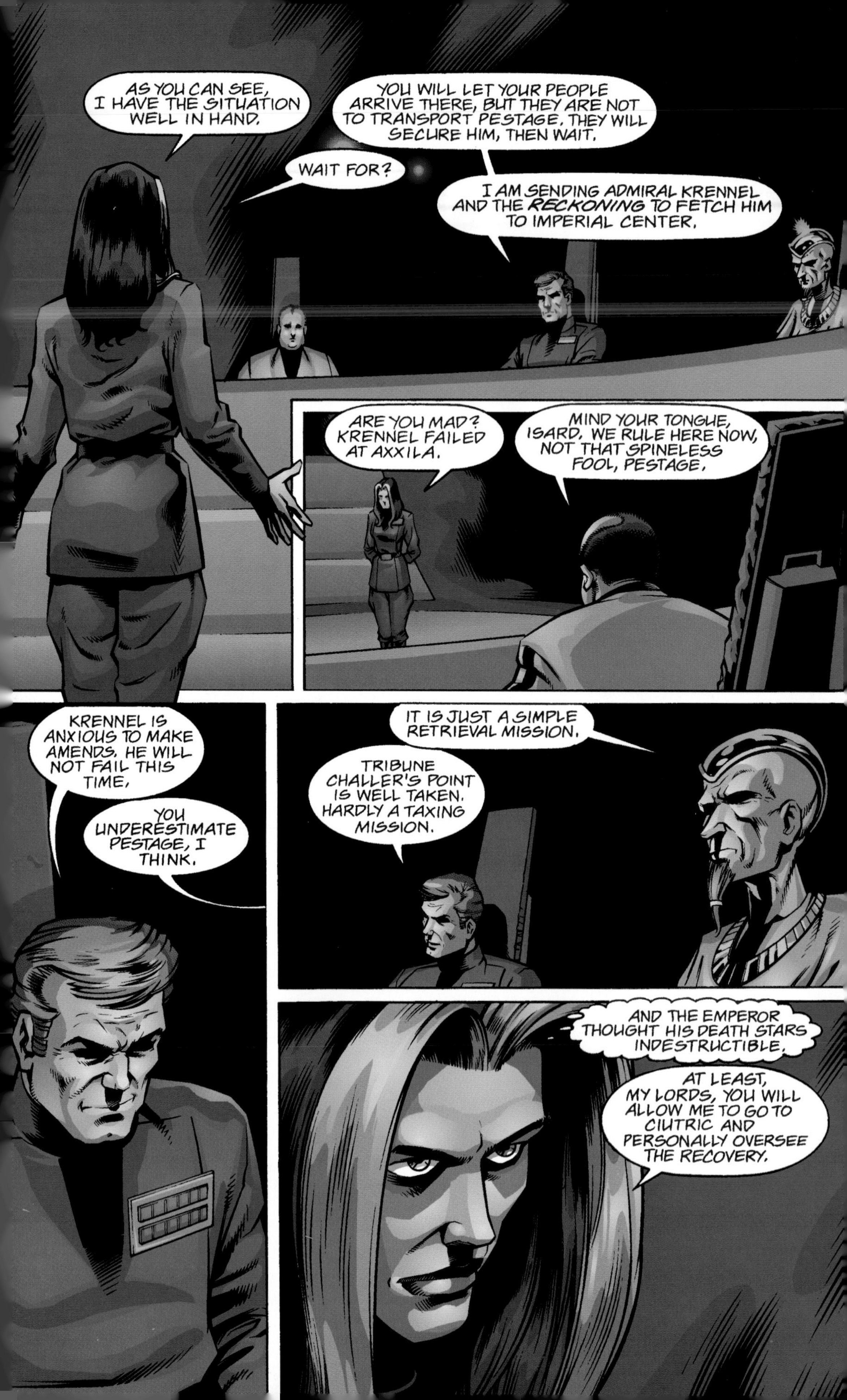
AS YOU CAN SEE, I HAVE THE SITUATION WELL IN HAND.
YOU WILL LET YOUR PEOPLE ARRIVE THERE, BUT THEY ARE NOT TO TRANSPORT PESTAGE. THEY WILL SECURE HIM, THEN WAIT.
WAIT FOR?
I AM SENDING ADMIRAL KRENNEL AND THE *RECKONING* TO FETCH HIM TO IMPERIAL CENTER.
ARE YOU MAD? KRENNEL FAILED AT AXXILA.
MIND YOUR TONGUE, ISARD. WE RULE HERE NOW, NOT THAT SPINELESS FOOL, PESTAGE.
KRENNEL IS ANXIOUS TO MAKE AMENDS. HE WILL NOT FAIL THIS TIME.
YOU UNDERESTIMATE PESTAGE, I THINK.
IT IS JUST A SIMPLE RETRIEVAL MISSION.
TRIBUNE CHALLER'S POINT IS WELL TAKEN. HARDLY A TAXING MISSION.
AND THE EMPEROR THOUGHT HIS DEATH STARS INDESTRUCTIBLE.
AT LEAST, MY LORDS, YOU WILL ALLOW ME TO GO TO CIUTRIC AND PERSONALLY OVERSEE THE RECOVERY.

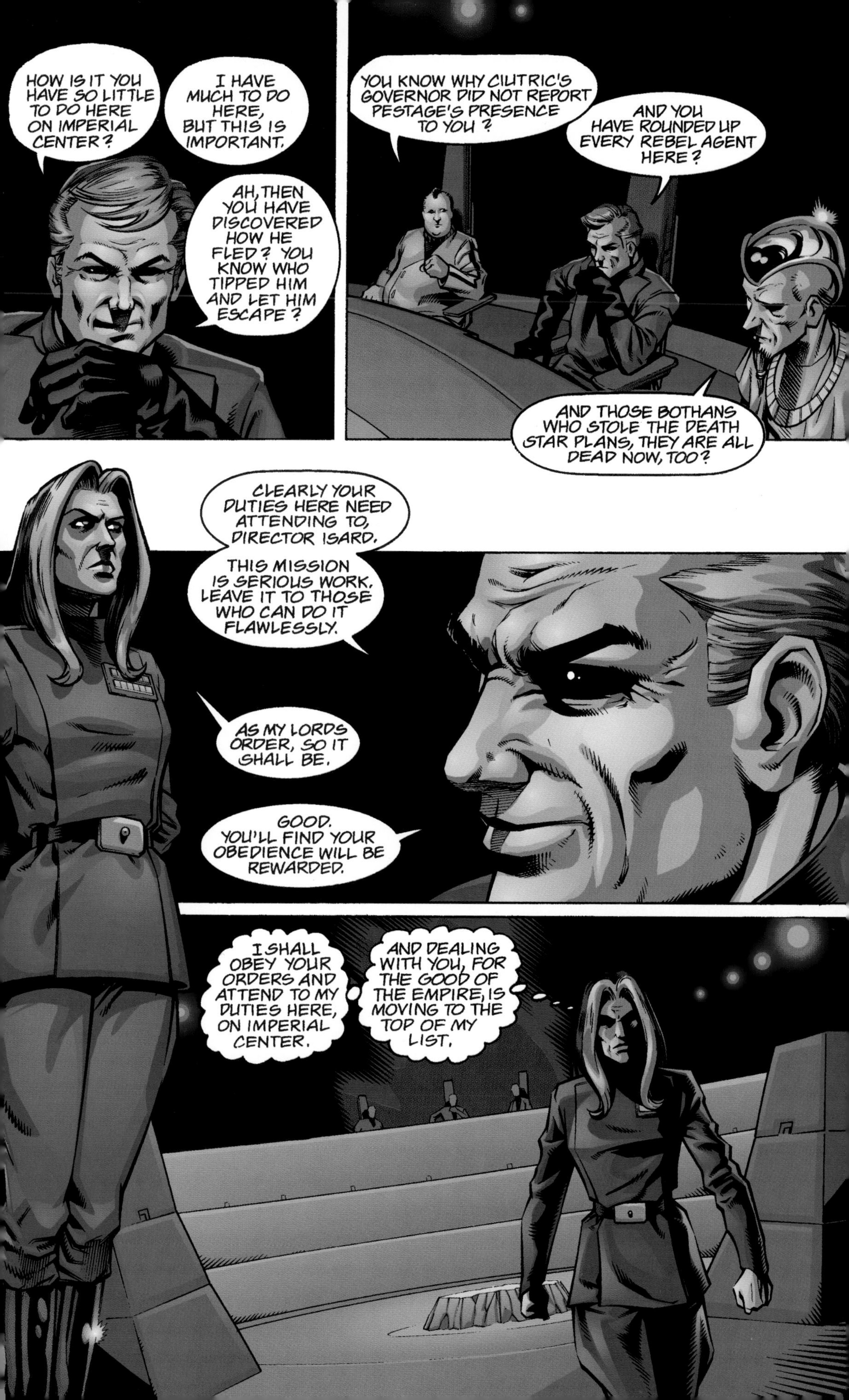
HOW IS IT YOU HAVE SO LITTLE TO DO HERE ON IMPERIAL CENTER?
I HAVE MUCH TO DO HERE, BUT THIS IS IMPORTANT.
AH, THEN YOU HAVE DISCOVERED HOW HE FLED? YOU KNOW WHO TIPPED HIM AND LET HIM ESCAPE?
YOU KNOW WHY CIUTRIC'S GOVERNOR DID NOT REPORT PESTAGE'S PRESENCE TO YOU?
AND YOU HAVE ROUNDED UP EVERY REBEL AGENT HERE?
AND THOSE BOTHANS WHO STOLE THE DEATH STAR PLANS, THEY ARE ALL DEAD NOW, TOO?
CLEARLY YOUR DUTIES HERE NEED ATTENDING TO, DIRECTOR ISARD.
THIS MISSION IS SERIOUS WORK. LEAVE IT TO THOSE WHO CAN DO IT FLAWLESSLY.
AS MY LORDS ORDER, SO IT SHALL BE.
GOOD. YOU'LL FIND YOUR OBEDIENCE WILL BE REWARDED.
I SHALL OBEY YOUR ORDERS AND ATTEND TO MY DUTIES HERE, ON IMPERIAL CENTER.
AND DEALING WITH YOU, FOR THE GOOD OF THE EMPIRE, IS MOVING TO THE TOP OF MY LIST.

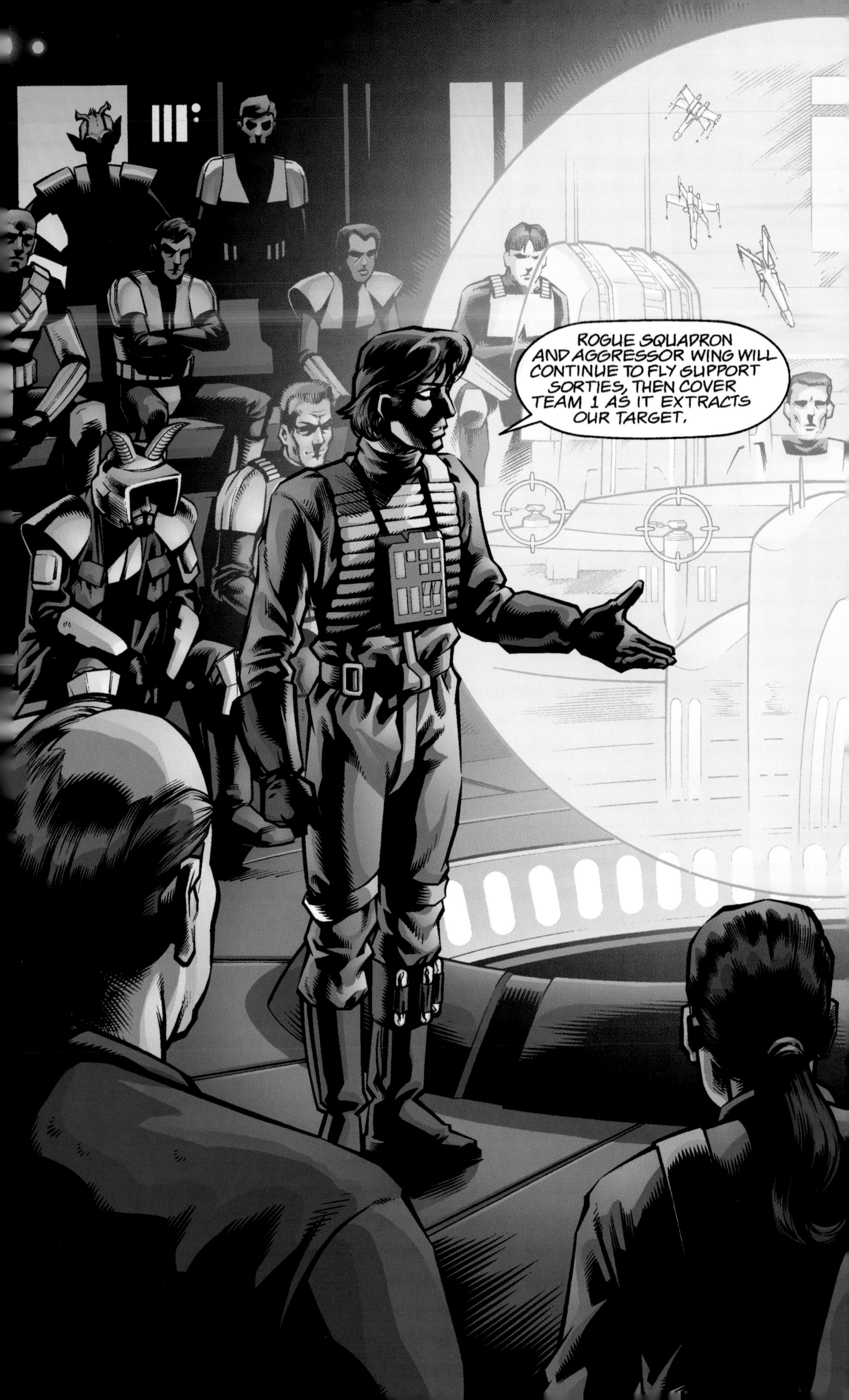
ROGUE SQUADRON AND AGGRESSOR WING WILL CONTINUE TO FLY SUPPORT SORTIES, THEN COVER TEAM 1 AS IT EXTRACTS OUR TARGET.

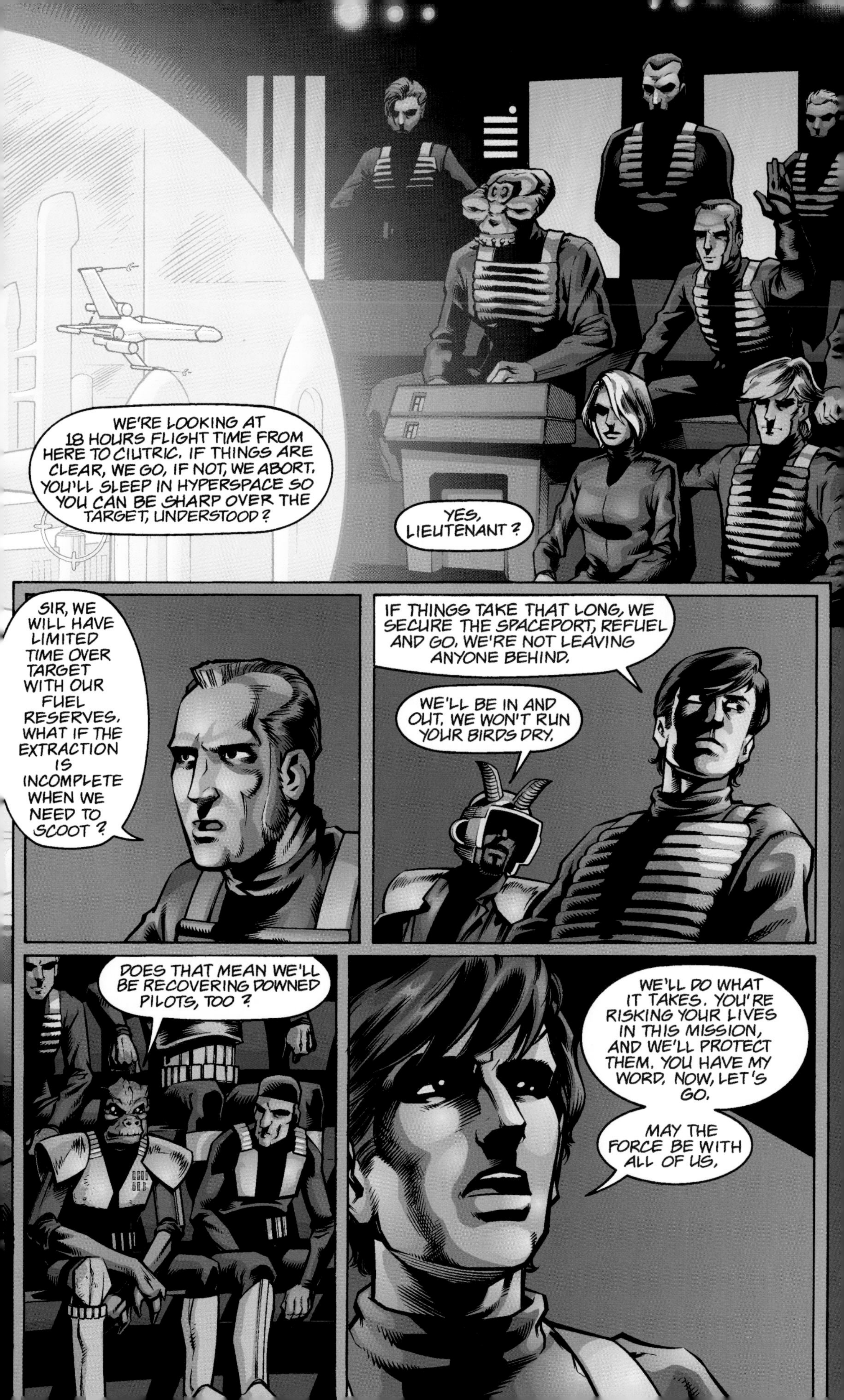
WE'RE LOOKING AT 18 HOURS FLIGHT TIME FROM HERE TO CIUTRIC. IF THINGS ARE CLEAR, WE GO, IF NOT, WE ABORT. YOU'LL SLEEP IN HYPERSPACE SO YOU CAN BE SHARP OVER THE TARGET, UNDERSTOOD?
YES, LIEUTENANT?
SIR, WE WILL HAVE LIMITED TIME OVER TARGET WITH OUR FUEL RESERVES, WHAT IF THE EXTRACTION IS INCOMPLETE WHEN WE NEED TO SCOOT?
IF THINGS TAKE THAT LONG, WE SECURE THE SPACEPORT, REFUEL AND GO, WE'RE NOT LEAVING ANYONE BEHIND.
WE'LL BE IN AND OUT, WE WON'T RUN YOUR BIRDS DRY.
DOES THAT MEAN WE'LL BE RECOVERING DOWNED PILOTS, TOO?
WE'LL DO WHAT IT TAKES. YOU'RE RISKING YOUR LIVES IN THIS MISSION, AND WE'LL PROTECT THEM. YOU HAVE MY WORD. NOW, LET'S GO.
MAY THE FORCE BE WITH ALL OF US.

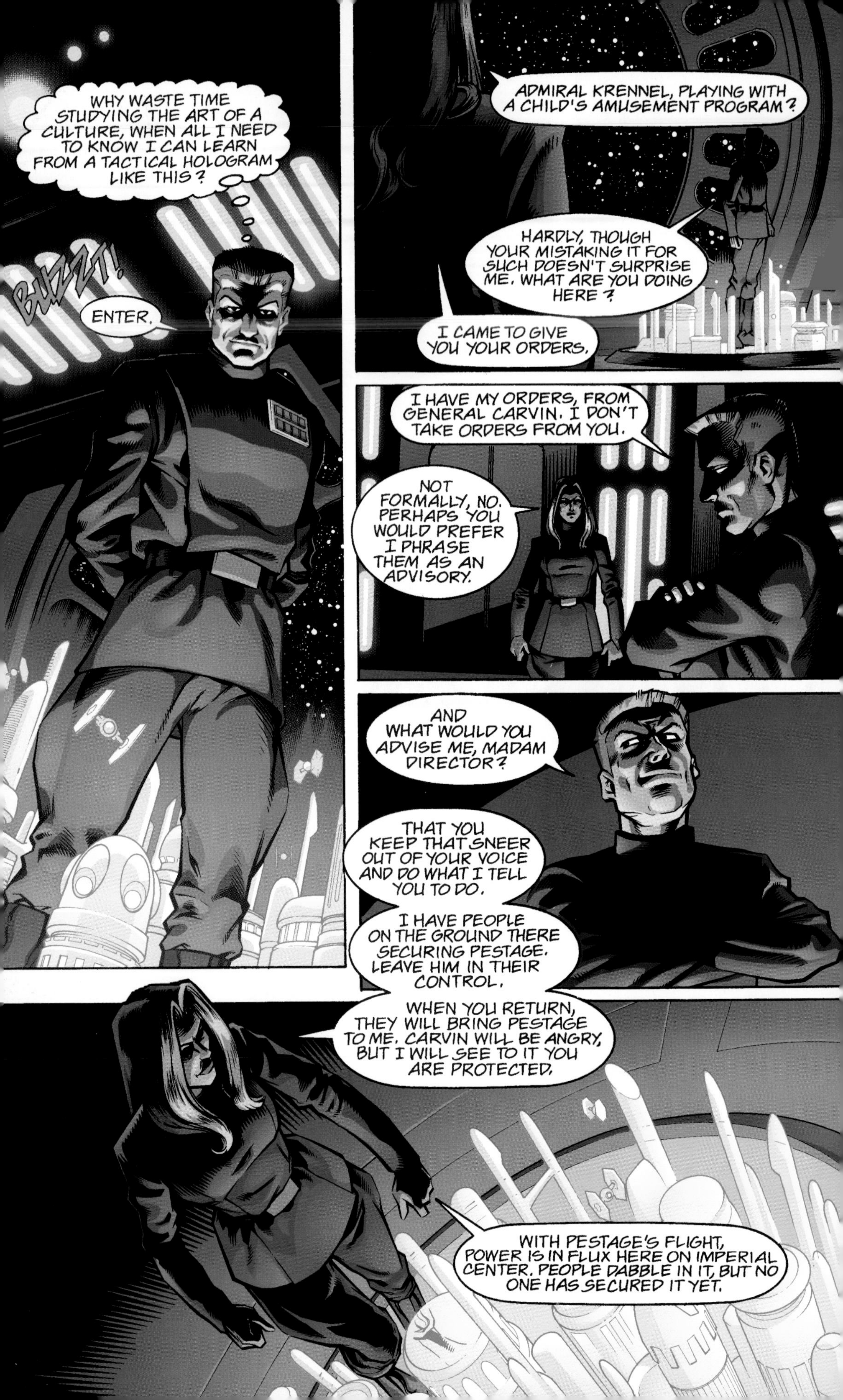
WHY WASTE TIME STUDYING THE ART OF A CULTURE, WHEN ALL I NEED TO KNOW I CAN LEARN FROM A TACTICAL HOLOGRAM LIKE THIS?
BUZZT!
ENTER.
ADMIRAL KRENNEL, PLAYING WITH A CHILD'S AMUSEMENT PROGRAM?
HARDLY, THOUGH YOUR MISTAKING IT FOR SUCH DOESN'T SURPRISE ME. WHAT ARE YOU DOING HERE?
I CAME TO GIVE YOU YOUR ORDERS.
I HAVE MY ORDERS, FROM GENERAL CARVIN. I DON'T TAKE ORDERS FROM YOU.
NOT FORMALLY, NO. PERHAPS YOU WOULD PREFER I PHRASE THEM AS AN ADVISORY.
AND WHAT WOULD YOU ADVISE ME, MADAM DIRECTOR?
THAT YOU KEEP THAT SNEER OUT OF YOUR VOICE AND DO WHAT I TELL YOU TO DO.
I HAVE PEOPLE ON THE GROUND THERE SECURING PESTAGE. LEAVE HIM IN THEIR CONTROL.
WHEN YOU RETURN, THEY WILL BRING PESTAGE TO ME. CARVIN WILL BE ANGRY, BUT I WILL SEE TO IT YOU ARE PROTECTED.
WITH PESTAGE'S FLIGHT, POWER IS IN FLUX HERE ON IMPERIAL CENTER. PEOPLE DABBLE IN IT, BUT NO ONE HAS SECURED IT YET.

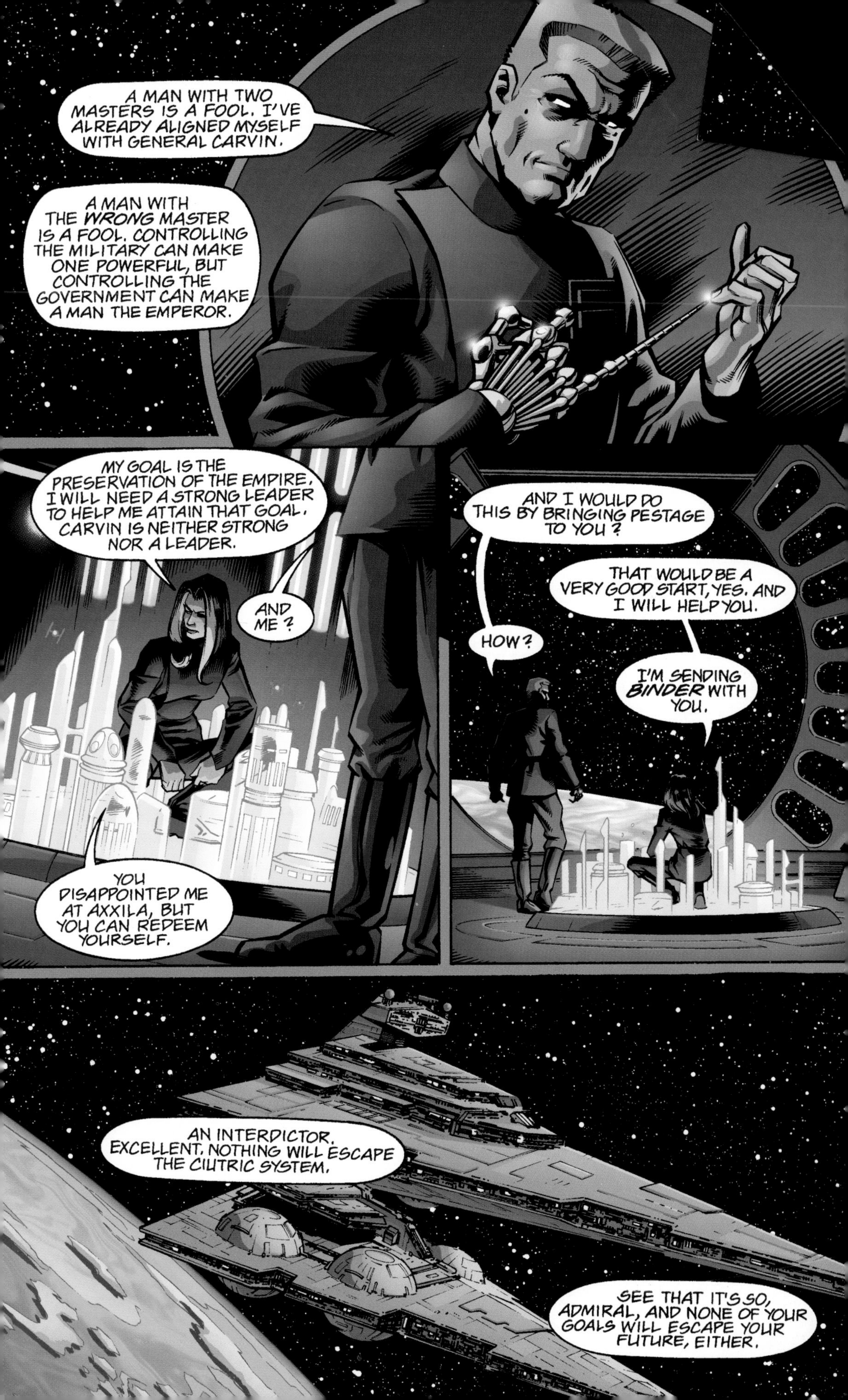
A MAN WITH TWO MASTERS IS A FOOL. I'VE ALREADY ALIGNED MYSELF WITH GENERAL CARVIN.
A MAN WITH THE *WRONG* MASTER IS A FOOL. CONTROLLING THE MILITARY CAN MAKE ONE POWERFUL, BUT CONTROLLING THE GOVERNMENT CAN MAKE A MAN THE EMPEROR.
MY GOAL IS THE PRESERVATION OF THE EMPIRE. I WILL NEED A STRONG LEADER TO HELP ME ATTAIN THAT GOAL. CARVIN IS NEITHER STRONG NOR A LEADER.
AND ME?
YOU DISAPPOINTED ME AT AXXILA, BUT YOU CAN REDEEM YOURSELF.
AND I WOULD DO THIS BY BRINGING PESTAGE TO YOU?
THAT WOULD BE A VERY GOOD START, YES. AND I WILL HELP YOU.
HOW?
I'M SENDING *BINDER* WITH YOU.
AN INTERDICTOR. EXCELLENT. NOTHING WILL ESCAPE THE CIUTRIC SYSTEM.
SEE THAT IT'S SO, ADMIRAL, AND NONE OF YOUR GOALS WILL ESCAPE YOUR FUTURE, EITHER.

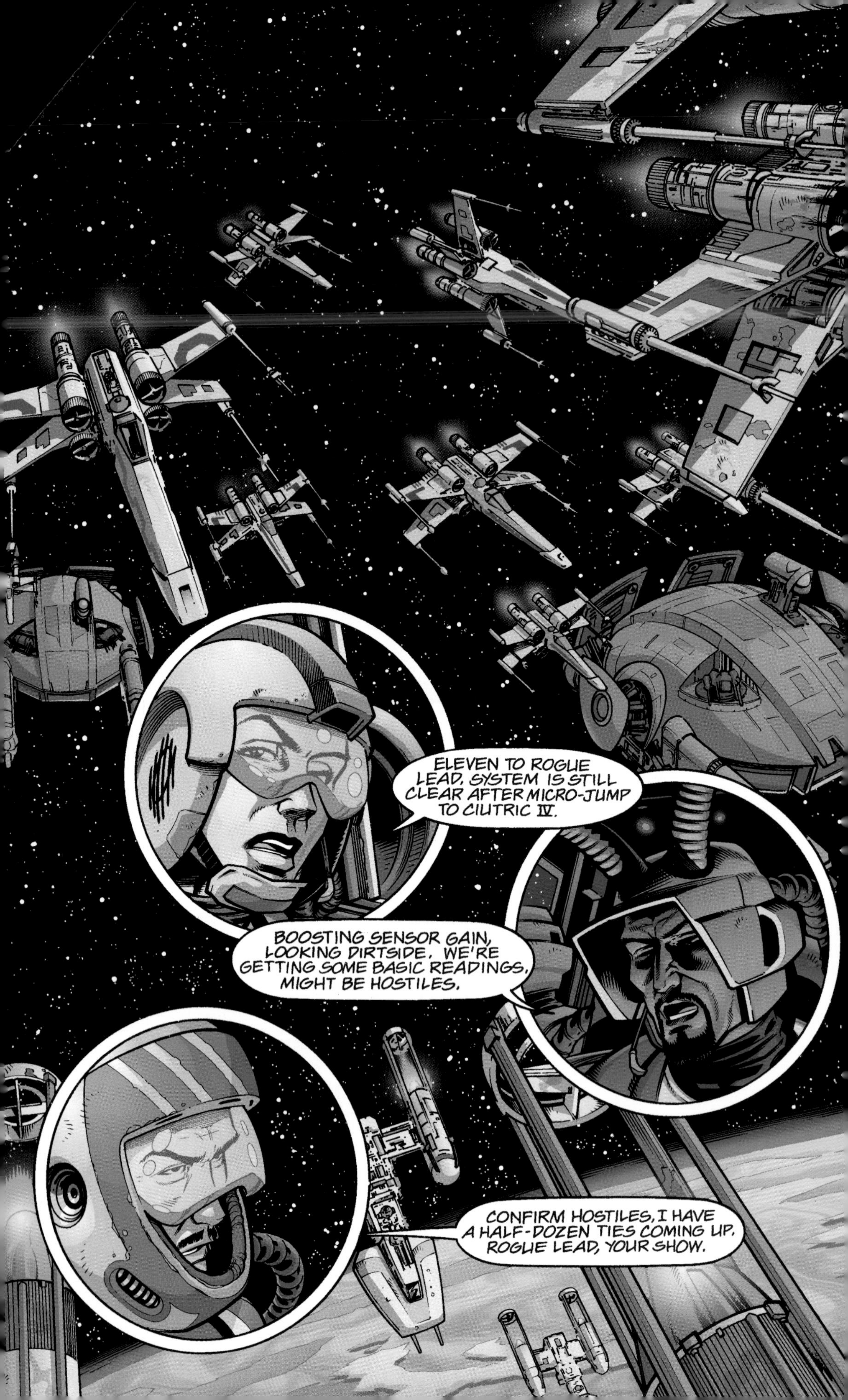
ELEVEN TO ROGUE LEAD, SYSTEM IS STILL CLEAR AFTER MICRO-JUMP TO CIUTRIC IV.
BOOSTING SENSOR GAIN, LOOKING DIRTSIDE. WE'RE GETTING SOME BASIC READINGS, MIGHT BE HOSTILES.
CONFIRM HOSTILES, I HAVE A HALF-DOZEN TIES COMING UP, ROGUE LEAD, YOUR SHOW.

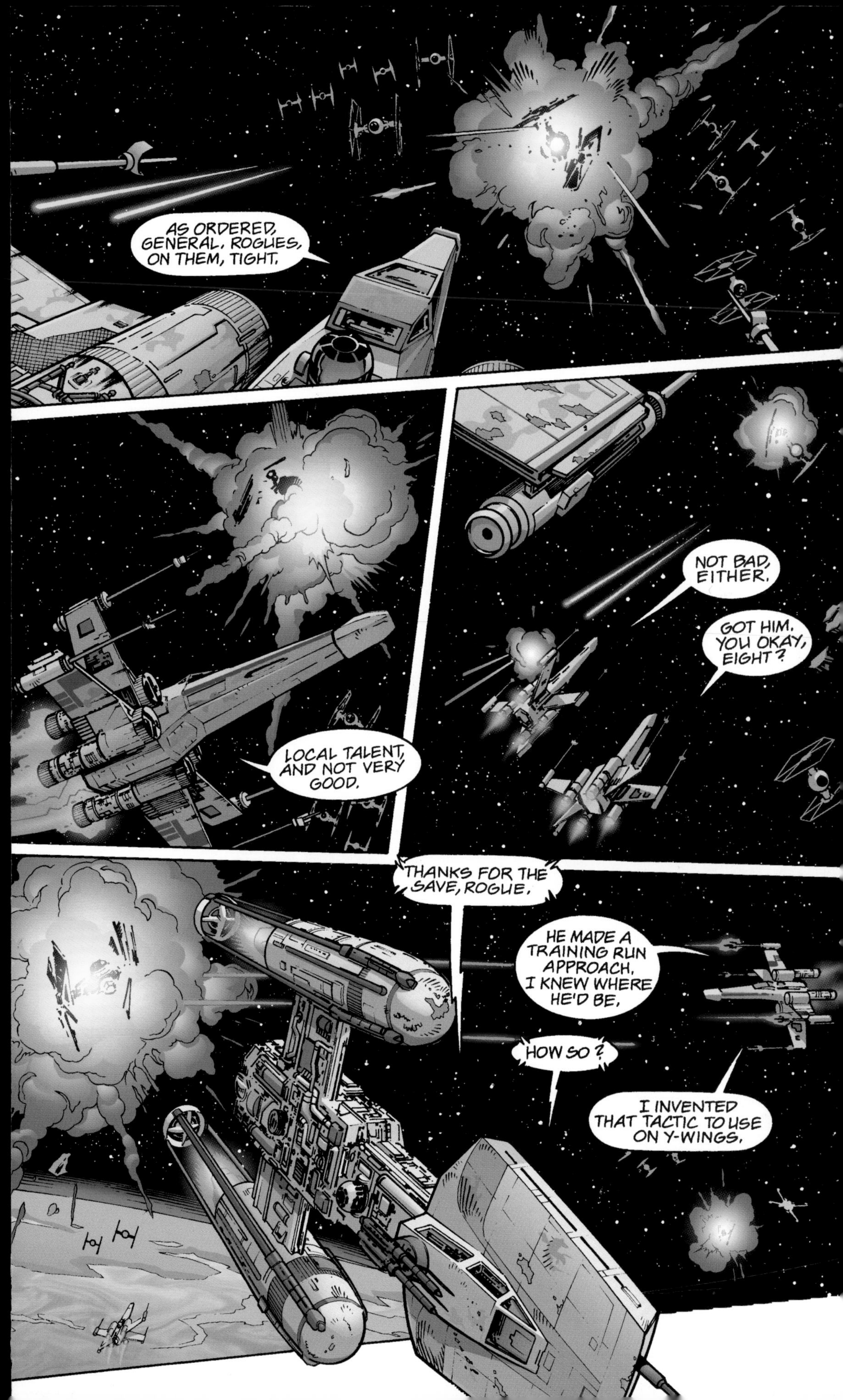
AS ORDERED, GENERAL, ROGUES, ON THEM, TIGHT.
LOCAL TALENT, AND NOT VERY GOOD.
NOT BAD, EITHER.
GOT HIM. YOU OKAY, EIGHT?
THANKS FOR THE SAVE, ROGUE.
HE MADE A TRAINING RUN APPROACH, I KNEW WHERE HE'D BE.
HOW SO?
I INVENTED THAT TACTIC TO USE ON Y-WINGS.

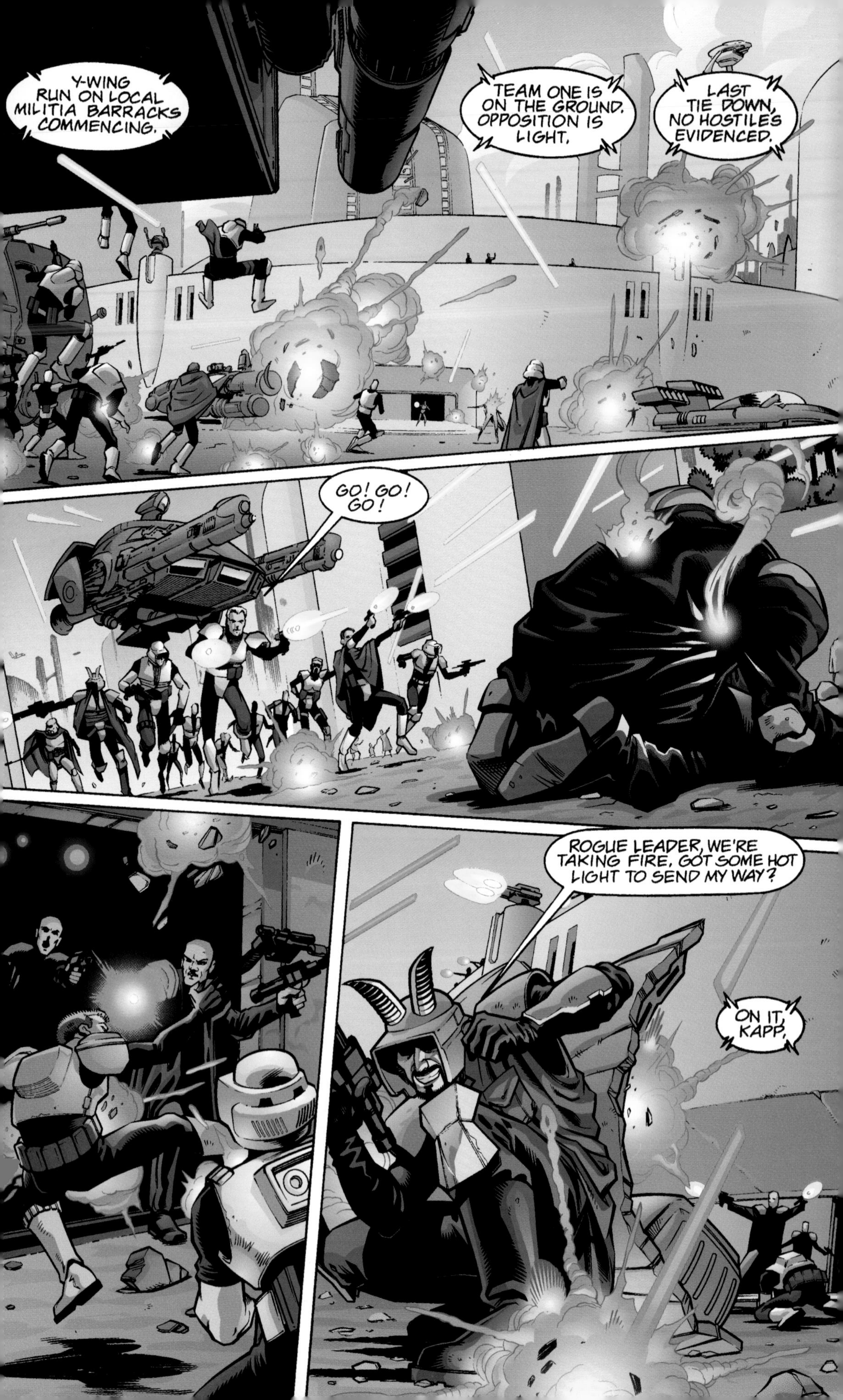
Y-WING RUN ON LOCAL MILITIA BARRACKS COMMENCING.
TEAM ONE IS ON THE GROUND. OPPOSITION IS LIGHT.
LAST TIE DOWN, NO HOSTILES EVIDENCED.
GO! GO! GO!
ROGUE LEADER, WE'RE TAKING FIRE, GOT SOME HOT LIGHT TO SEND MY WAY?
ON IT, KAPP.

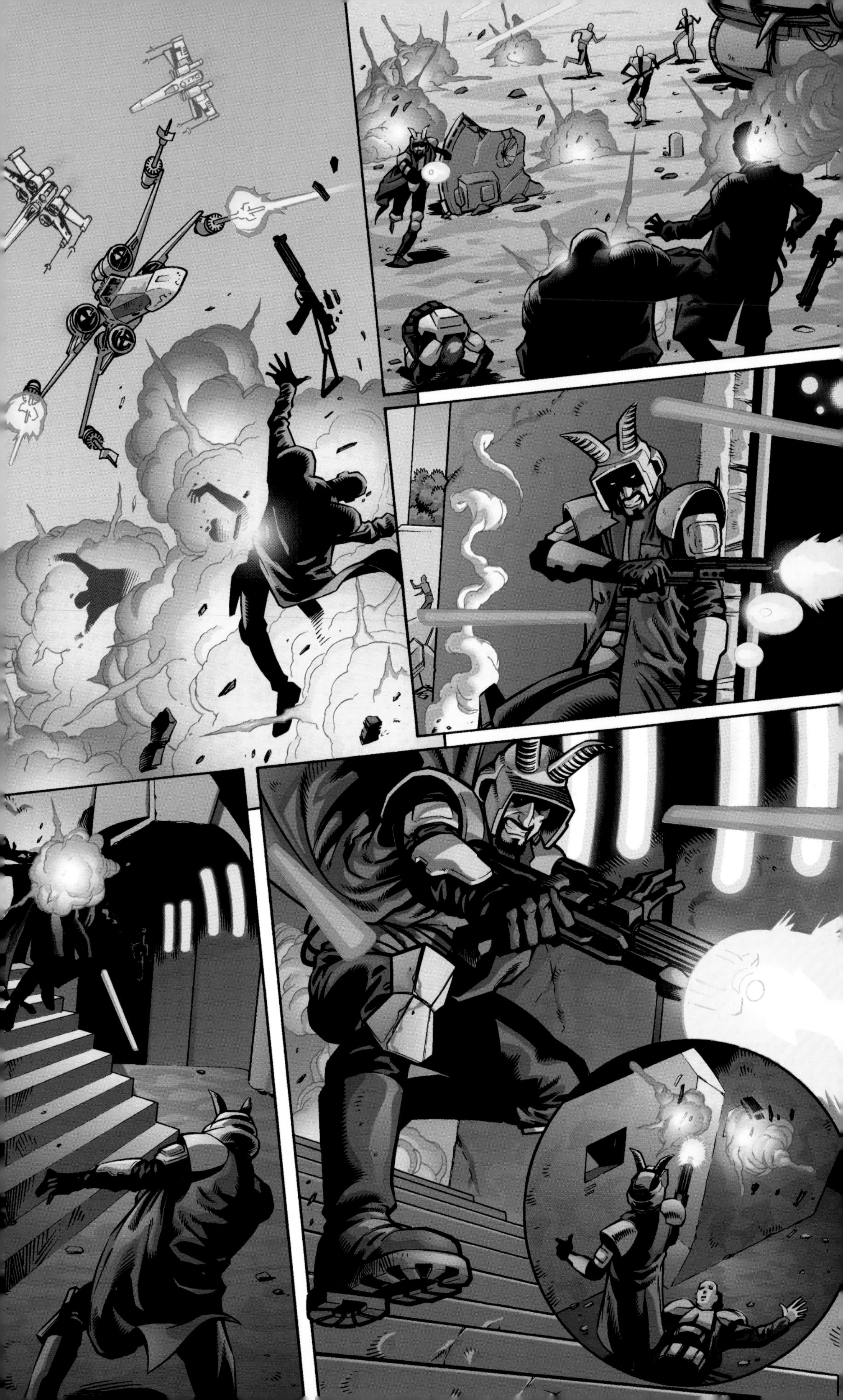

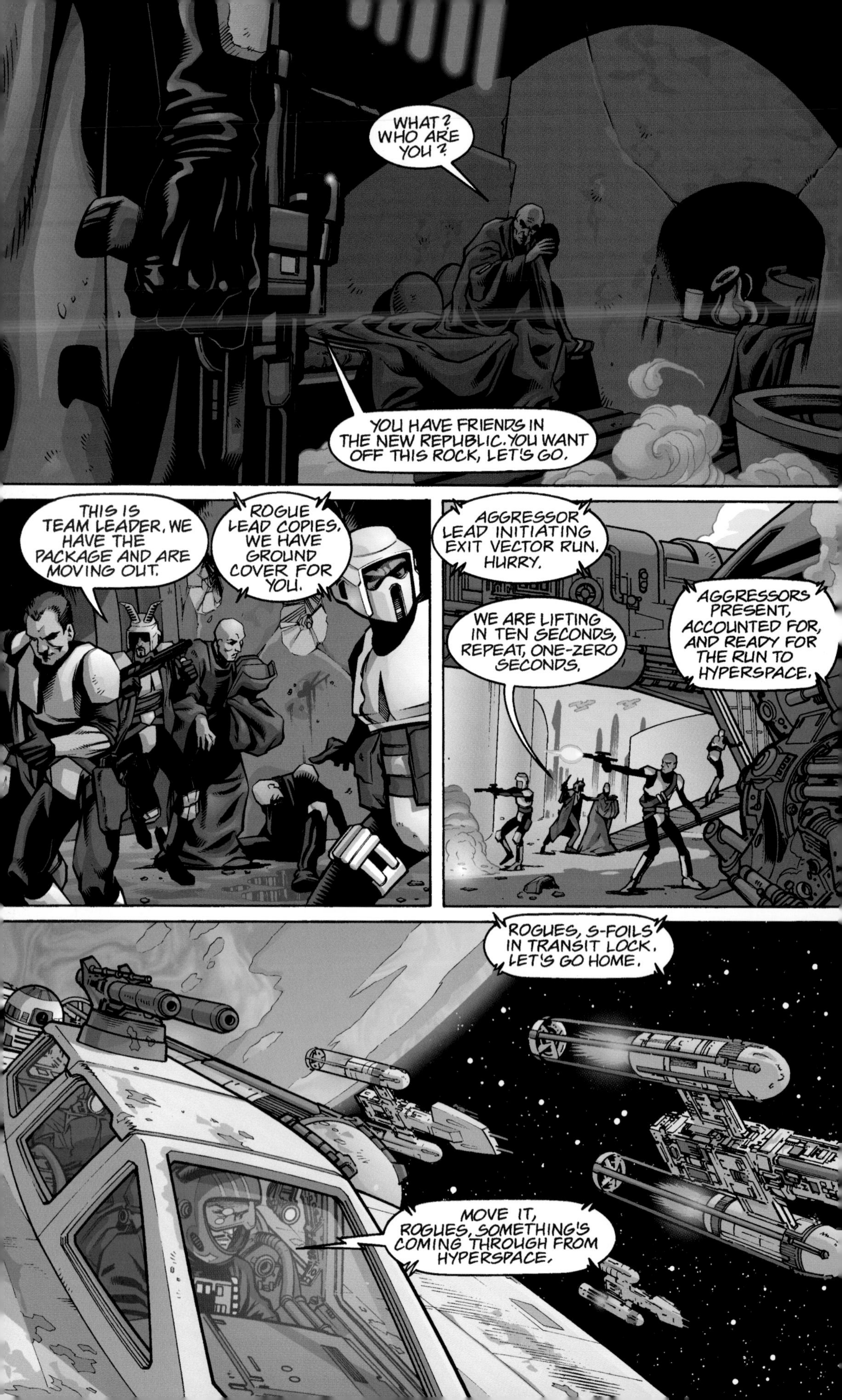
WHAT? WHO ARE YOU?
YOU HAVE FRIENDS IN THE NEW REPUBLIC. YOU WANT OFF THIS ROCK, LET'S GO.
THIS IS TEAM LEADER, WE HAVE THE PACKAGE AND ARE MOVING OUT.
ROGUE LEAD COPIES. WE HAVE GROUND COVER FOR YOU.
AGGRESSOR LEAD INITIATING EXIT VECTOR RUN. HURRY.
WE ARE LIFTING IN TEN SECONDS, REPEAT, ONE-ZERO SECONDS.
AGGRESSORS PRESENT, ACCOUNTED FOR, AND READY FOR THE RUN TO HYPERSPACE.
ROGUES, S-FOILS IN TRANSIT LOCK. LET'S GO HOME.
MOVE IT, ROGUES, SOMETHING'S COMING THROUGH FROM HYPERSPACE.

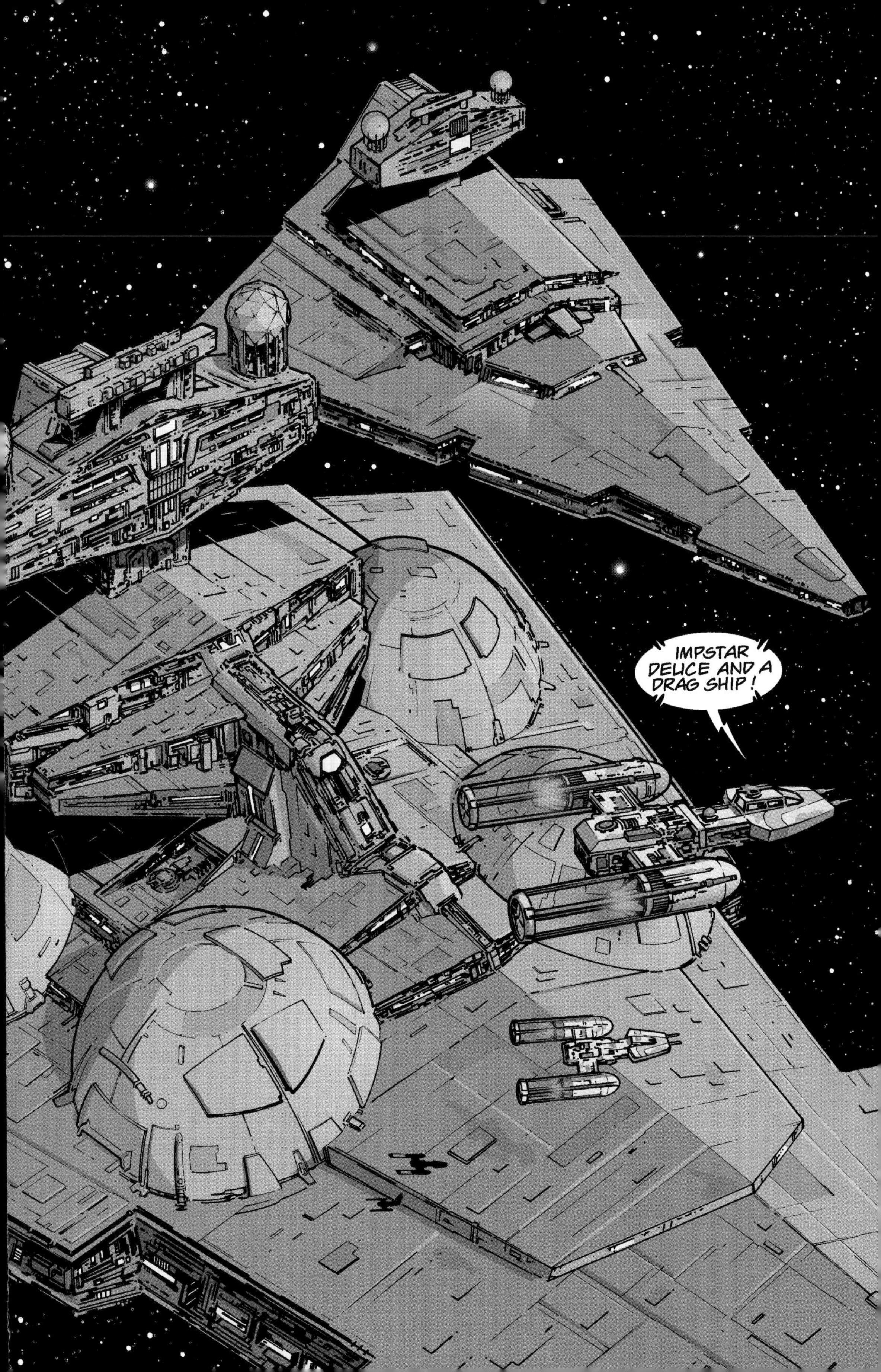
IMPSTAR DEUCE AND A DRAG SHIP!

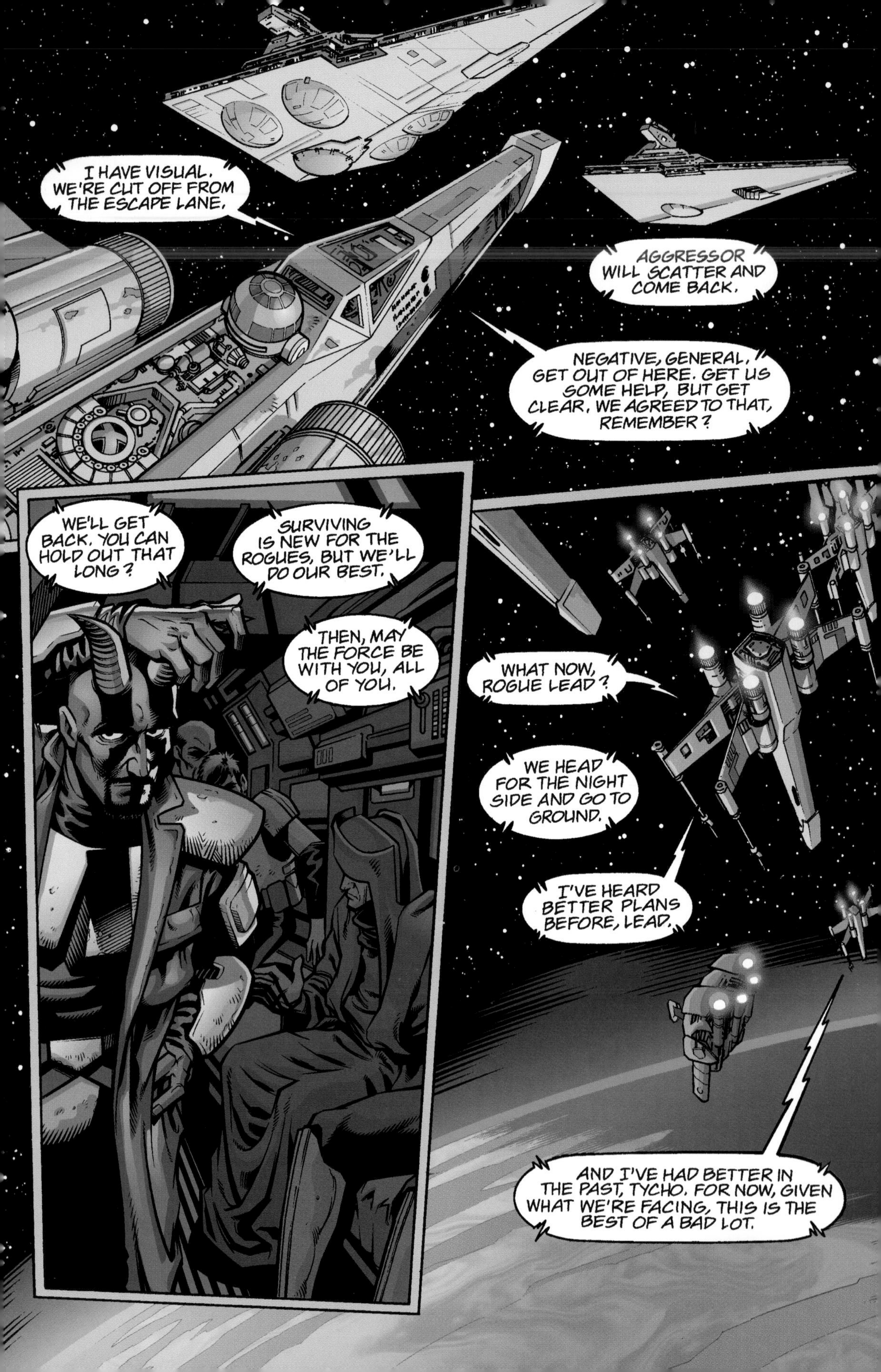
I HAVE VISUAL. WE'RE CUT OFF FROM THE ESCAPE LANE.
AGGRESSOR WILL SCATTER AND COME BACK.
NEGATIVE, GENERAL. GET OUT OF HERE. GET US SOME HELP, BUT GET CLEAR. WE AGREED TO THAT, REMEMBER?
WE'LL GET BACK. YOU CAN HOLD OUT THAT LONG?
SURVIVING IS NEW FOR THE ROGUES, BUT WE'LL DO OUR BEST.
THEN, MAY THE FORCE BE WITH YOU, ALL OF YOU.
WHAT NOW, ROGUE LEAD?
WE HEAD FOR THE NIGHT SIDE AND GO TO GROUND.
I'VE HEARD BETTER PLANS BEFORE, LEAD.
AND I'VE HAD BETTER IN THE PAST, TYCHO. FOR NOW, GIVEN WHAT WE'RE FACING, THIS IS THE BEST OF A BAD LOT.

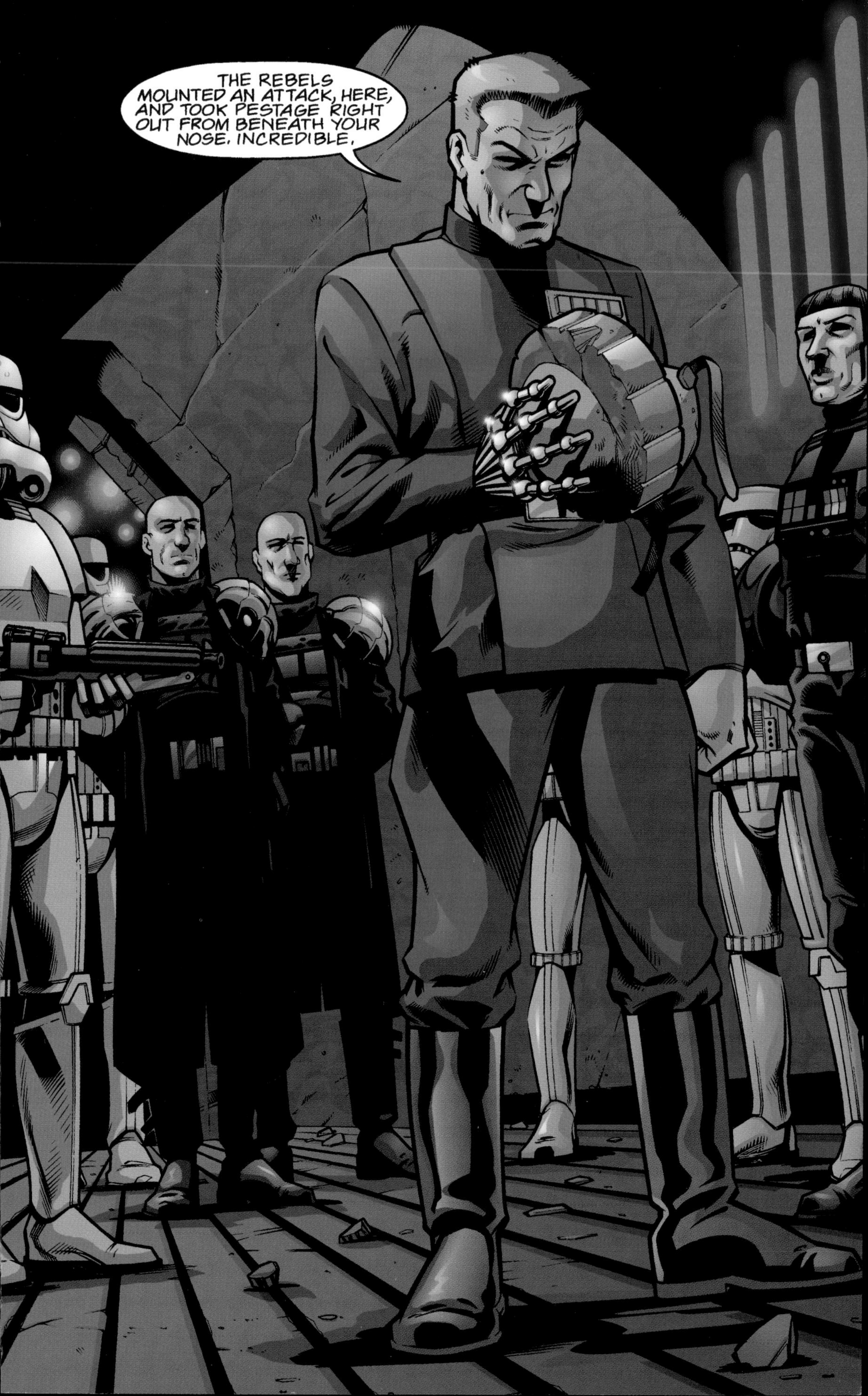
THE REBELS MOUNTED AN ATTACK, HERE, AND TOOK PESTAGE RIGHT OUT FROM BENEATH YOUR NOSE. INCREDIBLE.

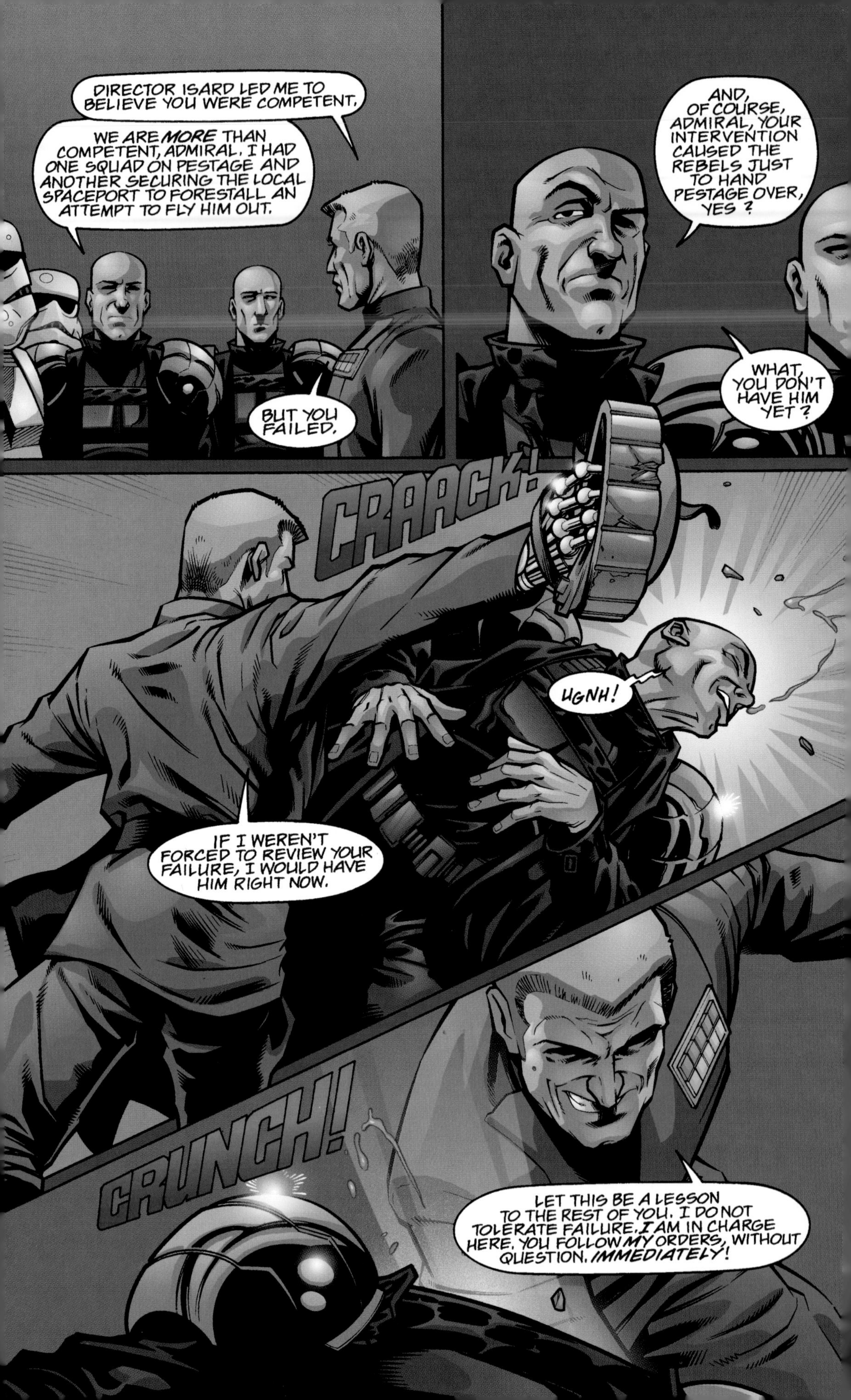
DIRECTOR ISARD LED ME TO BELIEVE YOU WERE COMPETENT.
WE ARE MORE THAN COMPETENT, ADMIRAL. I HAD ONE SQUAD ON PESTAGE AND ANOTHER SECURING THE LOCAL SPACEPORT TO FORESTALL AN ATTEMPT TO FLY HIM OUT.
BUT YOU FAILED.
AND, OF COURSE, ADMIRAL, YOUR INTERVENTION CAUSED THE REBELS JUST TO HAND PESTAGE OVER, YES ?
WHAT, YOU DON'T HAVE HIM YET ?
CRAACK!
UGNH!
IF I WEREN'T FORCED TO REVIEW YOUR FAILURE, I WOULD HAVE HIM RIGHT NOW.
CRUNCH!
LET THIS BE A LESSON TO THE REST OF YOU. I DO NOT TOLERATE FAILURE. I AM IN CHARGE HERE. YOU FOLLOW MY ORDERS, WITHOUT QUESTION. IMMEDIATELY!

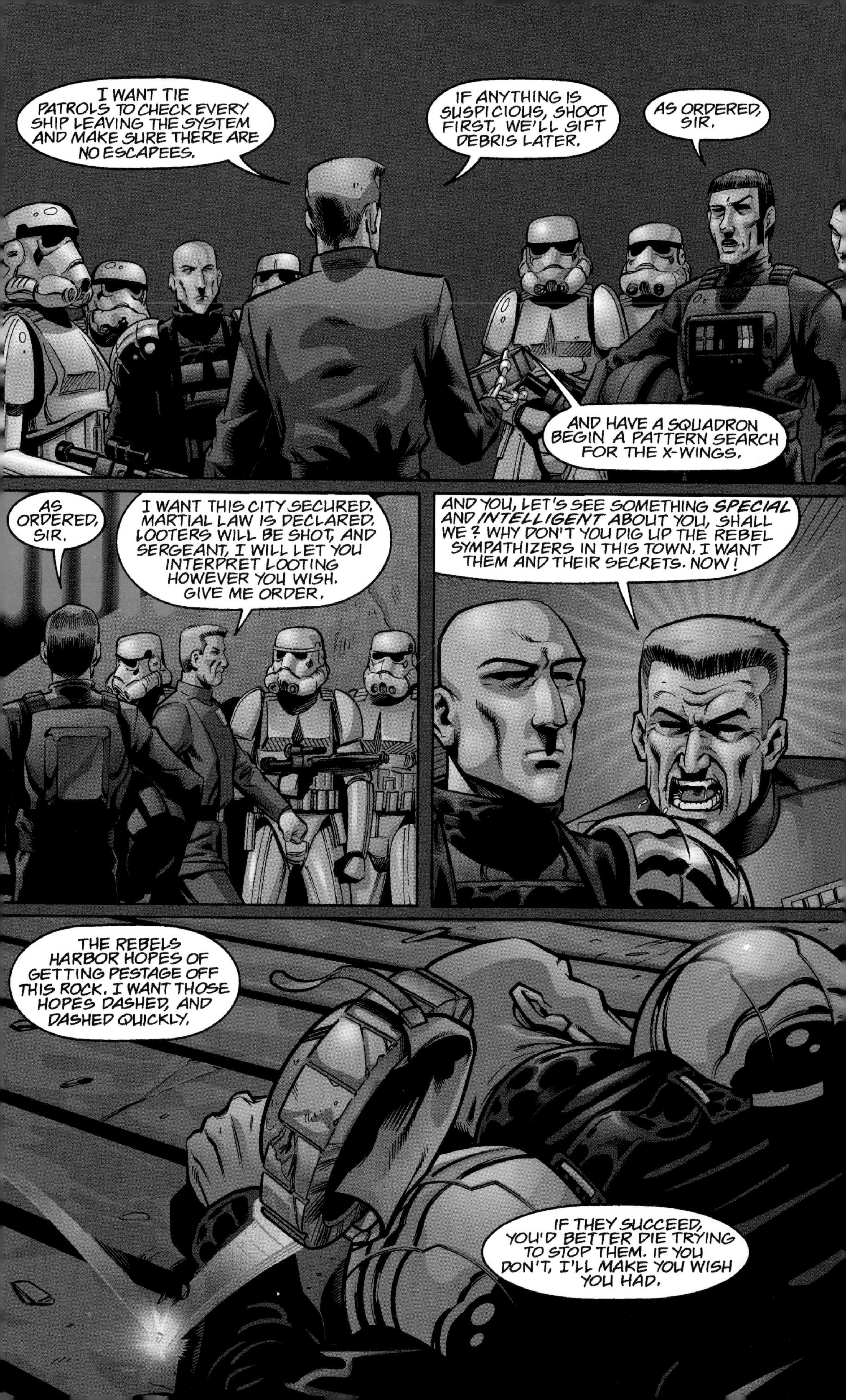

I WANT TIE PATROLS TO CHECK EVERY SHIP LEAVING THE SYSTEM AND MAKE SURE THERE ARE NO ESCAPEES.
IF ANYTHING IS SUSPICIOUS, SHOOT FIRST, WE'LL SIFT DEBRIS LATER.
AS ORDERED, SIR.
AND HAVE A SQUADRON BEGIN A PATTERN SEARCH FOR THE X-WINGS.
AS ORDERED, SIR.
I WANT THIS CITY SECURED. MARTIAL LAW IS DECLARED. LOOTERS WILL BE SHOT, AND SERGEANT, I WILL LET YOU INTERPRET LOOTING HOWEVER YOU WISH. GIVE ME ORDER.
AND YOU, LET'S SEE SOMETHING SPECIAL AND INTELLIGENT ABOUT YOU, SHALL WE? WHY DON'T YOU DIG UP THE REBEL SYMPATHIZERS IN THIS TOWN. I WANT THEM AND THEIR SECRETS. NOW!
THE REBELS HARBOR HOPES OF GETTING PESTAGE OFF THIS ROCK. I WANT THOSE HOPES DASHED, AND DASHED QUICKLY.
IF THEY SUCCEED, YOU'D BETTER DIE TRYING TO STOP THEM. IF YOU DON'T, I'LL MAKE YOU WISH YOU HAD.

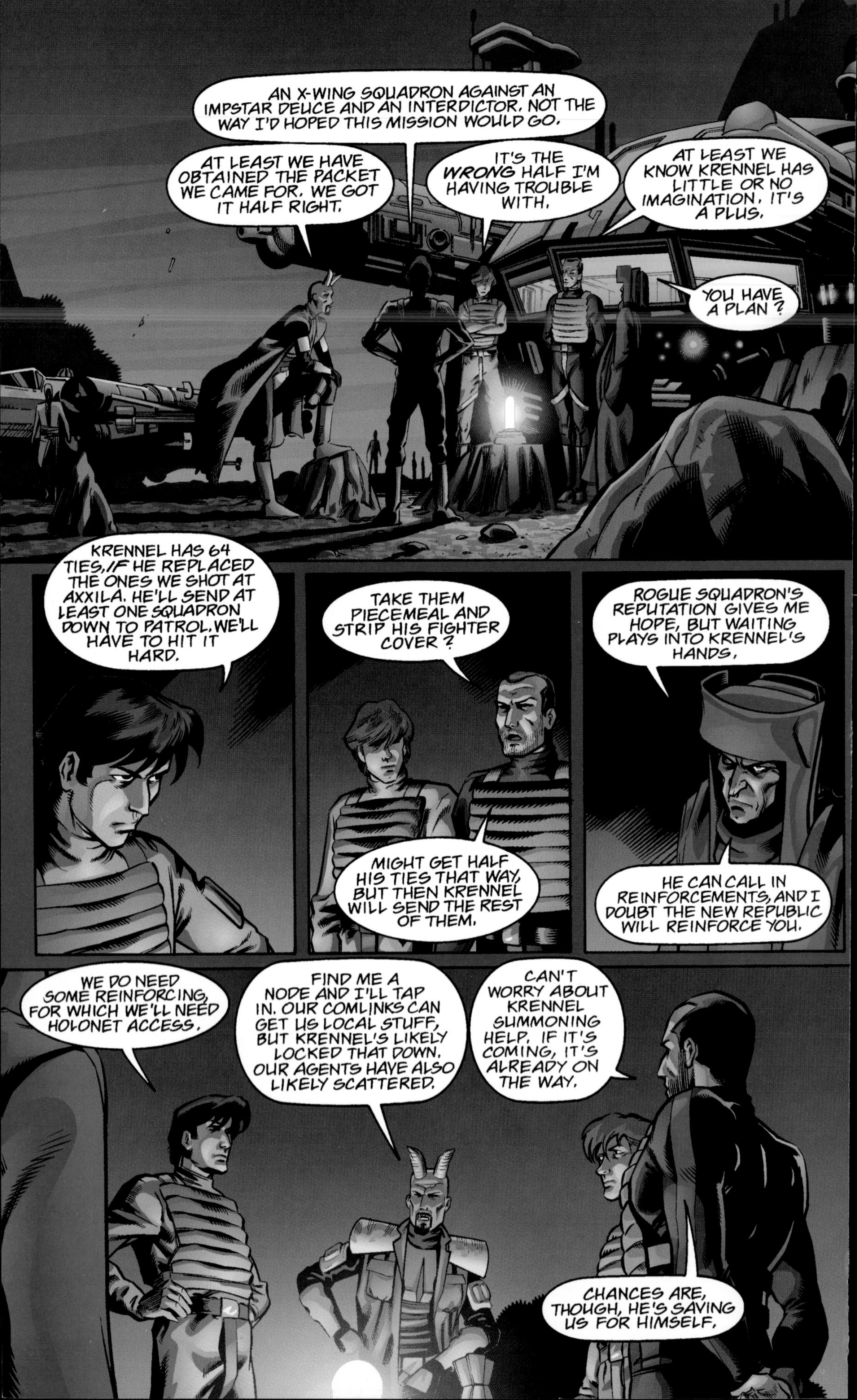
AN X-WING SQUADRON AGAINST AN IMPSTAR DEUCE AND AN INTERDICTOR. NOT THE WAY I'D HOPED THIS MISSION WOULD GO.
AT LEAST WE HAVE OBTAINED THE PACKET WE CAME FOR. WE GOT IT HALF RIGHT.
IT'S THE WRONG HALF I'M HAVING TROUBLE WITH.
AT LEAST WE KNOW KRENNEL HAS LITTLE OR NO IMAGINATION. IT'S A PLUS.
YOU HAVE A PLAN?
KRENNEL HAS 64 TIES, IF HE REPLACED THE ONES WE SHOT AT AXXILA. HE'LL SEND AT LEAST ONE SQUADRON DOWN TO PATROL. WE'LL HAVE TO HIT IT HARD.
TAKE THEM PIECEMEAL AND STRIP HIS FIGHTER COVER?
MIGHT GET HALF HIS TIES THAT WAY, BUT THEN KRENNEL WILL SEND THE REST OF THEM.
ROGUE SQUADRON'S REPUTATION GIVES ME HOPE, BUT WAITING PLAYS INTO KRENNEL'S HANDS.
HE CAN CALL IN REINFORCEMENTS, AND I DOUBT THE NEW REPUBLIC WILL REINFORCE YOU.
WE DO NEED SOME REINFORCING, FOR WHICH WE'LL NEED HOLONET ACCESS.
FIND ME A NODE AND I'LL TAP IN. OUR COMLINKS CAN GET US LOCAL STUFF, BUT KRENNEL'S LIKELY LOCKED THAT DOWN. OUR AGENTS HAVE ALSO LIKELY SCATTERED.
CAN'T WORRY ABOUT KRENNEL SUMMONING HELP. IF IT'S COMING, IT'S ALREADY ON THE WAY.
CHANCES ARE, THOUGH, HE'S SAVING US FOR HIMSELF.

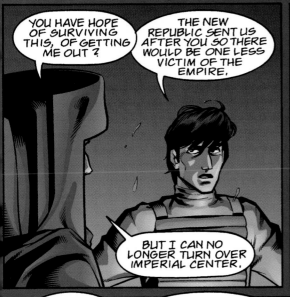

YOU HAVE HOPE OF SURVIVING THIS, OF GETTING ME OUT?

THE NEW REPUBLIC SENT US AFTER YOU SO THERE WOULD BE ONE LESS VICTIM OF THE EMPIRE.

BUT I CAN NO LONGER TURN OVER IMPERIAL CENTER.

THAT'S WHAT YOU IMPS ALWAYS MISSED. THE REBELLION WASN'T ABOUT PLANETS, IT WAS ABOUT PEOPLE...

...IT WASN'T ABOUT POWER, BUT ABOUT FREEDOM. PEOPLE WILL DO A LOT TO WIN FREEDOM, FOR THEMSELVES AND FOR THOSE THEY HOLD DEAR.

I DOUBT MANY OF YOUR CONFEDERATES WOULD HOLD ME DEAR.

YOU'RE ON THE RUN FROM THE EMPIRE. YOU'RE ONE OF US WHETHER YOU LIKE IT OR NOT.

BACK TO THE KEY POINT HERE, GUYS. WE VAPE TIES, THEN TAKE OUR PROTON TORPS TO THE DRAG-SHIP. ONCE IT'S DOWN, THE SHUTTLES RUN AND WE'LL FOLLOW.

THAT'S THE PLAN, RIGHT?

IT'S OUR WORKING PLAN FOR THE MOMENT, ANYWAY. HAVE PILOTS STANDING BY FOR DEALING WITH ANY TIE PATROL.

I'LL SET THE WATCHES, WEDGE.

SUCH CONFIDENCE IN THE FACE OF OVERWHELMING ODDS...

...IF THE EMPEROR HAD ANY IDEA OF HIS FOES' DEDICATION...

WE'D JUST HAVE KILLED THAT MANY MORE DEATH STARS IS ALL. THERE'S NO STOPPING FREEDOM.

WE'VE BEEN INFORMED BY GENERAL SALM THAT AN IMPERIAL STAR DESTROYER AND AN INTERDICTOR CRUISER HAVE TRAPPED ROGUE SQUADRON AND COMMANDO TEAM ONE ON CLIITRIC, THEY DO HAVE PESTAGE, THOUGH.

THIS IS NOT GOOD.

I KNEW THIS WOULD HAPPEN.

WE'LL HAVE TO REINFORCE THEM. IT WILL TAKE 18 HOURS TO GET MORE TROOPS THERE, AS I RECALL.

MIGHT AS WELL BE A MONTH, LEIA, WE CAN SEND NO ONE.

HOW CAN YOU SAY THAT? YOUR...

...MY GREAT-NEPHEW IS THERE? I KNOW THAT, BUT MY CONCERN IS FOR THE NEW REPUBLIC. IF WE ESCALATE THIS SITUATION, WE COULD BE BADLY HURT.

WE MADE A RUN AND WE FAILED.

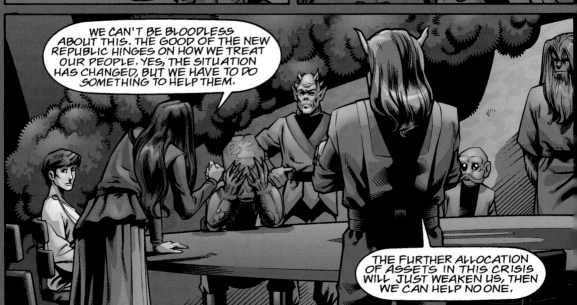

WE CAN'T BE BLOODLESS ABOUT THIS. THE GOOD OF THE NEW REPUBLIC HINGES ON HOW WE TREAT OUR PEOPLE. YES, THE SITUATION HAS CHANGED, BUT WE HAVE TO DO SOMETHING TO HELP THEM.

THE FURTHER ALLOCATION OF ASSETS IN THIS CRISIS WILL JUST WEAKEN US, THEN WE CAN HELP NO ONE.

IF WE DON'T DO SOMETHING TO SAVE THEM, NO ONE WILL EVER COME TO US FOR HELP AGAIN.

IF YOU DON'T AUTHORIZE A RESCUE EFFORT...

...YOU'LL DO WHAT, LEIA?

I'LL CALL LUKE, I'LL GET HAN AND THE **FALCON** AND LANDO...

AND RESCUE THEM YOURSELF, LEIA? PUT YOURSELF IN JEOPARDY?

I'M NOT AFRAID TO FIGHT.

WE KNOW THAT, LEIA, BUT IT IS NO LONGER YOUR PLACE TO FIGHT.

YOU HAVE OTHER DUTIES NOW, THINGS THAT YOU DO BETTER THAN FIGHTING.

...BUT...

YES, WEDGE IS A FRIEND AND, IF HE DIES, WE WILL MOURN. GONE ARE THE DAYS, MY DEAR, WHEN ONE MORE BLASTER WILL WIN A FIGHT FOR US. WE HAVE OUR ROLES AND WE MUST ACCEPT THEM, AS WEDGE AND HIS PEOPLE HAVE.

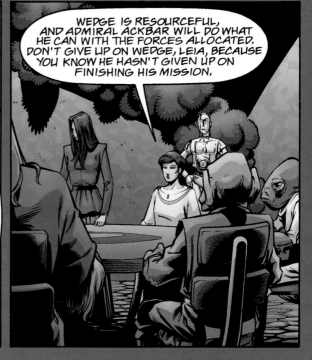

WEDGE IS RESOURCEFUL, AND ADMIRAL ACKBAR WILL DO WHAT HE CAN WITH THE FORCES ALLOCATED. DON'T GIVE UP ON WEDGE, LEIA, BECAUSE YOU KNOW HE HASN'T GIVEN UP ON FINISHING HIS MISSION.

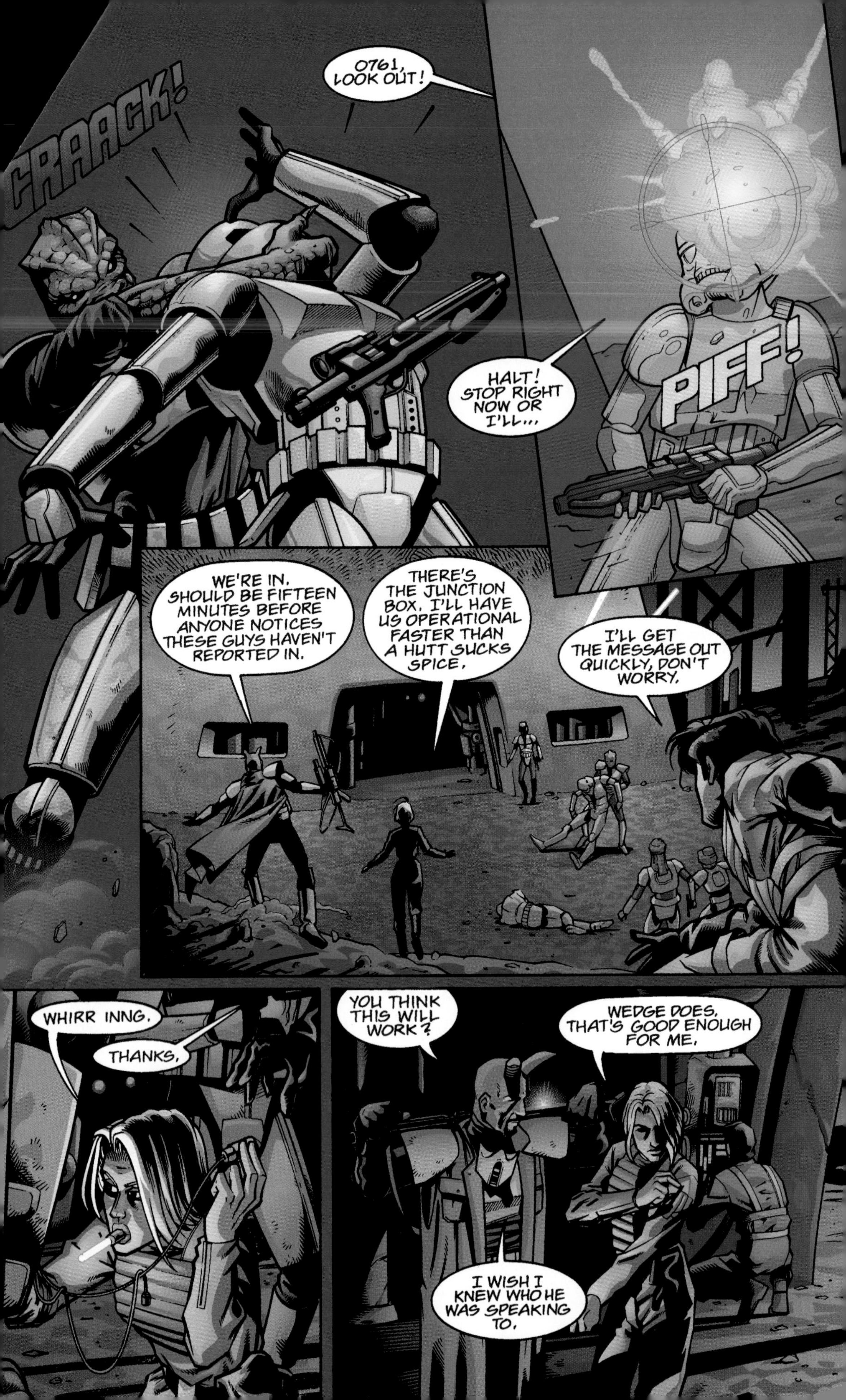
CRAACK!
0761, LOOK OUT!
HALT! STOP RIGHT NOW OR I'LL...
PIFF!
WE'RE IN. SHOULD BE FIFTEEN MINUTES BEFORE ANYONE NOTICES THESE GUYS HAVEN'T REPORTED IN.
THERE'S THE JUNCTION BOX. I'LL HAVE US OPERATIONAL FASTER THAN A HUTT SUCKS SPICE.
I'LL GET THE MESSAGE OUT QUICKLY, DON'T WORRY.
WHIRR INNG.
THANKS.
YOU THINK THIS WILL WORK?
WEDGE DOES. THAT'S GOOD ENOUGH FOR ME.
I WISH I KNEW WHO HE WAS SPEAKING TO.

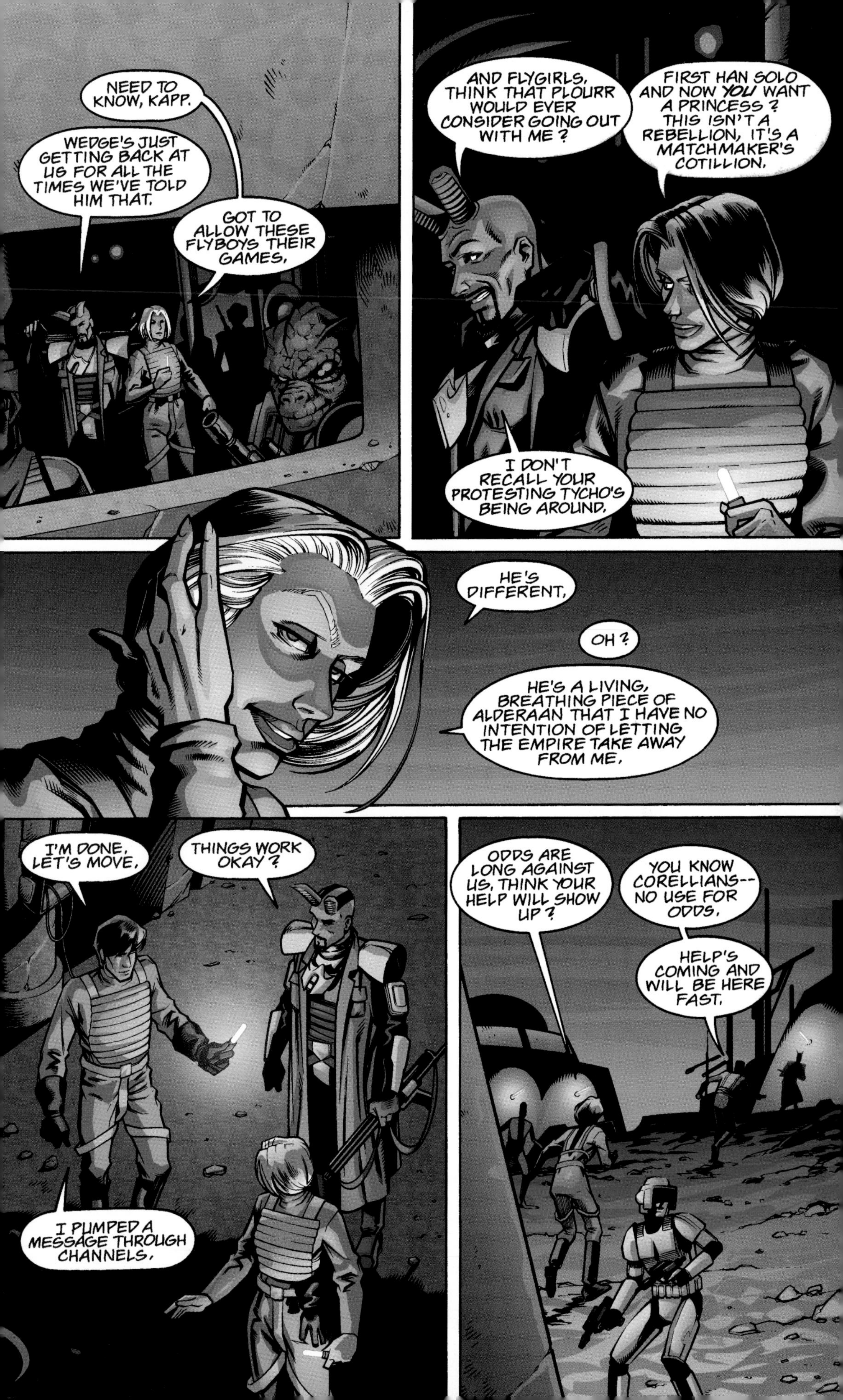

WEDGE'S JUST GETTING BACK AT US FOR ALL THE TIMES WE'VE TOLD HIM THAT.
NEED TO KNOW, KAPP.
GOT TO ALLOW THESE FLYBOYS THEIR GAMES.
AND FLYGIRLS. THINK THAT PLOURR WOULD EVER CONSIDER GOING OUT WITH ME?
FIRST HAN SOLO AND NOW YOU WANT A PRINCESS? THIS ISN'T A REBELLION, IT'S A MATCHMAKER'S COTILLION.
I DON'T RECALL YOUR PROTESTING TYCHO'S BEING AROUND.
HE'S DIFFERENT.
OH?
HE'S A LIVING, BREATHING PIECE OF ALDERAAN THAT I HAVE NO INTENTION OF LETTING THE EMPIRE TAKE AWAY FROM ME.
I'M DONE. LET'S MOVE.
THINGS WORK OKAY?
I PUMPED A MESSAGE THROUGH CHANNELS.
ODDS ARE LONG AGAINST US. THINK YOUR HELP WILL SHOW UP?
YOU KNOW CORELLIANS-- NO USE FOR ODDS.
HELP'S COMING AND WILL BE HERE FAST.

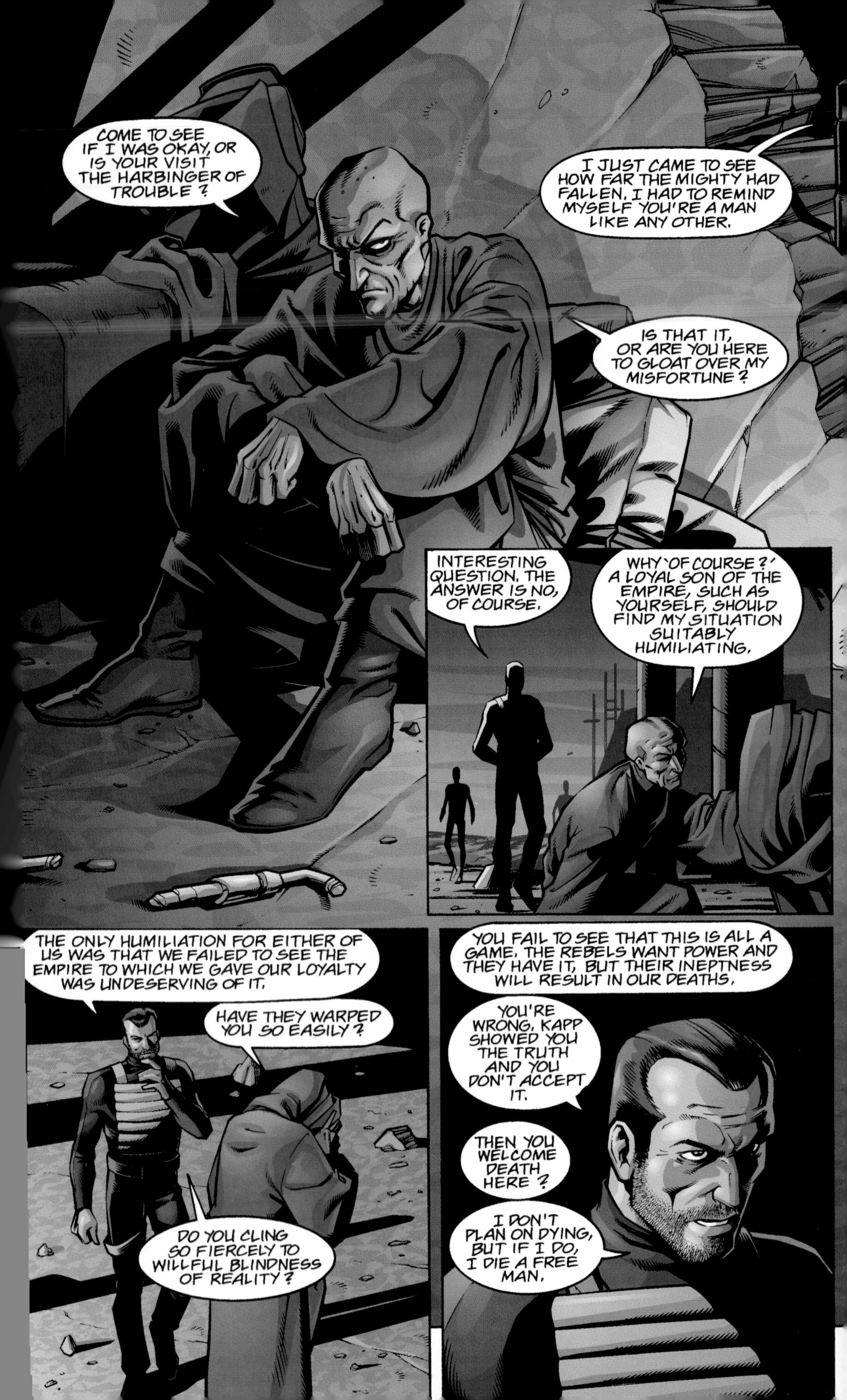
COME TO SEE IF I WAS OKAY, OR IS YOUR VISIT THE HARBINGER OF TROUBLE ?
I JUST CAME TO SEE HOW FAR THE MIGHTY HAD FALLEN. I HAD TO REMIND MYSELF YOU'RE A MAN LIKE ANY OTHER.
IS THAT IT, OR ARE YOU HERE TO GLOAT OVER MY MISFORTUNE ?
INTERESTING QUESTION. THE ANSWER IS NO, OF COURSE.
WHY 'OF COURSE ?' A LOYAL SON OF THE EMPIRE, SUCH AS YOURSELF, SHOULD FIND MY SITUATION SUITABLY HUMILIATING.
THE ONLY HUMILIATION FOR EITHER OF US WAS THAT WE FAILED TO SEE THE EMPIRE TO WHICH WE GAVE OUR LOYALTY WAS UNDESERVING OF IT.
HAVE THEY WARPED YOU SO EASILY ?
DO YOU CLING SO FIERCELY TO WILLFUL BLINDNESS OF REALITY ?
YOU FAIL TO SEE THAT THIS IS ALL A GAME. THE REBELS WANT POWER AND THEY HAVE IT, BUT THEIR INEPTNESS WILL RESULT IN OUR DEATHS.
YOU'RE WRONG. KAPP SHOWED YOU THE TRUTH AND YOU DON'T ACCEPT IT.
THEN YOU WELCOME DEATH HERE ?
I DON'T PLAN ON DYING, BUT IF I DO, I DIE A FREE MAN.

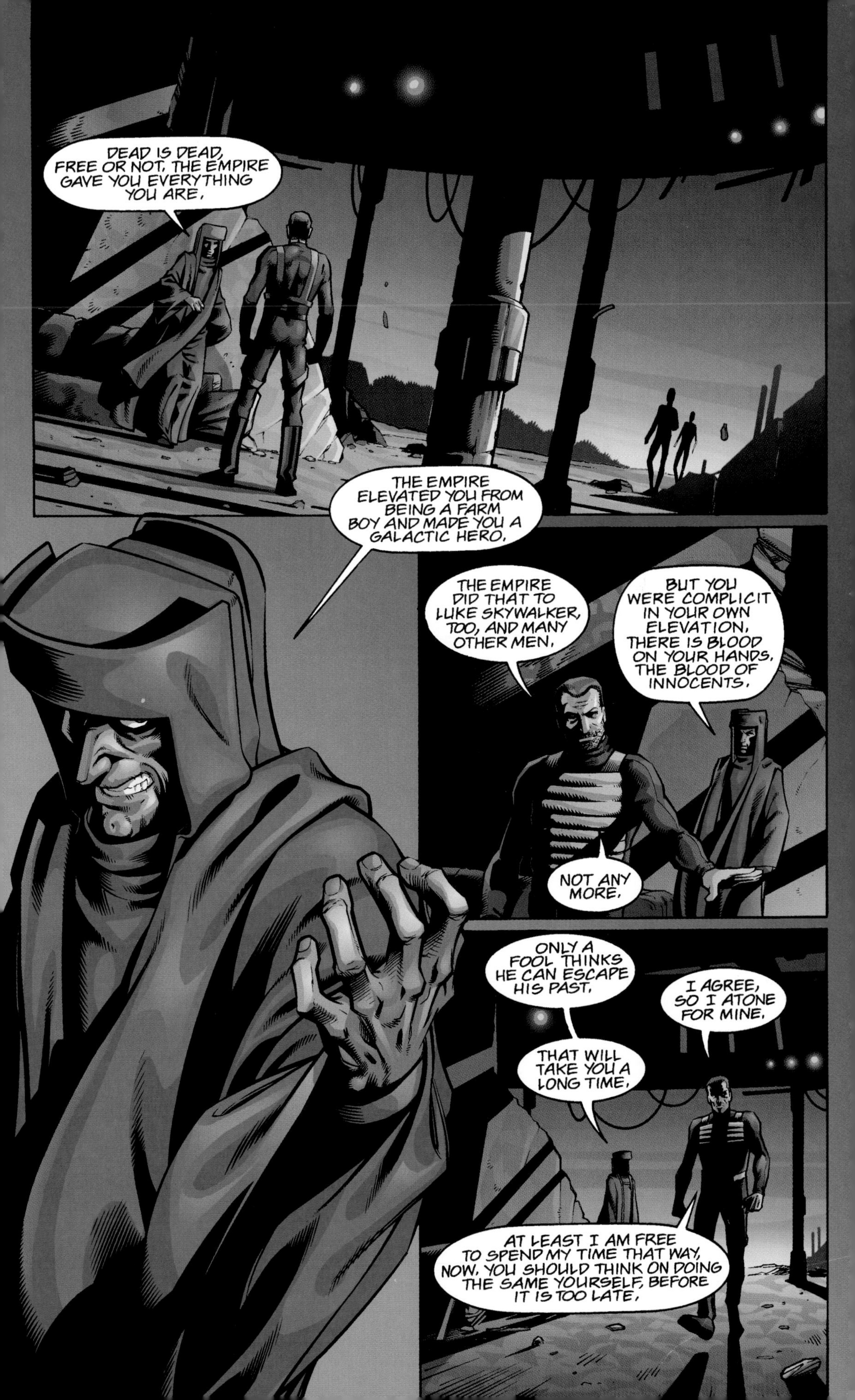
DEAD IS DEAD, FREE OR NOT. THE EMPIRE GAVE YOU EVERYTHING YOU ARE.
THE EMPIRE ELEVATED YOU FROM BEING A FARM BOY AND MADE YOU A GALACTIC HERO.
THE EMPIRE DID THAT TO LUKE SKYWALKER, TOO, AND MANY OTHER MEN.
BUT YOU WERE COMPLICIT IN YOUR OWN ELEVATION. THERE IS BLOOD ON YOUR HANDS. THE BLOOD OF INNOCENTS.
NOT ANY MORE.
ONLY A FOOL THINKS HE CAN ESCAPE HIS PAST.
I AGREE. SO I ATONE FOR MINE.
THAT WILL TAKE YOU A LONG TIME.
AT LEAST I AM FREE TO SPEND MY TIME THAT WAY, NOW. YOU SHOULD THINK ON DOING THE SAME YOURSELF, BEFORE IT IS TOO LATE.

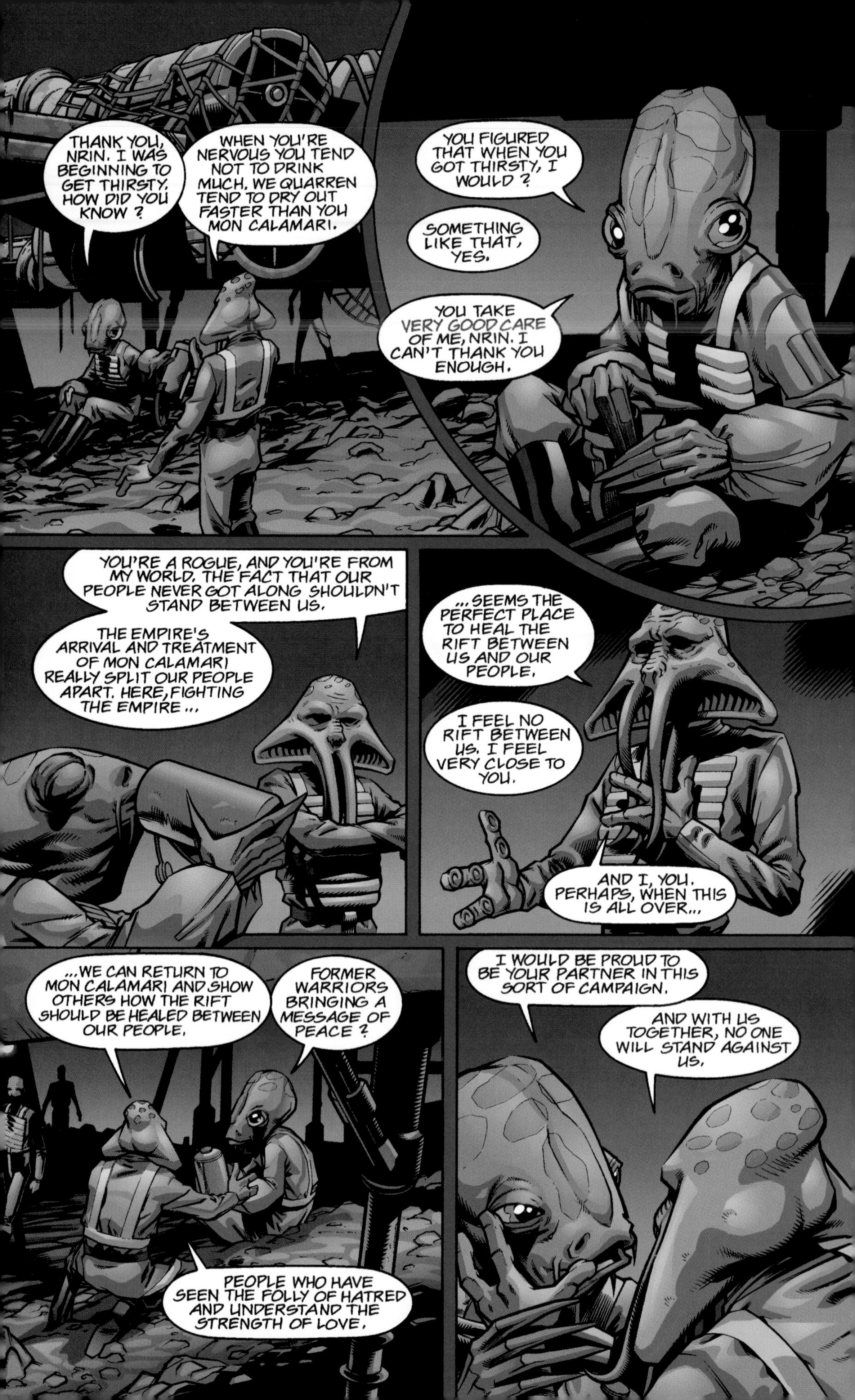
THANK YOU, NRIN. I WAS BEGINNING TO GET THIRSTY. HOW DID YOU KNOW ?
WHEN YOU'RE NERVOUS YOU TEND NOT TO DRINK MUCH. WE QUARREN TEND TO DRY OUT FASTER THAN YOU MON CALAMARI.
YOU FIGURED THAT WHEN YOU GOT THIRSTY, I WOULD ?
SOMETHING LIKE THAT, YES.
YOU TAKE VERY GOOD CARE OF ME, NRIN. I CAN'T THANK YOU ENOUGH.
YOU'RE A ROGUE, AND YOU'RE FROM MY WORLD. THE FACT THAT OUR PEOPLE NEVER GOT ALONG SHOULDN'T STAND BETWEEN US.
THE EMPIRE'S ARRIVAL AND TREATMENT OF MON CALAMARI REALLY SPLIT OUR PEOPLE APART. HERE, FIGHTING THE EMPIRE...
...SEEMS THE PERFECT PLACE TO HEAL THE RIFT BETWEEN US AND OUR PEOPLE.
I FEEL NO RIFT BETWEEN US. I FEEL VERY CLOSE TO YOU.
AND I, YOU. PERHAPS, WHEN THIS IS ALL OVER...
...WE CAN RETURN TO MON CALAMARI AND SHOW OTHERS HOW THE RIFT SHOULD BE HEALED BETWEEN OUR PEOPLE.
FORMER WARRIORS BRINGING A MESSAGE OF PEACE ?
PEOPLE WHO HAVE SEEN THE FOLLY OF HATRED AND UNDERSTAND THE STRENGTH OF LOVE.
I WOULD BE PROUD TO BE YOUR PARTNER IN THIS SORT OF CAMPAIGN.
AND WITH US TOGETHER, NO ONE WILL STAND AGAINST US.

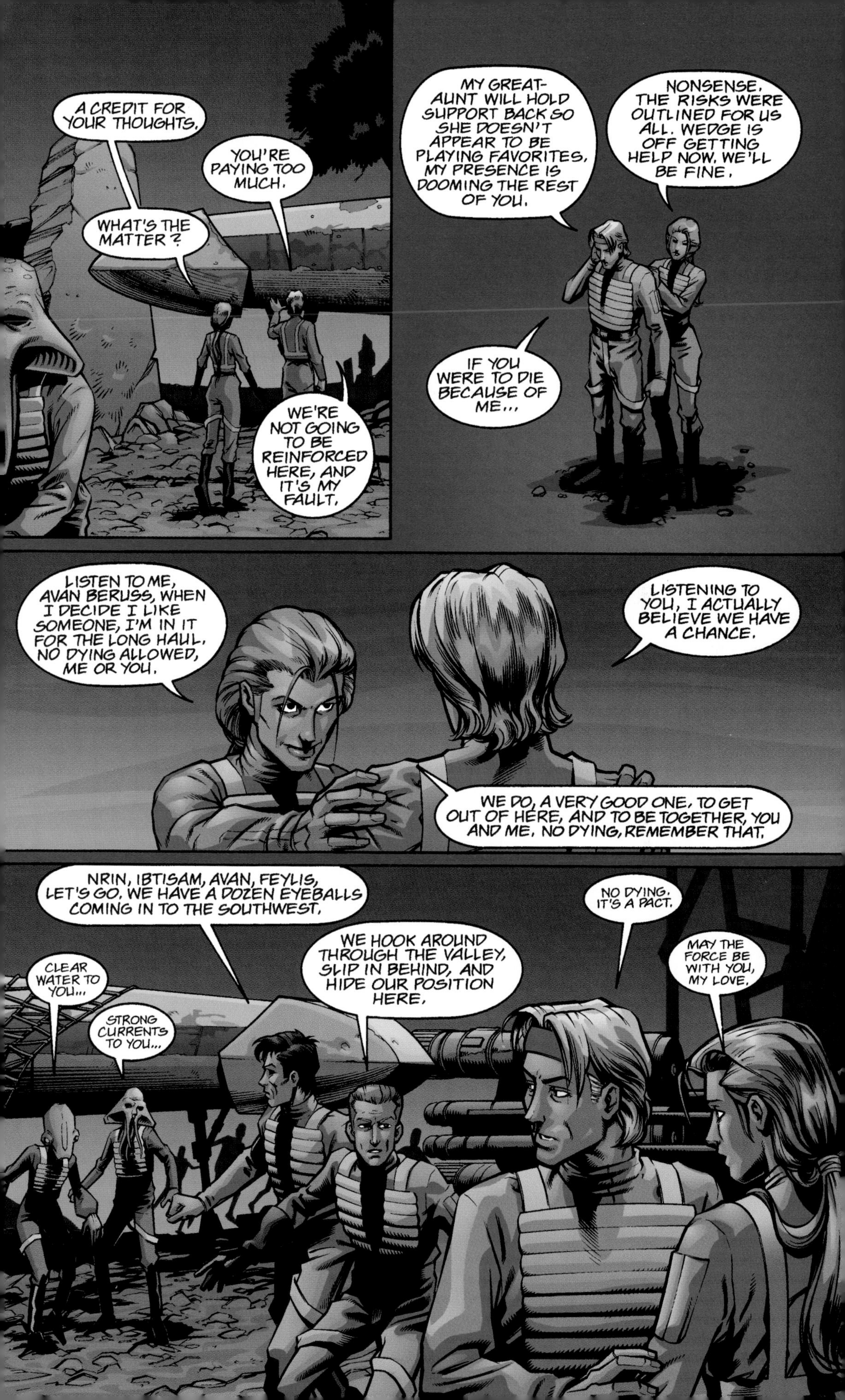
A CREDIT FOR YOUR THOUGHTS.
YOU'RE PAYING TOO MUCH.
WHAT'S THE MATTER?
WE'RE NOT GOING TO BE REINFORCED HERE, AND IT'S MY FAULT.
MY GREAT-AUNT WILL HOLD SUPPORT BACK SO SHE DOESN'T APPEAR TO BE PLAYING FAVORITES. MY PRESENCE IS DOOMING THE REST OF YOU.
NONSENSE. THE RISKS WERE OUTLINED FOR US ALL. WEDGE IS OFF GETTING HELP NOW. WE'LL BE FINE.
IF YOU WERE TO DIE BECAUSE OF ME...
LISTEN TO ME, AVAN BERUSS. WHEN I DECIDE I LIKE SOMEONE, I'M IN IT FOR THE LONG HAUL. NO DYING ALLOWED, ME OR YOU.
LISTENING TO YOU, I ACTUALLY BELIEVE WE HAVE A CHANCE.
WE DO, A VERY GOOD ONE, TO GET OUT OF HERE, AND TO BE TOGETHER, YOU AND ME. NO DYING, REMEMBER THAT.
NRIN, IBTISAM, AVAN, FEYLIS, LET'S GO. WE HAVE A DOZEN EYEBALLS COMING IN TO THE SOUTHWEST.
WE HOOK AROUND THROUGH THE VALLEY, SLIP IN BEHIND, AND HIDE OUR POSITION HERE.
CLEAR WATER TO YOU...
STRONG CURRENTS TO YOU...
NO DYING. IT'S A PACT.
MAY THE FORCE BE WITH YOU, MY LOVE.

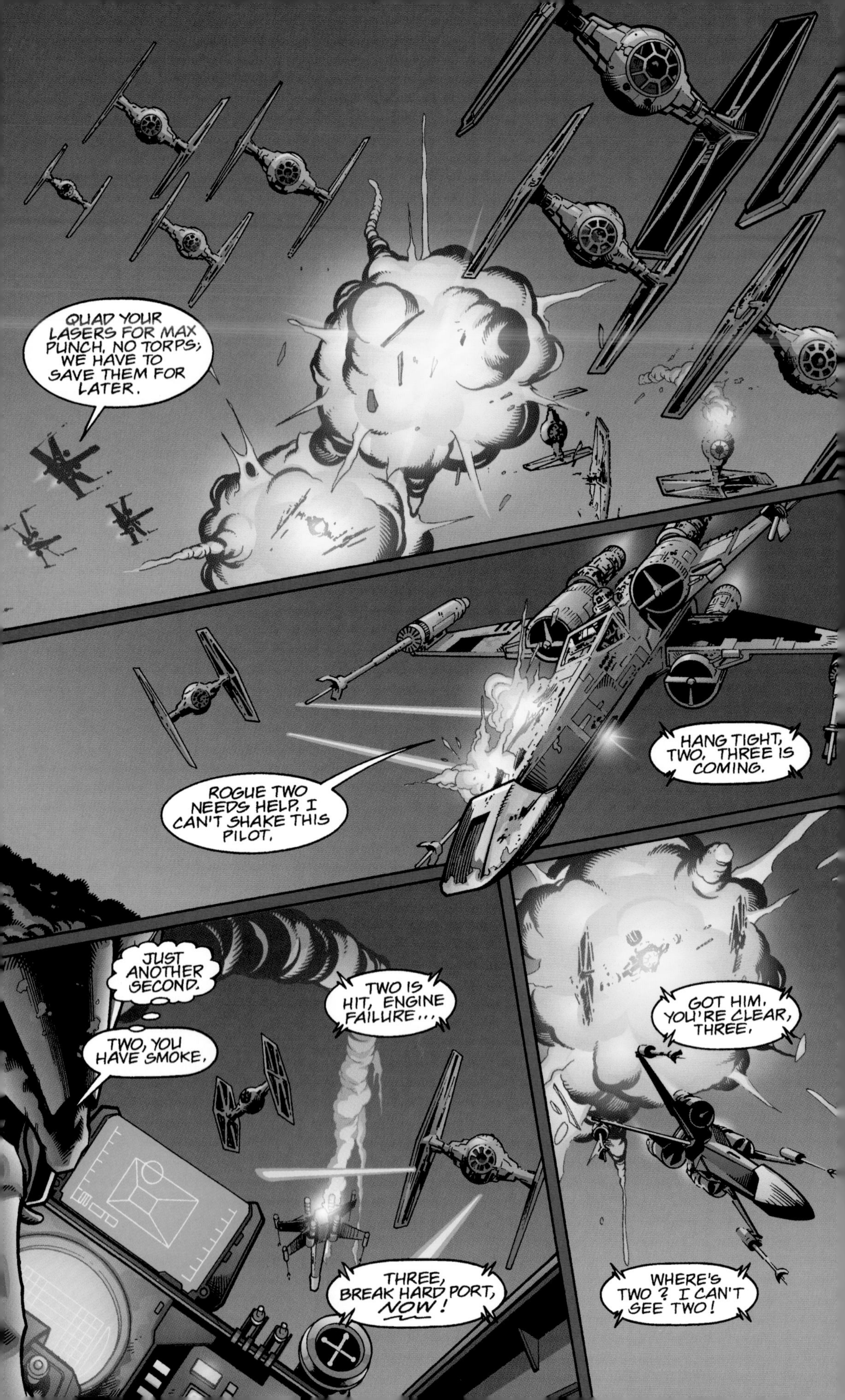
QUAD YOUR LASERS FOR MAX PUNCH, NO TORPS; WE HAVE TO SAVE THEM FOR LATER.
ROGUE TWO NEEDS HELP. I CAN'T SHAKE THIS PILOT.
HANG TIGHT, TWO, THREE IS COMING.
JUST ANOTHER SECOND.
TWO, YOU HAVE SMOKE.
TWO IS HIT, ENGINE FAILURE...
THREE, BREAK HARD PORT, NOW!
GOT HIM, YOU'RE CLEAR, THREE.
WHERE'S TWO? I CAN'T SEE TWO!

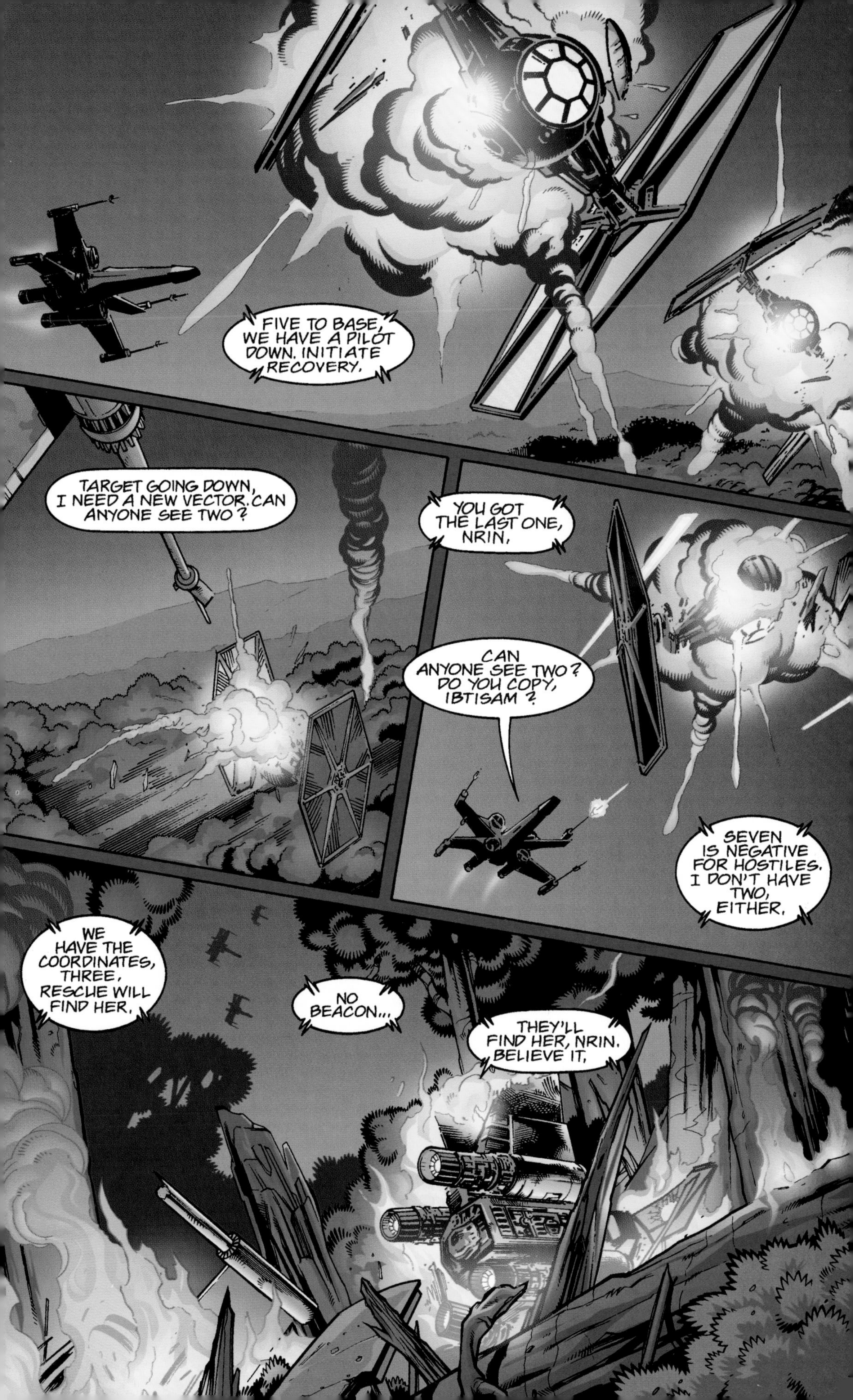
FIVE TO BASE, WE HAVE A PILOT DOWN. INITIATE RECOVERY.
TARGET GOING DOWN, I NEED A NEW VECTOR. CAN ANYONE SEE TWO ?
YOU GOT THE LAST ONE, NRIN.
CAN ANYONE SEE TWO ? DO YOU COPY, IBTISAM ?
SEVEN IS NEGATIVE FOR HOSTILES. I DON'T HAVE TWO, EITHER.
WE HAVE THE COORDINATES, THREE. RESCUE WILL FIND HER.
NO BEACON...
THEY'LL FIND HER, NRIN. BELIEVE IT.

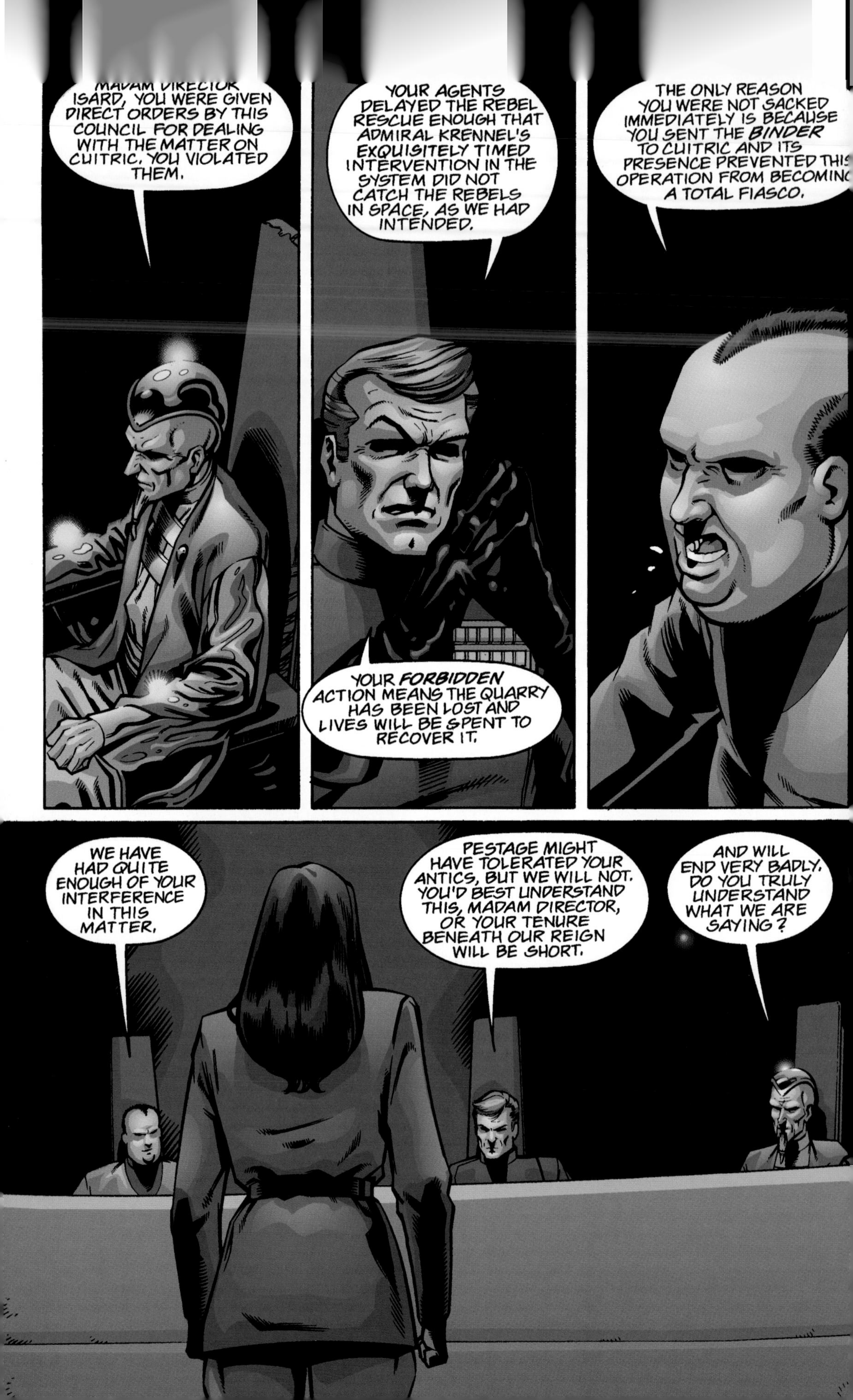
MADAM DIRECTOR ISARD, YOU WERE GIVEN DIRECT ORDERS BY THIS COUNCIL FOR DEALING WITH THE MATTER ON CUITRIC. YOU VIOLATED THEM.
YOUR AGENTS DELAYED THE REBEL RESCUE ENOUGH THAT ADMIRAL KRENNEL'S EXQUISITELY TIMED INTERVENTION IN THE SYSTEM DID NOT CATCH THE REBELS IN SPACE, AS WE HAD INTENDED.
YOUR FORBIDDEN ACTION MEANS THE QUARRY HAS BEEN LOST AND LIVES WILL BE SPENT TO RECOVER IT.
THE ONLY REASON YOU WERE NOT SACKED IMMEDIATELY IS BECAUSE YOU SENT THE BINDER TO CUITRIC AND ITS PRESENCE PREVENTED THIS OPERATION FROM BECOMING A TOTAL FIASCO.
WE HAVE HAD QUITE ENOUGH OF YOUR INTERFERENCE IN THIS MATTER.
PESTAGE MIGHT HAVE TOLERATED YOUR ANTICS, BUT WE WILL NOT. YOU'D BEST UNDERSTAND THIS, MADAM DIRECTOR, OR YOUR TENURE BENEATH OUR REIGN WILL BE SHORT.
AND WILL END VERY BADLY. DO YOU TRULY UNDERSTAND WHAT WE ARE SAYING?

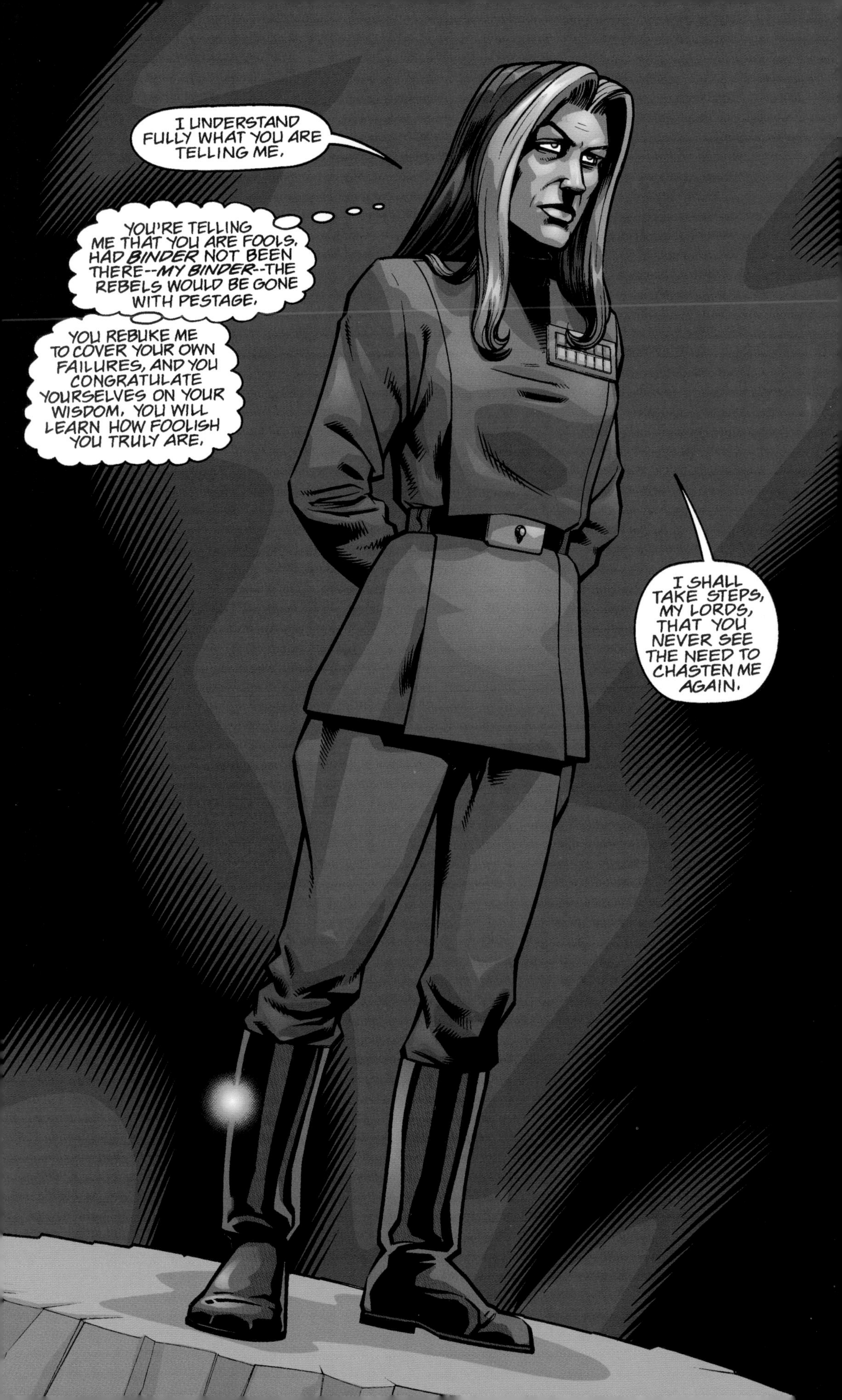
I UNDERSTAND FULLY WHAT YOU ARE TELLING ME.
YOU'RE TELLING ME THAT YOU ARE FOOLS. HAD *BINDER* NOT BEEN THERE--*MY BINDER*--THE REBELS WOULD BE GONE WITH PESTAGE.
YOU REBUKE ME TO COVER YOUR OWN FAILURES, AND YOU CONGRATULATE YOURSELVES ON YOUR WISDOM. YOU WILL LEARN HOW FOOLISH YOU TRULY ARE.
I SHALL TAKE STEPS, MY LORDS, THAT YOU NEVER SEE THE NEED TO CHASTEN ME AGAIN.

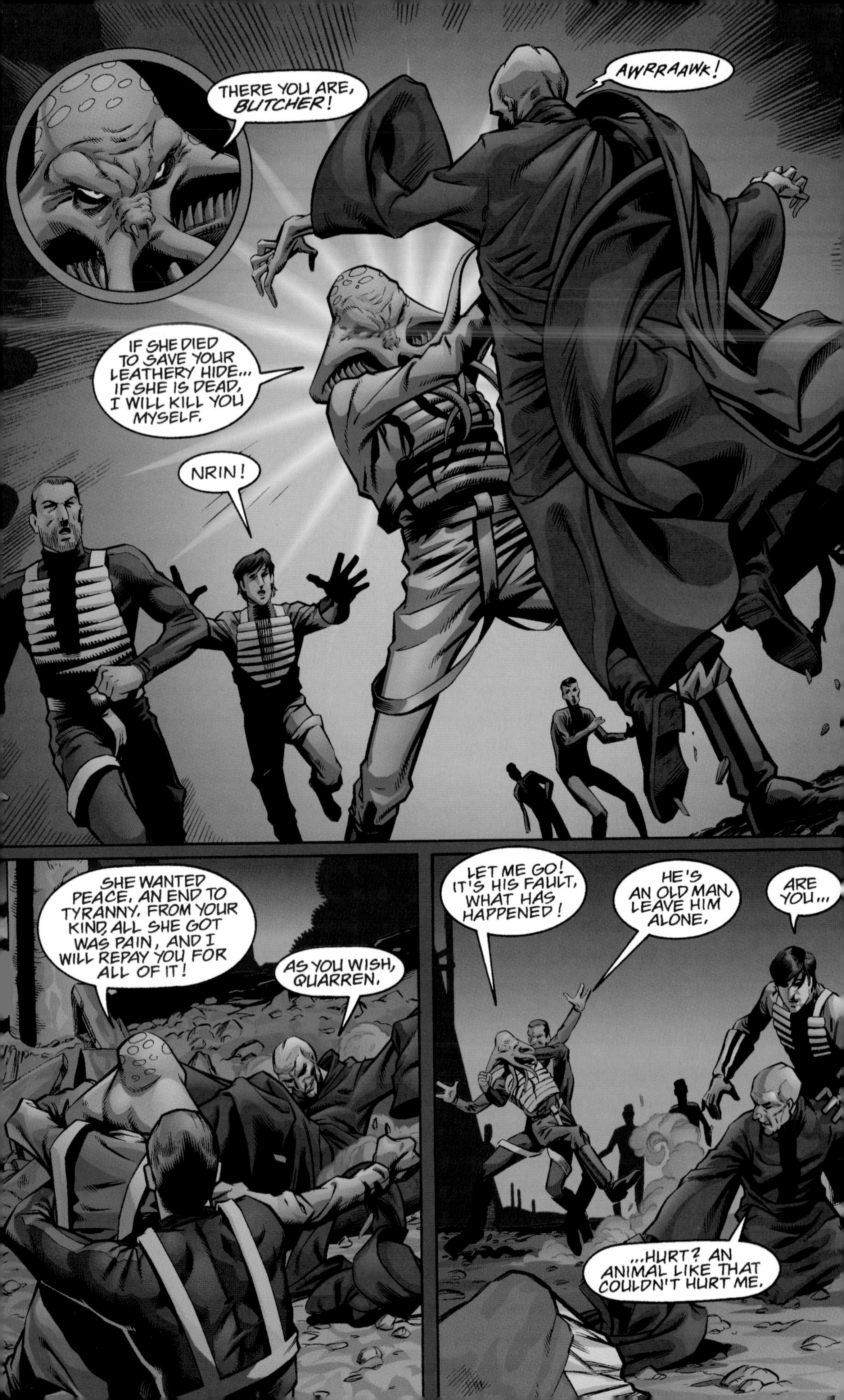
THERE YOU ARE, BUTCHER!
AWRRAAWK!
IF SHE DIED TO SAVE YOUR LEATHERY HIDE... IF SHE IS DEAD, I WILL KILL YOU MYSELF.
NRIN!
SHE WANTED PEACE, AN END TO TYRANNY. FROM YOUR KIND, ALL SHE GOT WAS PAIN, AND I WILL REPAY YOU FOR ALL OF IT!
AS YOU WISH, QUARREN.
LET ME GO! IT'S HIS FAULT, WHAT HAS HAPPENED!
HE'S AN OLD MAN, LEAVE HIM ALONE.
ARE YOU...
...HURT? AN ANIMAL LIKE THAT COULDN'T HURT ME.

A MAN, JUST LIKE YOU.

NO, A MAN AS I ONCE WAS, NO MORE.

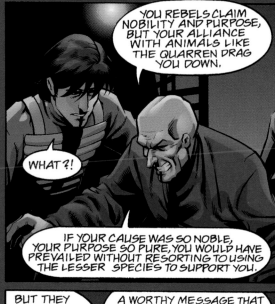

YOU REBELS CLAIM NOBILITY AND PURPOSE, BUT YOUR ALLIANCE WITH ANIMALS LIKE THE QUARREN DRAG YOU DOWN.

WHAT?!

IF YOUR CAUSE WAS SO NOBLE, YOUR PURPOSE SO PURE, YOU WOULD HAVE PREVAILED WITHOUT RESORTING TO USING THE LESSER SPECIES TO SUPPORT YOU.

YOU ARE FROM IMPERIAL STOCK. YOU CAN'T CHANGE.

I CAN CHANGE AND I HAVE CHANGED. I'VE CHANGED BECAUSE OF YOU.

WHAT?

YOU, THE REBELS, YOUR EFFORTS AGAINST ALL ODDS, YOUR BELIEF IN THE JUSTICE OF YOUR CAUSE.

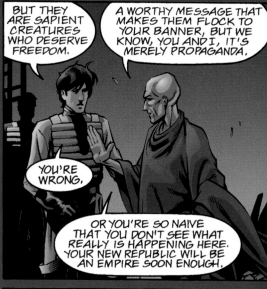

BUT THEY ARE SAPIENT CREATURES WHO DESERVE FREEDOM.

A WORTHY MESSAGE THAT MAKES THEM FLOCK TO YOUR BANNER, BUT WE KNOW, YOU AND I, IT'S MERELY PROPAGANDA.

YOU'RE WRONG.

OR YOU'RE SO NAIVE THAT YOU DON'T SEE WHAT REALLY IS HAPPENING HERE. YOUR NEW REPUBLIC WILL BE AN EMPIRE SOON ENOUGH.

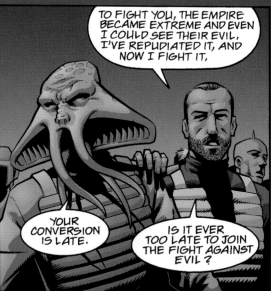

TO FIGHT YOU, THE EMPIRE BECAME EXTREME AND EVEN I COULD SEE THEIR EVIL. I'VE REPUDIATED IT, AND NOW I FIGHT IT.

YOUR CONVERSION IS LATE.

IS IT EVER TOO LATE TO JOIN THE FIGHT AGAINST EVIL?

IT IS ALL ABOUT POWER AND HOW IT CHANGES PEOPLE. YOUR LEADERS WILL SEE TO THAT, THEY WILL FALL PREY TO IT.

NEVER. YOUR EXAMPLE ALONE WILL WARN THEM AWAY FROM SUCCUMBING TO EVIL.

THE RESCUE TEAM IS BACK!

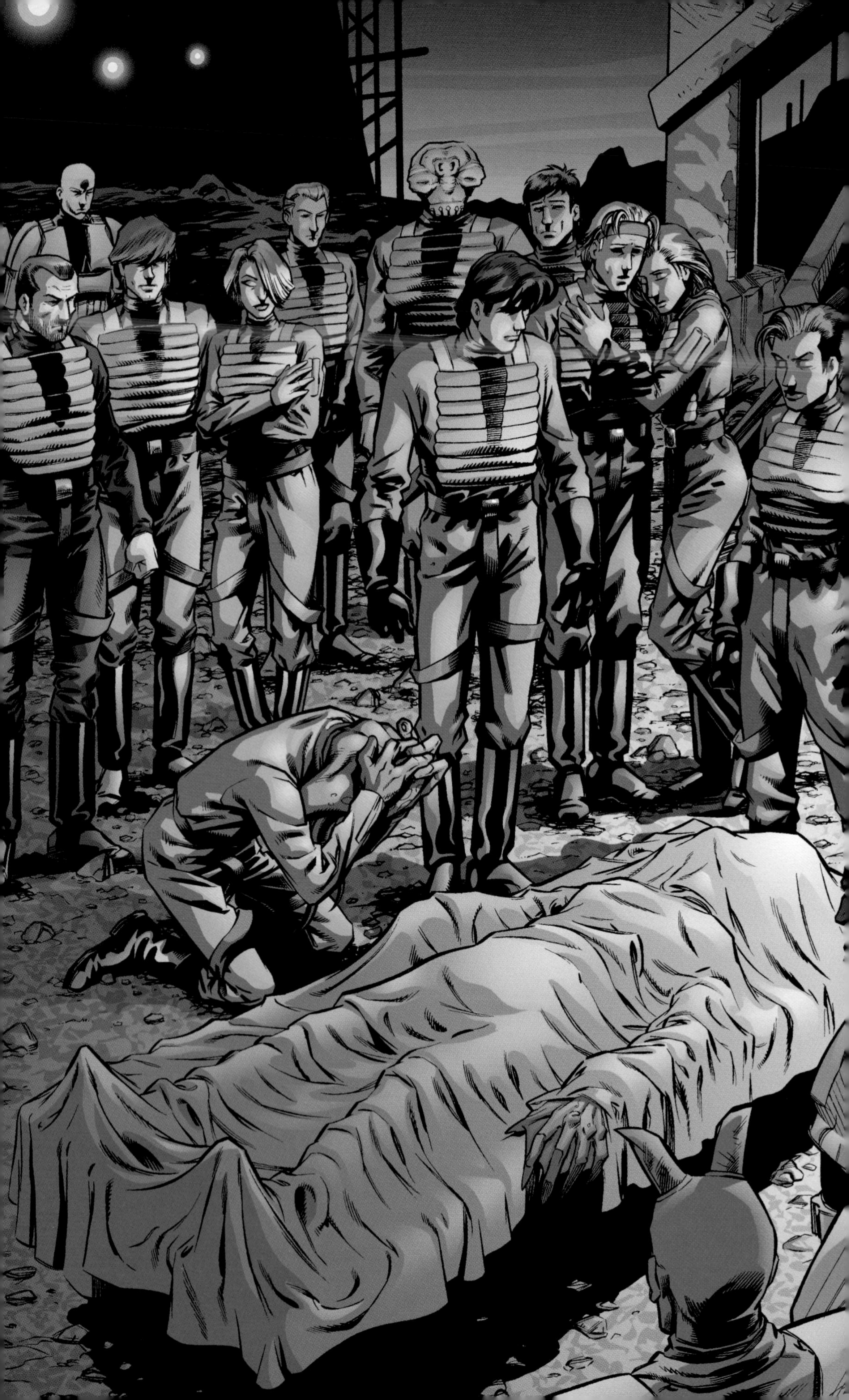

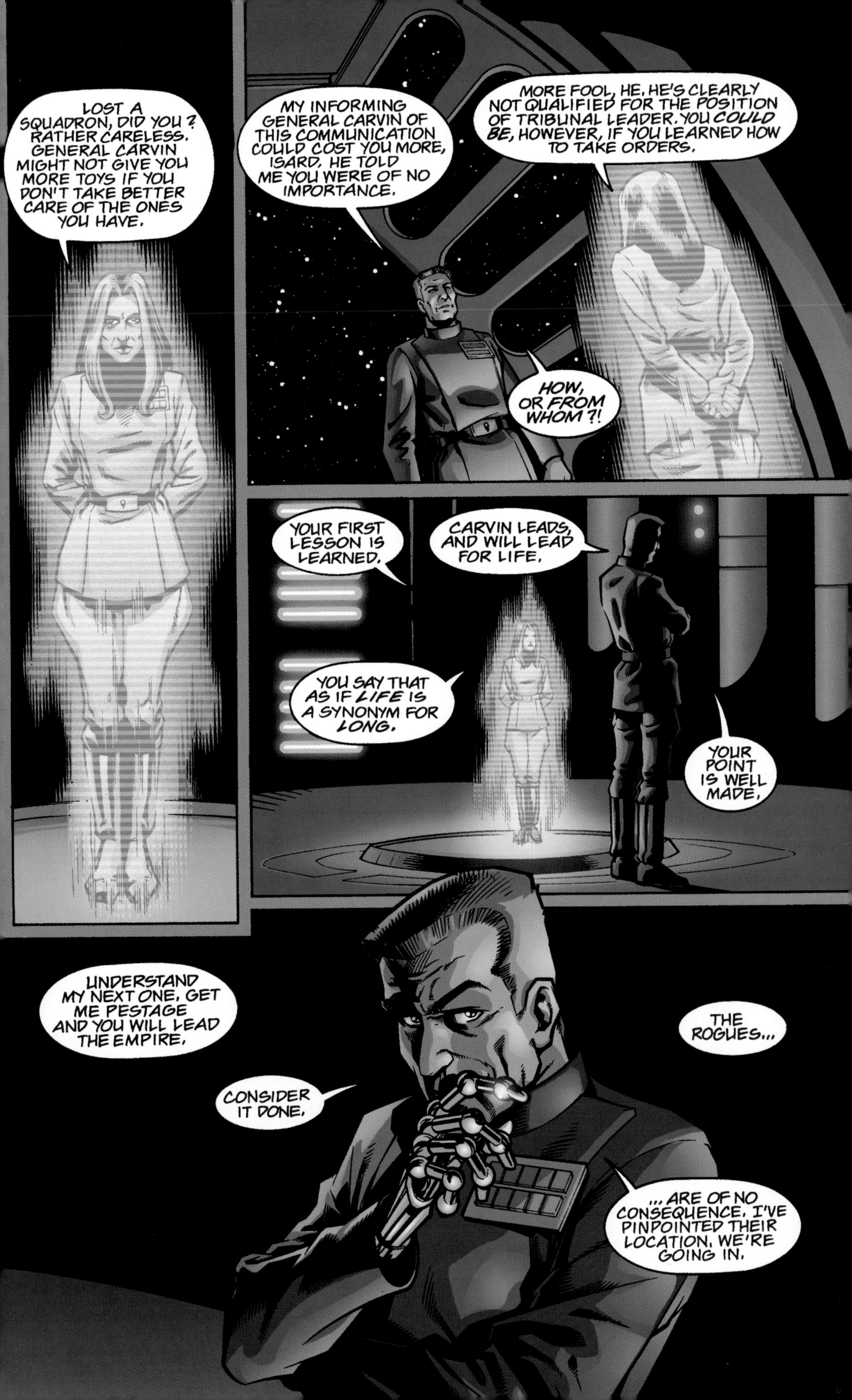
LOST A SQUADRON, DID YOU? RATHER CARELESS. GENERAL CARVIN MIGHT NOT GIVE YOU MORE TOYS IF YOU DON'T TAKE BETTER CARE OF THE ONES YOU HAVE.
MY INFORMING GENERAL CARVIN OF THIS COMMUNICATION COULD COST YOU MORE, ISARD. HE TOLD ME YOU WERE OF NO IMPORTANCE.
MORE FOOL, HE. HE'S CLEARLY NOT QUALIFIED FOR THE POSITION OF TRIBUNAL LEADER. YOU COULD BE, HOWEVER, IF YOU LEARNED HOW TO TAKE ORDERS.
HOW, OR FROM WHOM?!
YOUR FIRST LESSON IS LEARNED.
CARVIN LEADS, AND WILL LEAD FOR LIFE.
YOU SAY THAT AS IF LIFE IS A SYNONYM FOR LONG.
YOUR POINT IS WELL MADE.
UNDERSTAND MY NEXT ONE. GET ME PESTAGE AND YOU WILL LEAD THE EMPIRE.
CONSIDER IT DONE.
THE ROGUES...
...ARE OF NO CONSEQUENCE. I'VE PINPOINTED THEIR LOCATION. WE'RE GOING IN.

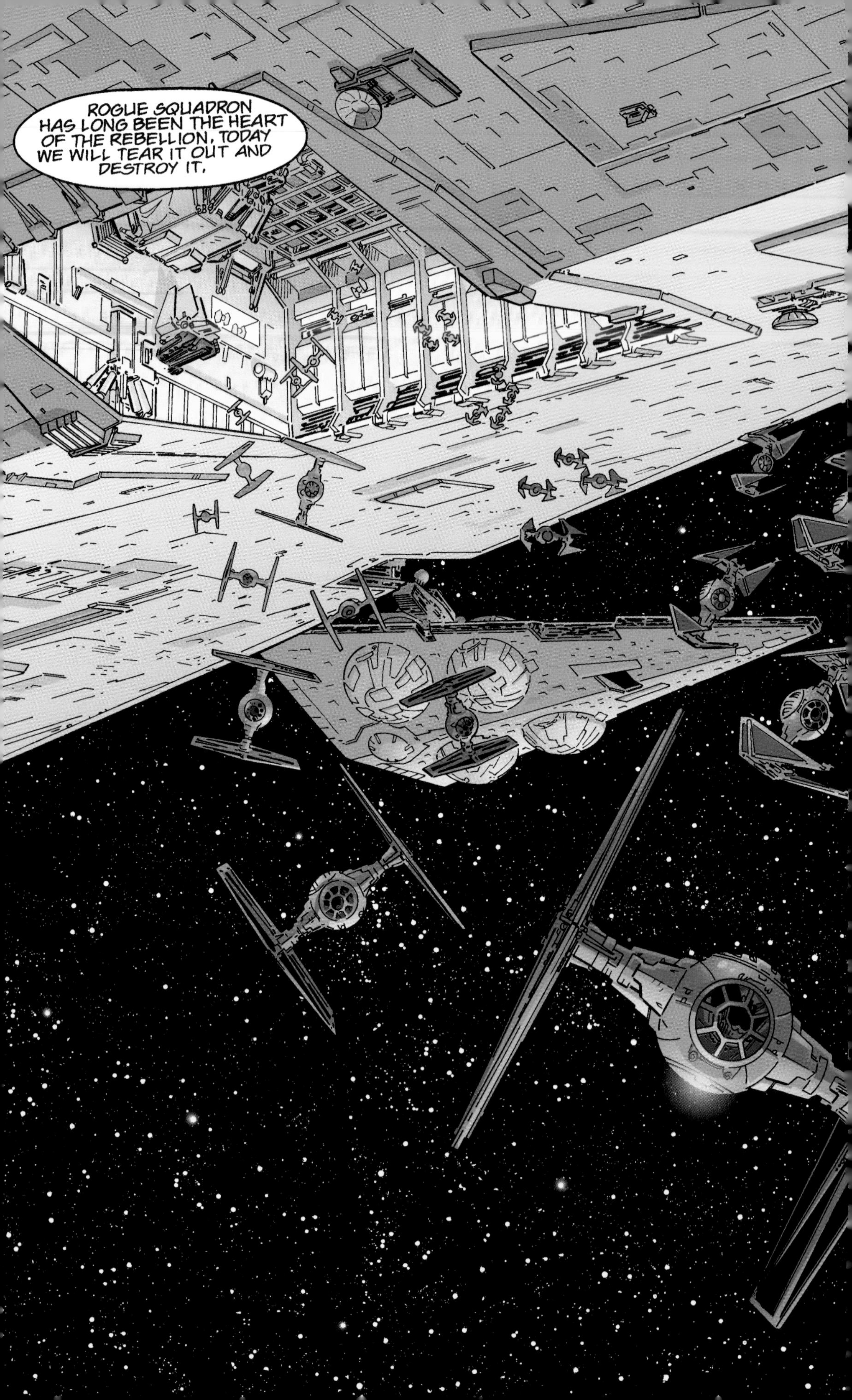
ROGUE SQUADRON HAS LONG BEEN THE HEART OF THE REBELLION, TODAY WE WILL TEAR IT OUT AND DESTROY IT.

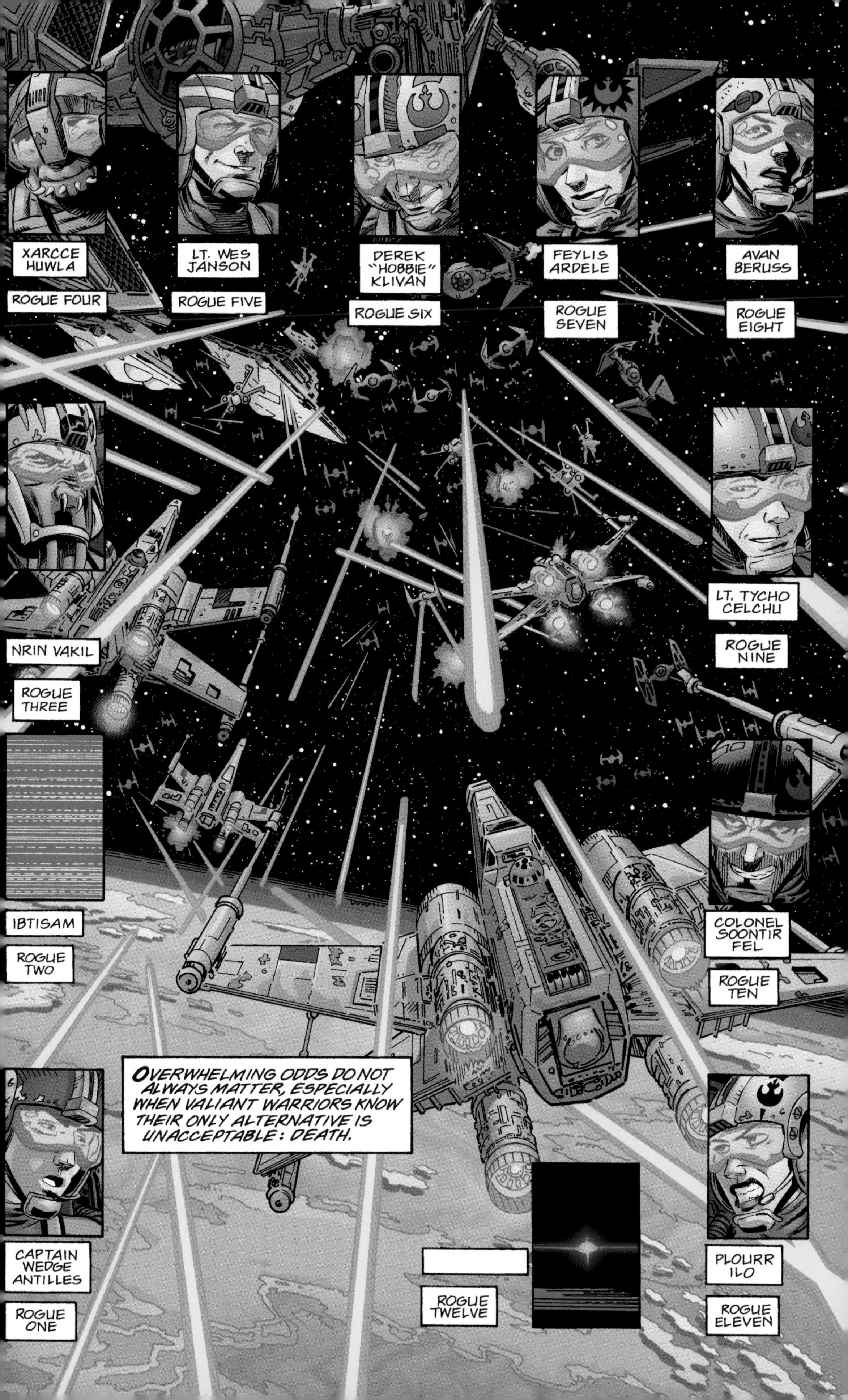
XARCCE HUWLA
ROGUE FOUR
LT. WES JANSON
ROGUE FIVE
DEREK "HOBBIE" KLIVAN
ROGUE SIX
FEYLIS ARDELE
ROGUE SEVEN
AVAN BERUSS
ROGUE EIGHT
NRIN VAKIL
ROGUE THREE
LT. TYCHO CELCHU
ROGUE NINE
IBTISAM
ROGUE TWO
COLONEL SOONTIR FEL
ROGUE TEN
OVERWHELMING ODDS DO NOT ALWAYS MATTER, ESPECIALLY WHEN VALIANT WARRIORS KNOW THEIR ONLY ALTERNATIVE IS UNACCEPTABLE: DEATH.
CAPTAIN WEDGE ANTILLES
ROGUE ONE
ROGUE TWELVE
PLOURR ILO
ROGUE ELEVEN

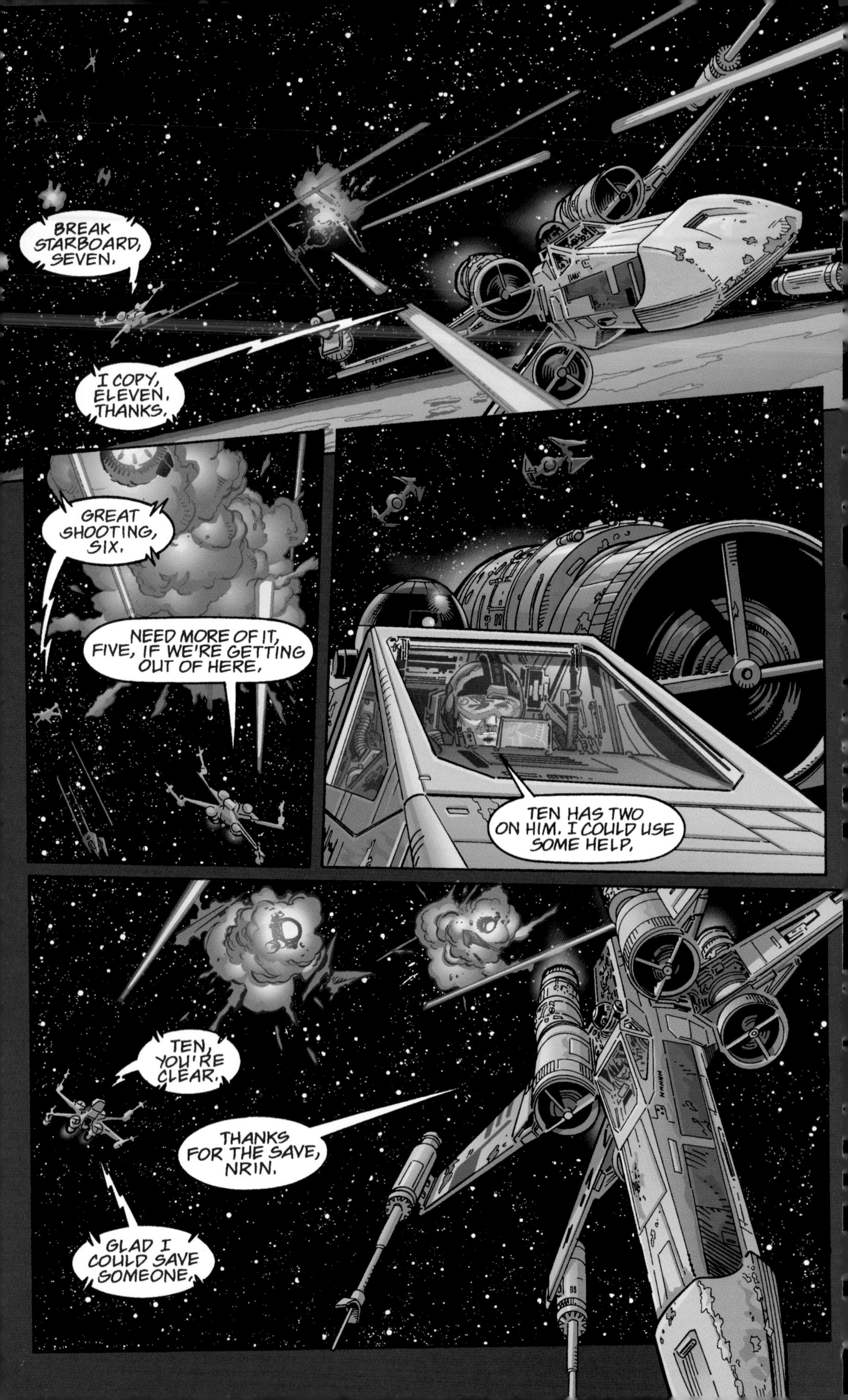
BREAK STARBOARD, SEVEN.
I COPY, ELEVEN. THANKS.
GREAT SHOOTING, SIX.
NEED MORE OF IT, FIVE, IF WE'RE GETTING OUT OF HERE.
TEN HAS TWO ON HIM. I COULD USE SOME HELP.
TEN, YOU'RE CLEAR.
THANKS FOR THE SAVE, NRIN.
GLAD I COULD SAVE SOMEONE.

SHIELDS AND EXPERIENCE ARE OUR ONLY ADVANTAGES, AND AGAINST THIS MANY TIES, THEY'LL ONLY WORK SO LONG.
ANOTHER ONE DOWN AND I'M CLEAR. ANYONE NEED HELP?
DON'T NEED HELP, NINE, BUT I'LL SPLIT THESE GUYS WITH YOU.
GLADLY, EIGHT, TAKE YOUR PICK.
NOT THE KIND OF WELCOME I WANTED TO GREET ME, WEDGE.
MIRAX! GET TO GROUND FAST. WE'LL BLIND THE EYEBALLS ON YOU.

THE TIES ARE SWARMING ON THE SKATE, WEDGE.
LET'S GO, ROGUES, HAVE TO SCRAPE THE TIES OFF.
MY R2 IS HIT, AND THEY'RE STILL COMING.
BREAK PORT, FIVE. I HAVE COVER FOR YOU.
GREAT. GOT A MIRACLE FOR THE REST OF US ?
THIS CLOSE ENOUGH, FIVE ?
WHAT ARE YOU DOING HERE, GENERAL ?
PAYING YOU BACK FOR SOME OF THE RESCUES IN THE PAST, ROGUE LEAD.

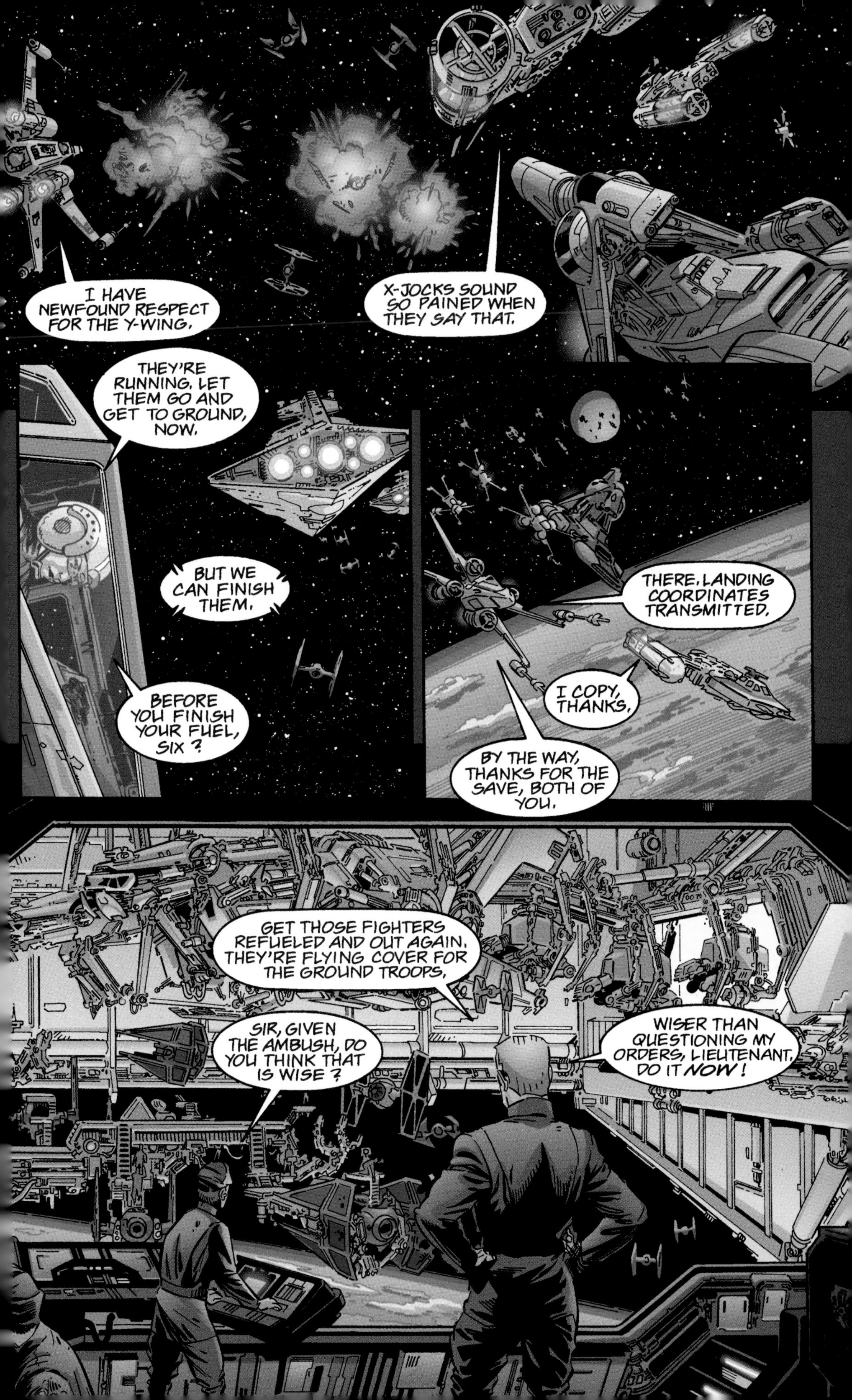
I HAVE NEWFOUND RESPECT FOR THE Y-WING.
X-JOCKS SOUND SO PAINED WHEN THEY SAY THAT.
THEY'RE RUNNING. LET THEM GO AND GET TO GROUND, NOW.
BUT WE CAN FINISH THEM.
BEFORE YOU FINISH YOUR FUEL, SIX ?
THERE. LANDING COORDINATES TRANSMITTED.
I COPY, THANKS.
BY THE WAY, THANKS FOR THE SAVE, BOTH OF YOU.
GET THOSE FIGHTERS REFUELED AND OUT AGAIN. THEY'RE FLYING COVER FOR THE GROUND TROOPS.
SIR, GIVEN THE AMBUSH, DO YOU THINK THAT IS WISE ?
WISER THAN QUESTIONING MY ORDERS, LIEUTENANT. DO IT NOW !

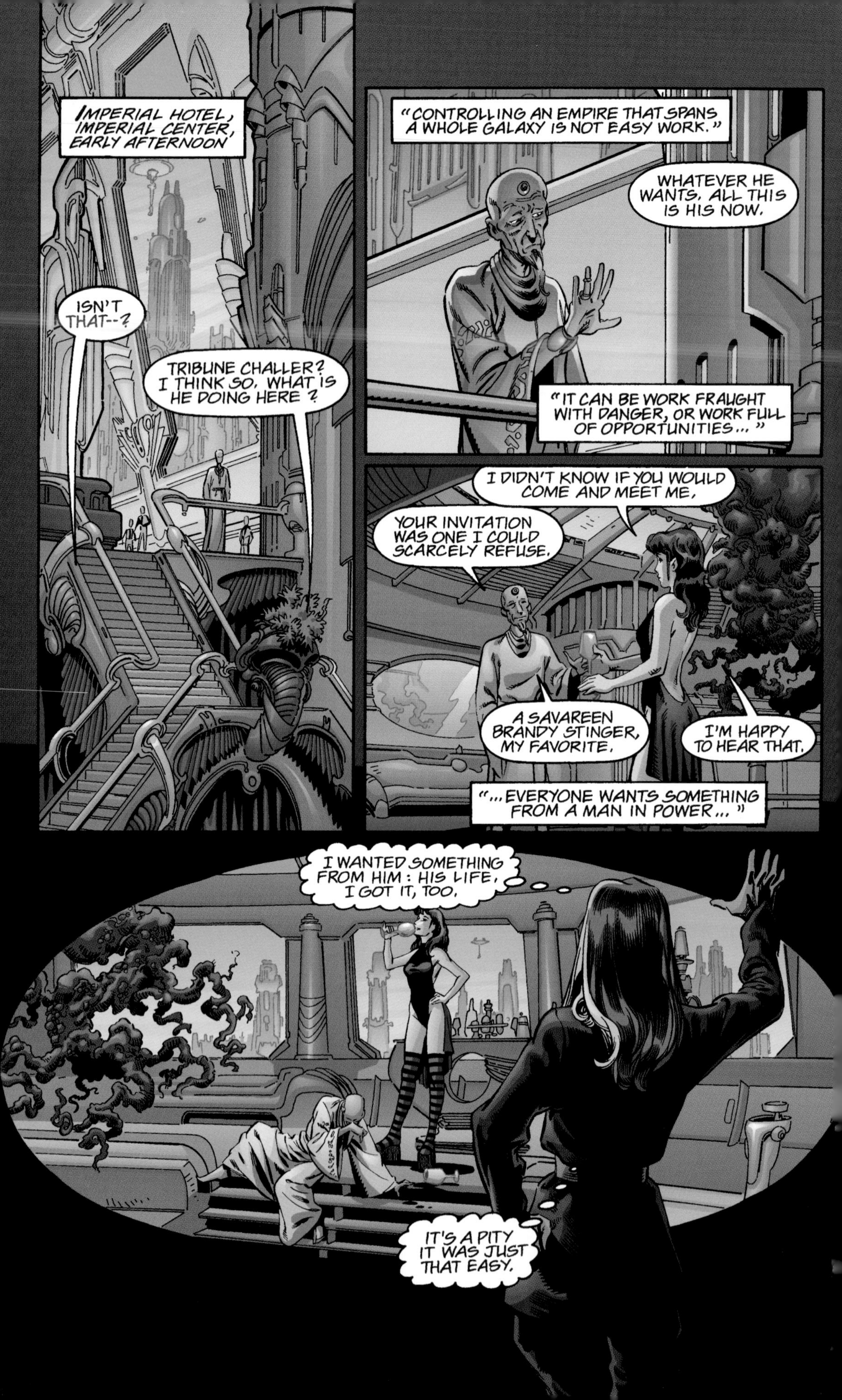

IMPERIAL HOTEL, IMPERIAL CENTER, EARLY AFTERNOON
ISN'T THAT--?
TRIBUNE CHALLER? I THINK SO. WHAT IS HE DOING HERE?
"CONTROLLING AN EMPIRE THAT SPANS A WHOLE GALAXY IS NOT EASY WORK."
WHATEVER HE WANTS, ALL THIS IS HIS NOW.
"IT CAN BE WORK FRAUGHT WITH DANGER, OR WORK FULL OF OPPORTUNITIES..."
I DIDN'T KNOW IF YOU WOULD COME AND MEET ME.
YOUR INVITATION WAS ONE I COULD SCARCELY REFUSE.
A SAVAREEN BRANDY STINGER, MY FAVORITE.
I'M HAPPY TO HEAR THAT.
"...EVERYONE WANTS SOMETHING FROM A MAN IN POWER..."
I WANTED SOMETHING FROM HIM: HIS LIFE. I GOT IT, TOO.
IT'S A PITY IT WAS JUST THAT EASY.

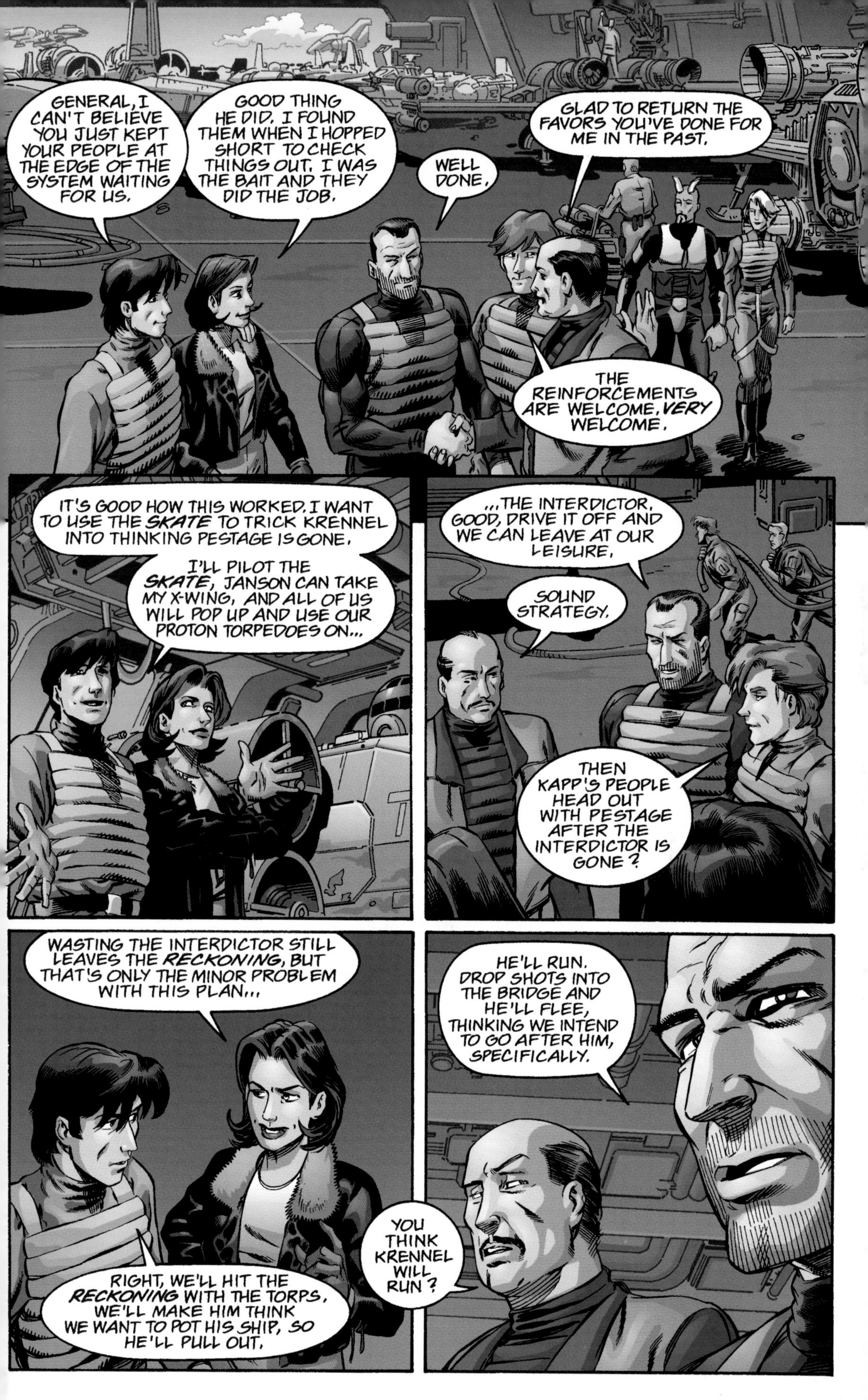
GENERAL, I CAN'T BELIEVE YOU JUST KEPT YOUR PEOPLE AT THE EDGE OF THE SYSTEM WAITING FOR US.
GOOD THING HE DID. I FOUND THEM WHEN I HOPPED SHORT TO CHECK THINGS OUT. I WAS THE BAIT AND THEY DID THE JOB.
WELL DONE.
GLAD TO RETURN THE FAVORS YOU'VE DONE FOR ME IN THE PAST.
THE REINFORCEMENTS ARE WELCOME. VERY WELCOME.
IT'S GOOD HOW THIS WORKED. I WANT TO USE THE SKATE TO TRICK KRENNEL INTO THINKING PESTAGE IS GONE.
I'LL PILOT THE SKATE, JANSON CAN TAKE MY X-WING, AND ALL OF US WILL POP UP AND USE OUR PROTON TORPEDOES ON...
...THE INTERDICTOR. GOOD, DRIVE IT OFF AND WE CAN LEAVE AT OUR LEISURE.
SOUND STRATEGY.
THEN KAPP'S PEOPLE HEAD OUT WITH PESTAGE AFTER THE INTERDICTOR IS GONE?
WASTING THE INTERDICTOR STILL LEAVES THE RECKONING, BUT THAT'S ONLY THE MINOR PROBLEM WITH THIS PLAN...
RIGHT, WE'LL HIT THE RECKONING WITH THE TORPS. WE'LL MAKE HIM THINK WE WANT TO POT HIS SHIP, SO HE'LL PULL OUT.
HE'LL RUN. DROP SHOTS INTO THE BRIDGE AND HE'LL FLEE, THINKING WE INTEND TO GO AFTER HIM, SPECIFICALLY.
YOU THINK KRENNEL WILL RUN?

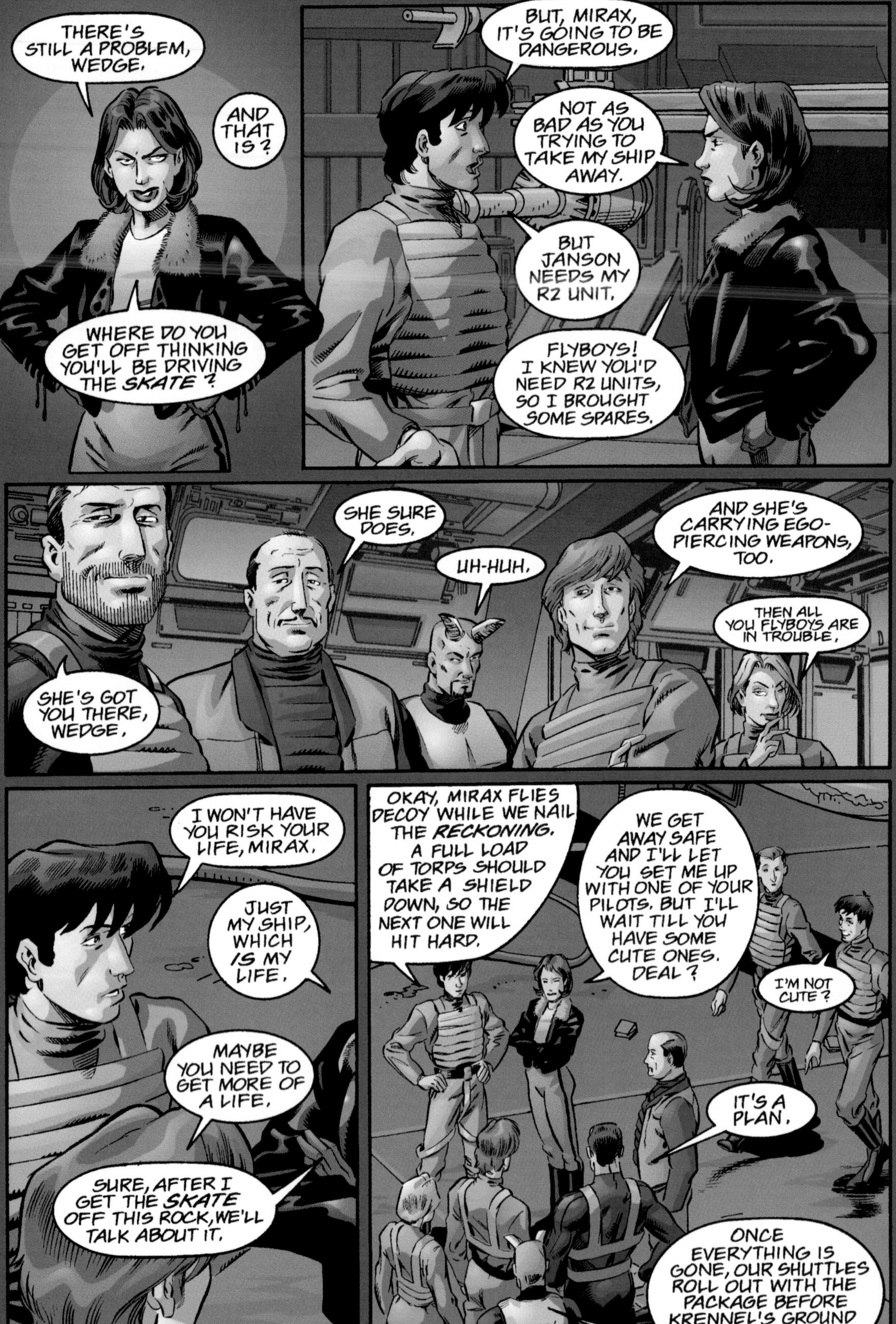
THERE'S STILL A PROBLEM, WEDGE.
AND THAT IS?
WHERE DO YOU GET OFF THINKING YOU'LL BE DRIVING THE *SKATE*?
BUT, MIRAX, IT'S GOING TO BE DANGEROUS.
NOT AS BAD AS YOU TRYING TO TAKE MY SHIP AWAY.
BUT JANSON NEEDS MY R2 UNIT.
FLYBOYS! I KNEW YOU'D NEED R2 UNITS, SO I BROUGHT SOME SPARES.
SHE'S GOT YOU THERE, WEDGE.
SHE SURE DOES.
UH-HUH.
AND SHE'S CARRYING EGO-PIERCING WEAPONS, TOO.
THEN ALL YOU FLYBOYS ARE IN TROUBLE.
I WON'T HAVE YOU RISK YOUR LIFE, MIRAX.
JUST MY SHIP, WHICH *IS* MY LIFE.
MAYBE YOU NEED TO GET MORE OF A LIFE.
SURE, AFTER I GET THE *SKATE* OFF THIS ROCK, WE'LL TALK ABOUT IT.
OKAY, MIRAX FLIES DECOY WHILE WE NAIL THE *RECKONING*. A FULL LOAD OF TORPS SHOULD TAKE A SHIELD DOWN, SO THE NEXT ONE WILL HIT HARD.
WE GET AWAY SAFE AND I'LL LET YOU SET ME UP WITH ONE OF YOUR PILOTS. BUT I'LL WAIT TILL YOU HAVE SOME CUTE ONES. DEAL?
I'M NOT CUTE?
IT'S A PLAN.
ONCE EVERYTHING IS GONE, OUR SHUTTLES ROLL OUT WITH THE PACKAGE BEFORE KRENNEL'S GROUND TROOPS GET HERE. GOT IT.

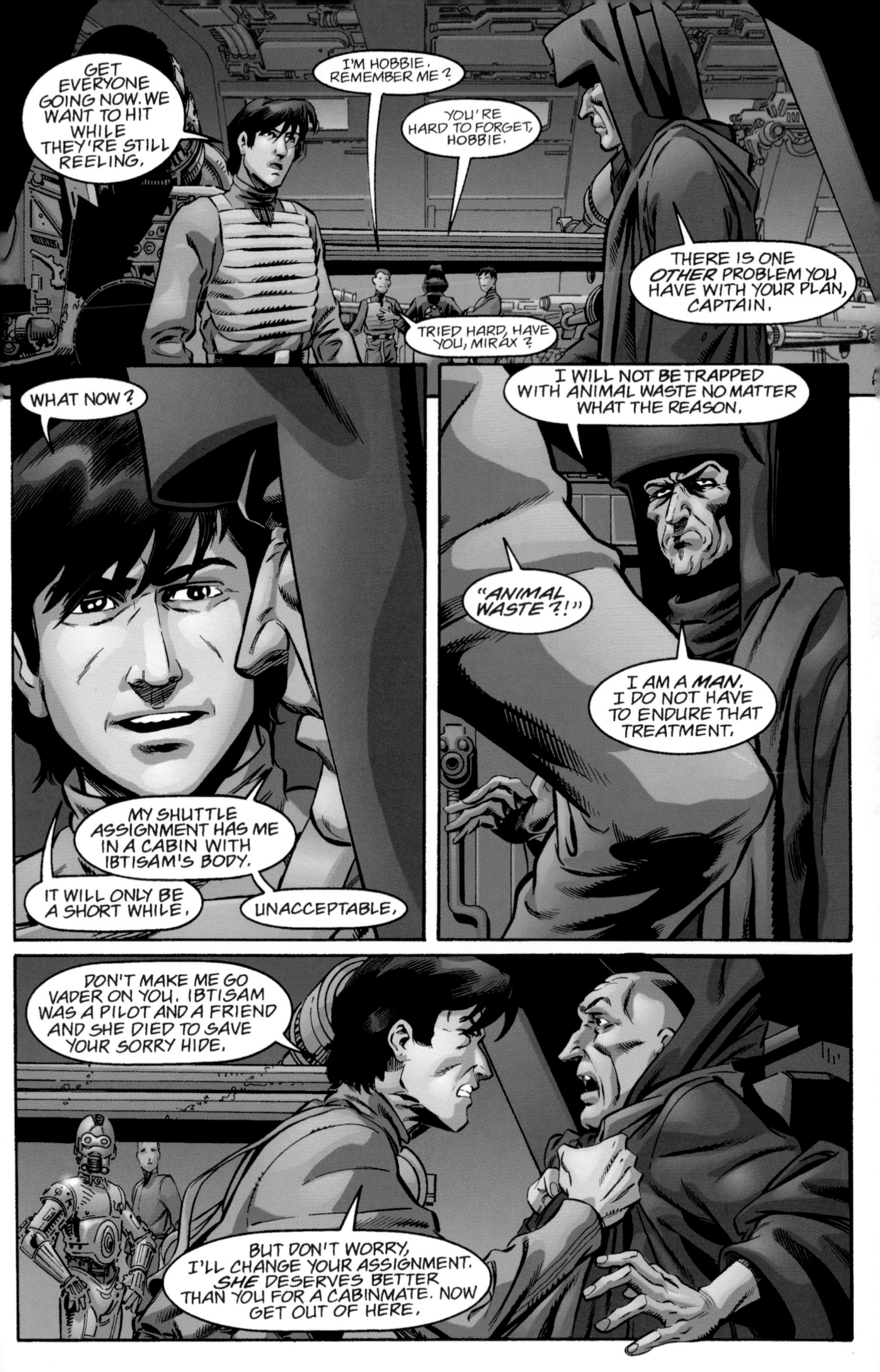
GET EVERYONE GOING NOW. WE WANT TO HIT WHILE THEY'RE STILL REELING.
I'M HOBBIE. REMEMBER ME?
YOU'RE HARD TO FORGET, HOBBIE.
TRIED HARD, HAVE YOU, MIRAX?
THERE IS ONE OTHER PROBLEM YOU HAVE WITH YOUR PLAN, CAPTAIN.
WHAT NOW?
MY SHUTTLE ASSIGNMENT HAS ME IN A CABIN WITH IBTISAM'S BODY.
IT WILL ONLY BE A SHORT WHILE.
UNACCEPTABLE.
I WILL NOT BE TRAPPED WITH ANIMAL WASTE NO MATTER WHAT THE REASON.
"ANIMAL WASTE?!"
I AM A MAN. I DO NOT HAVE TO ENDURE THAT TREATMENT.
DON'T MAKE ME GO VADER ON YOU. IBTISAM WAS A PILOT AND A FRIEND AND SHE DIED TO SAVE YOUR SORRY HIDE.
BUT DON'T WORRY, I'LL CHANGE YOUR ASSIGNMENT. SHE DESERVES BETTER THAN YOU FOR A CABINMATE. NOW GET OUT OF HERE.

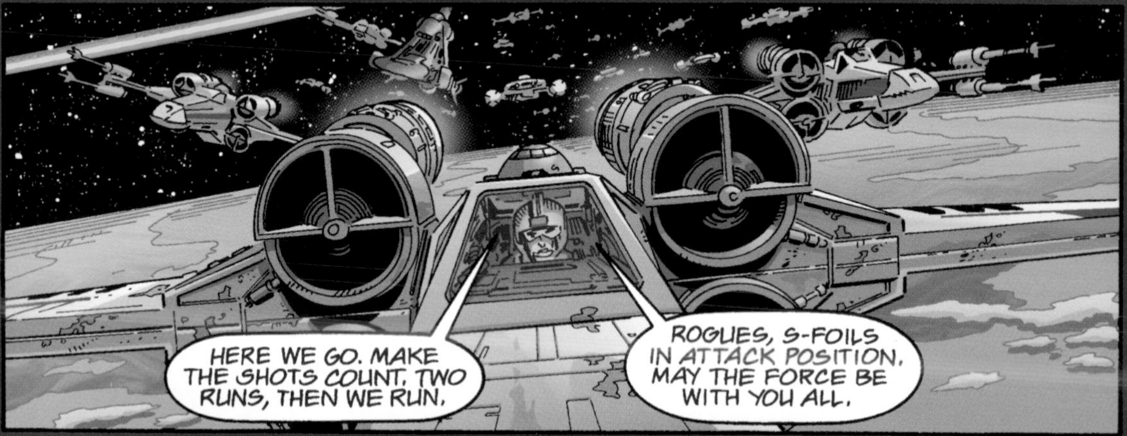
HERE WE GO. MAKE THE SHOTS COUNT. TWO RUNS, THEN WE RUN.
ROGUES, S-FOILS IN ATTACK POSITION. MAY THE FORCE BE WITH YOU ALL.

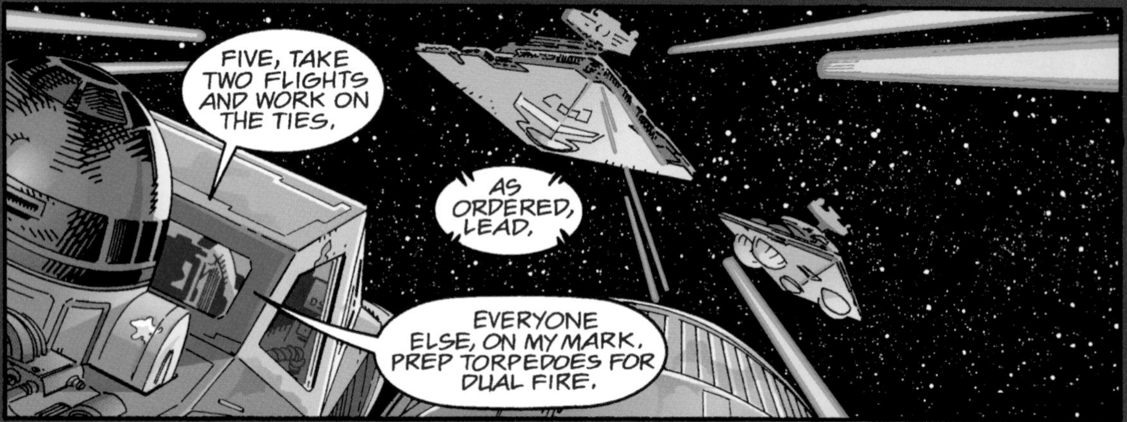
FIVE, TAKE TWO FLIGHTS AND WORK ON THE TIES.
AS ORDERED, LEAD.
EVERYONE ELSE, ON MY MARK. PREP TORPEDOES FOR DUAL FIRE.

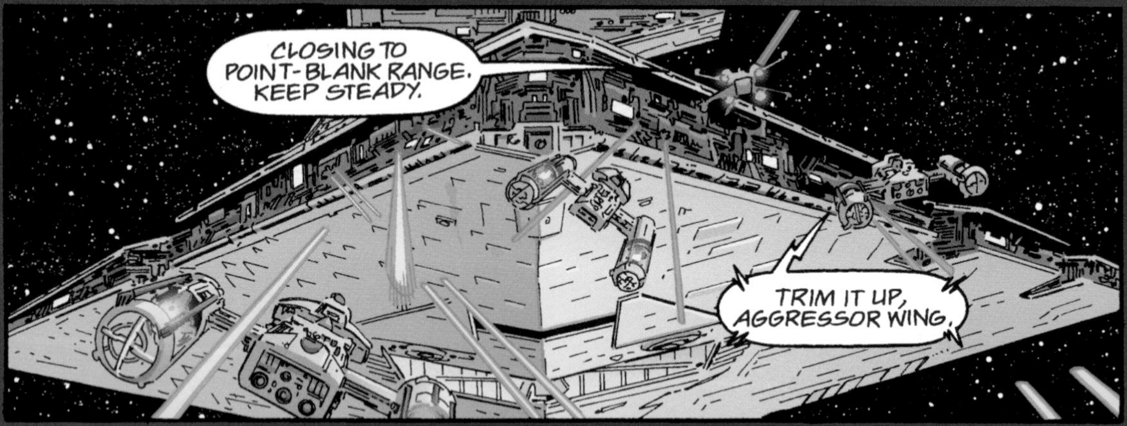
CLOSING TO POINT-BLANK RANGE. KEEP STEADY.
TRIM IT UP, AGGRESSOR WING.

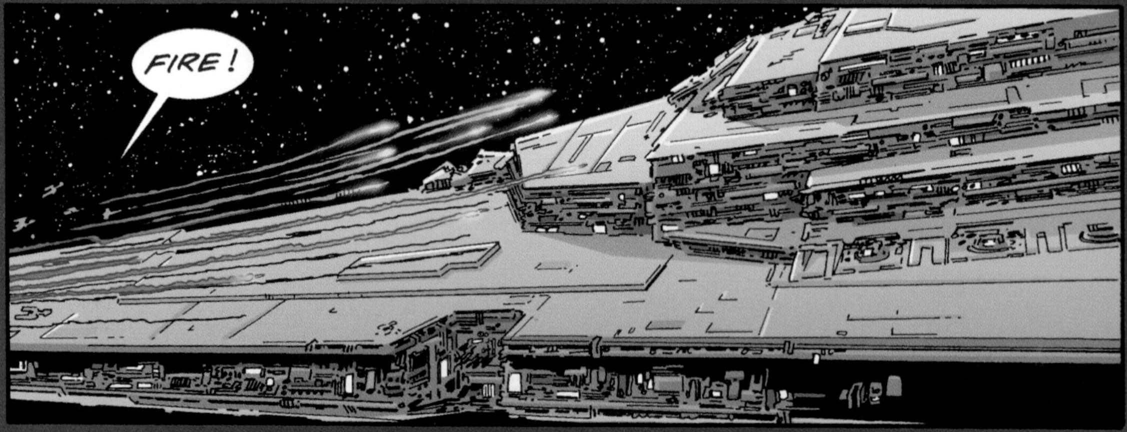
FIRE!

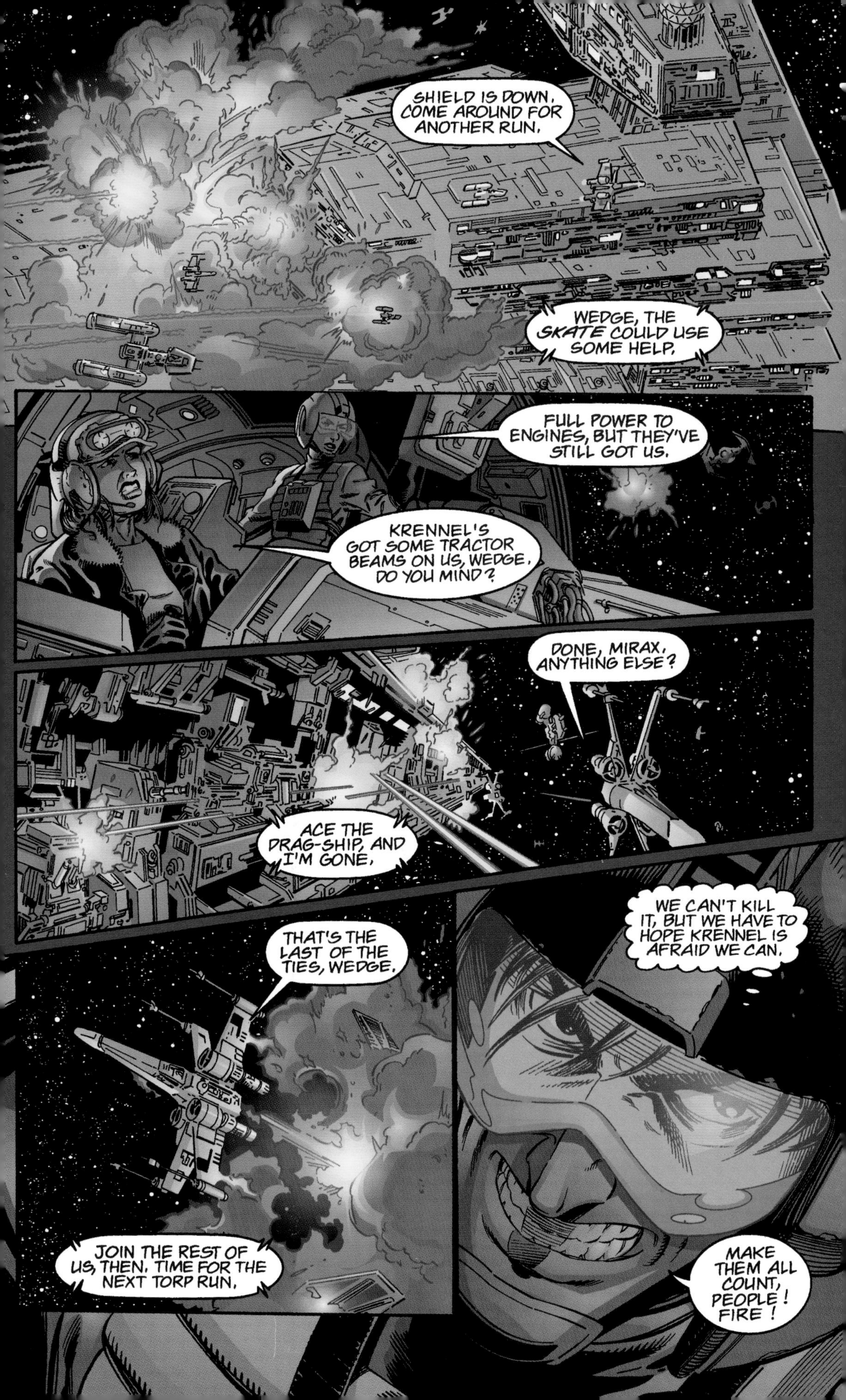

SHIELD IS DOWN, COME AROUND FOR ANOTHER RUN.
WEDGE, THE SKATE COULD USE SOME HELP.
FULL POWER TO ENGINES, BUT THEY'VE STILL GOT US.
KRENNEL'S GOT SOME TRACTOR BEAMS ON US, WEDGE. DO YOU MIND?
DONE, MIRAX, ANYTHING ELSE?
ACE THE DRAG-SHIP, AND I'M GONE.
THAT'S THE LAST OF THE TIES, WEDGE.
JOIN THE REST OF US, THEN. TIME FOR THE NEXT TORP RUN.
WE CAN'T KILL IT, BUT WE HAVE TO HOPE KRENNEL IS AFRAID WE CAN.
MAKE THEM ALL COUNT, PEOPLE! FIRE!

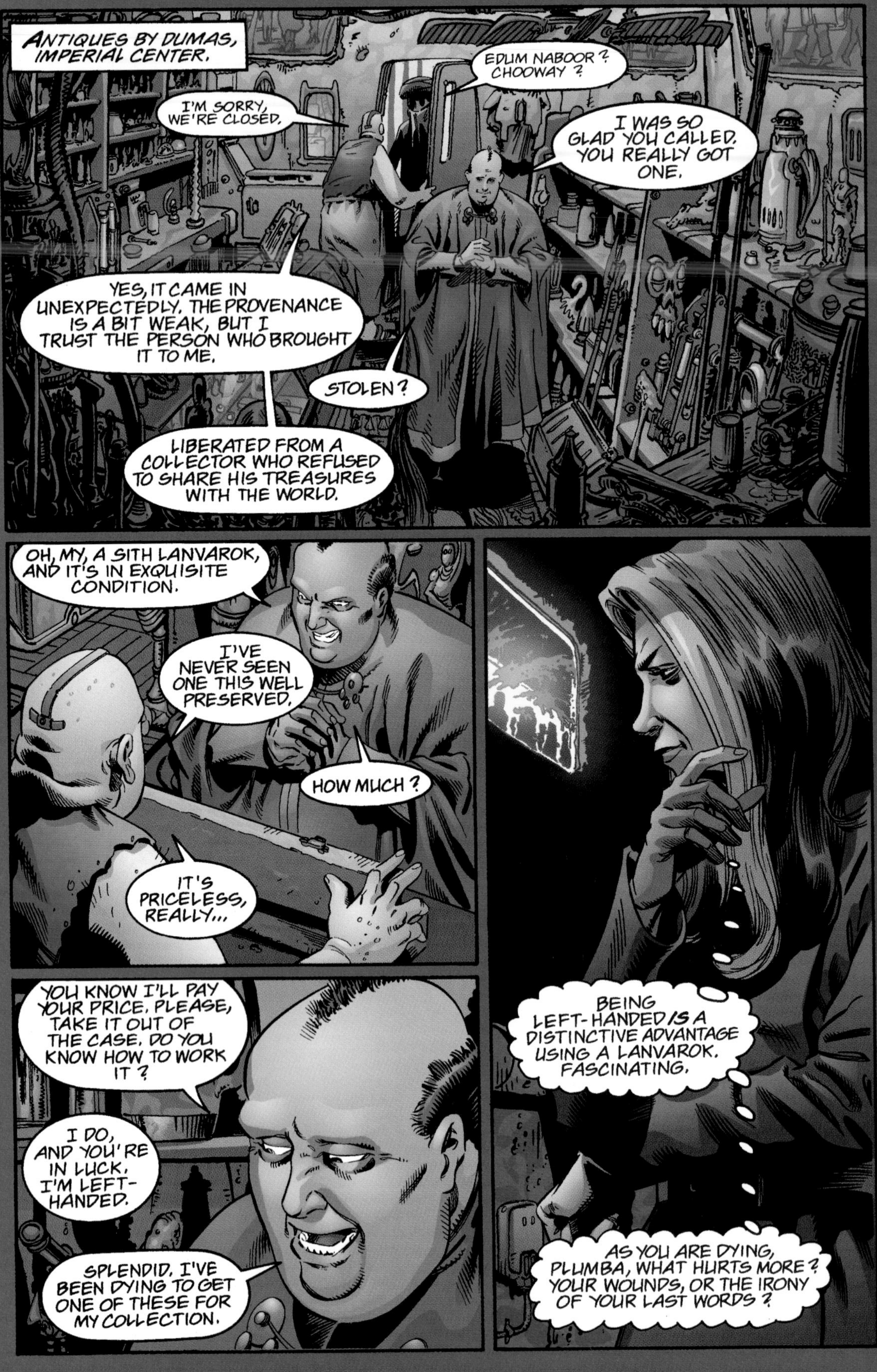
ANTIQUES BY DUMAS, IMPERIAL CENTER.
EDUM NABOOR? CHOOWAY?
I'M SORRY, WE'RE CLOSED.
I WAS SO GLAD YOU CALLED. YOU REALLY GOT ONE.
YES, IT CAME IN UNEXPECTEDLY. THE PROVENANCE IS A BIT WEAK, BUT I TRUST THE PERSON WHO BROUGHT IT TO ME.
STOLEN?
LIBERATED FROM A COLLECTOR WHO REFUSED TO SHARE HIS TREASURES WITH THE WORLD.
OH, MY, A SITH LANVAROK, AND IT'S IN EXQUISITE CONDITION.
I'VE NEVER SEEN ONE THIS WELL PRESERVED.
HOW MUCH?
IT'S PRICELESS, REALLY...
YOU KNOW I'LL PAY YOUR PRICE. PLEASE, TAKE IT OUT OF THE CASE. DO YOU KNOW HOW TO WORK IT?
I DO, AND YOU'RE IN LUCK, I'M LEFT-HANDED.
SPLENDID. I'VE BEEN DYING TO GET ONE OF THESE FOR MY COLLECTION.
BEING LEFT-HANDED IS A DISTINCTIVE ADVANTAGE USING A LANVAROK. FASCINATING.
AS YOU ARE DYING, PLUMBA, WHAT HURTS MORE? YOUR WOUNDS, OR THE IRONY OF YOUR LAST WORDS?

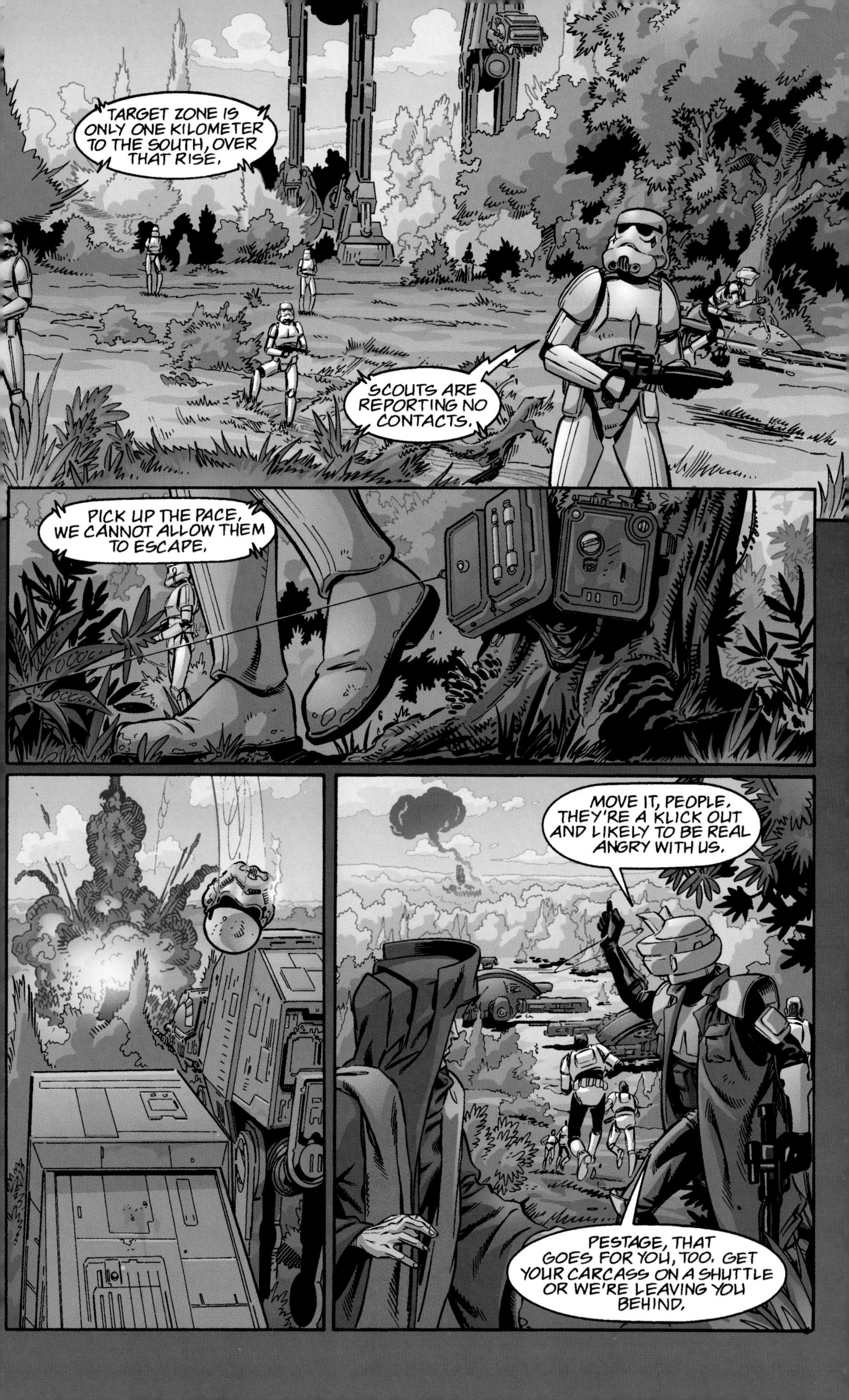
TARGET ZONE IS ONLY ONE KILOMETER TO THE SOUTH, OVER THAT RISE.
SCOUTS ARE REPORTING NO CONTACTS.
PICK UP THE PACE. WE CANNOT ALLOW THEM TO ESCAPE.
MOVE IT, PEOPLE. THEY'RE A KLICK OUT AND LIKELY TO BE REAL ANGRY WITH US.
PESTAGE, THAT GOES FOR YOU, TOO. GET YOUR CARCASS ON A SHUTTLE OR WE'RE LEAVING YOU BEHIND.

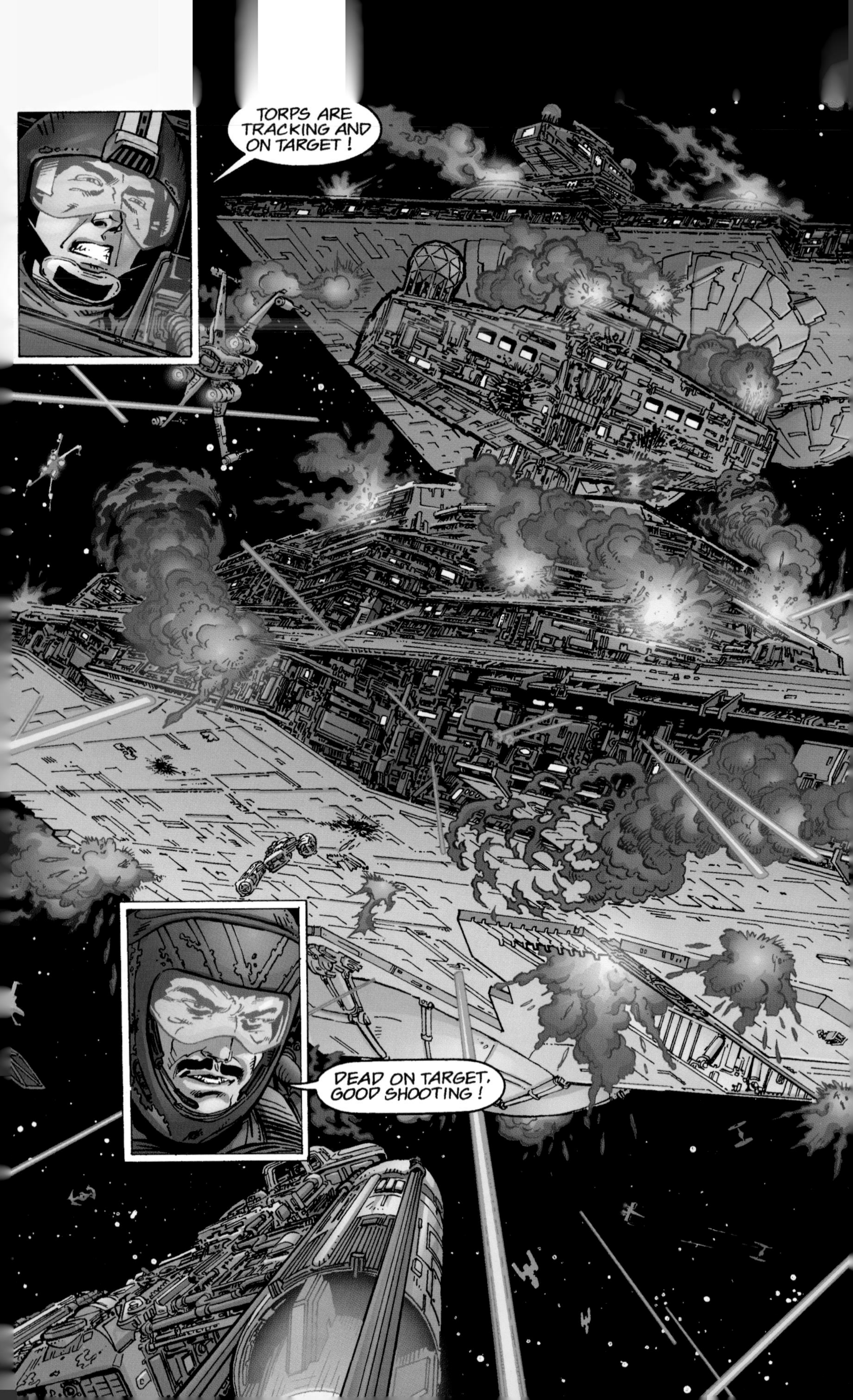
TORPS ARE TRACKING AND ON TARGET !
DEAD ON TARGET. GOOD SHOOTING !

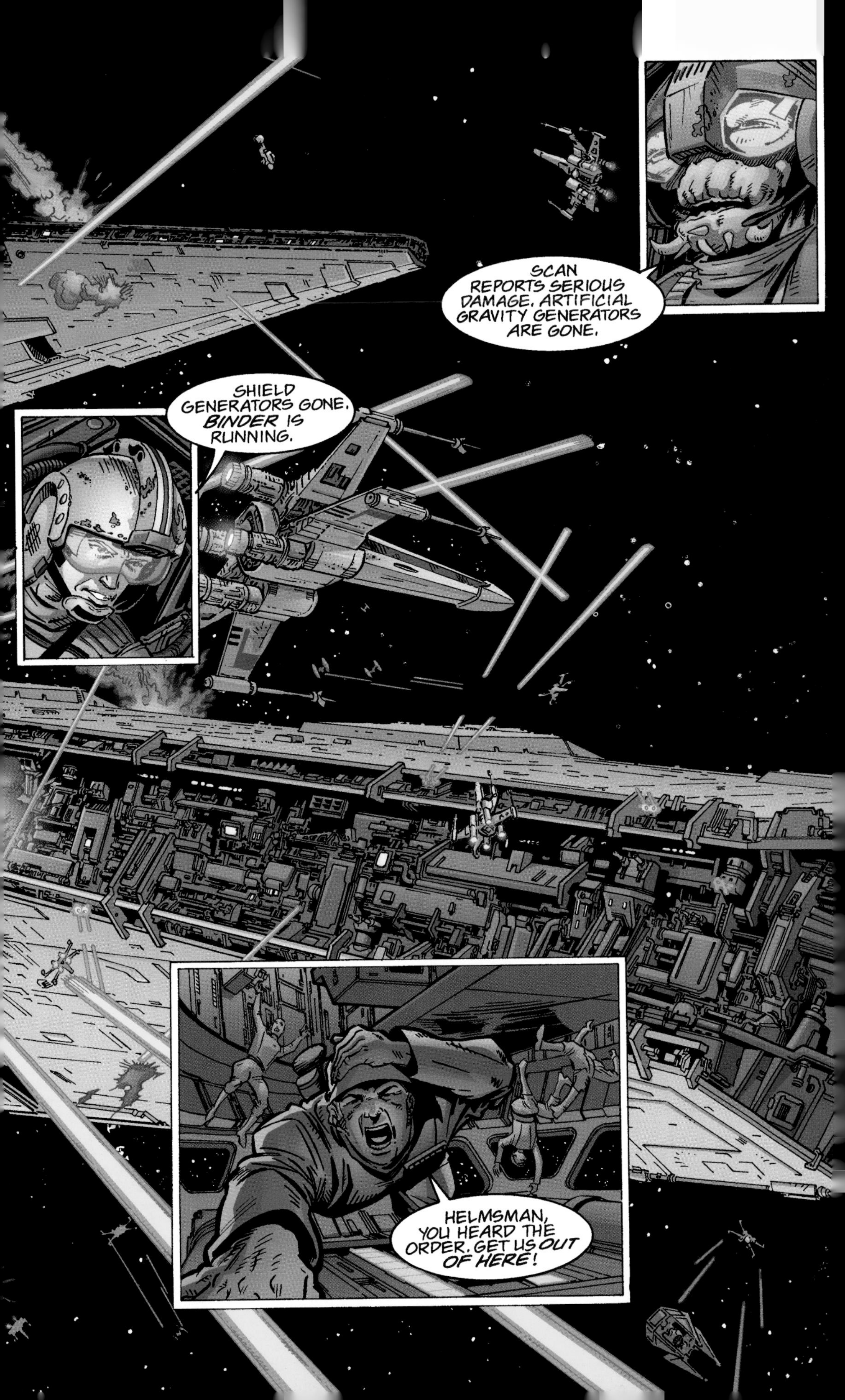
SCAN REPORTS SERIOUS DAMAGE. ARTIFICIAL GRAVITY GENERATORS ARE GONE.
SHIELD GENERATORS GONE. BINDER IS RUNNING.
HELMSMAN, YOU HEARD THE ORDER. GET US OUT OF HERE!

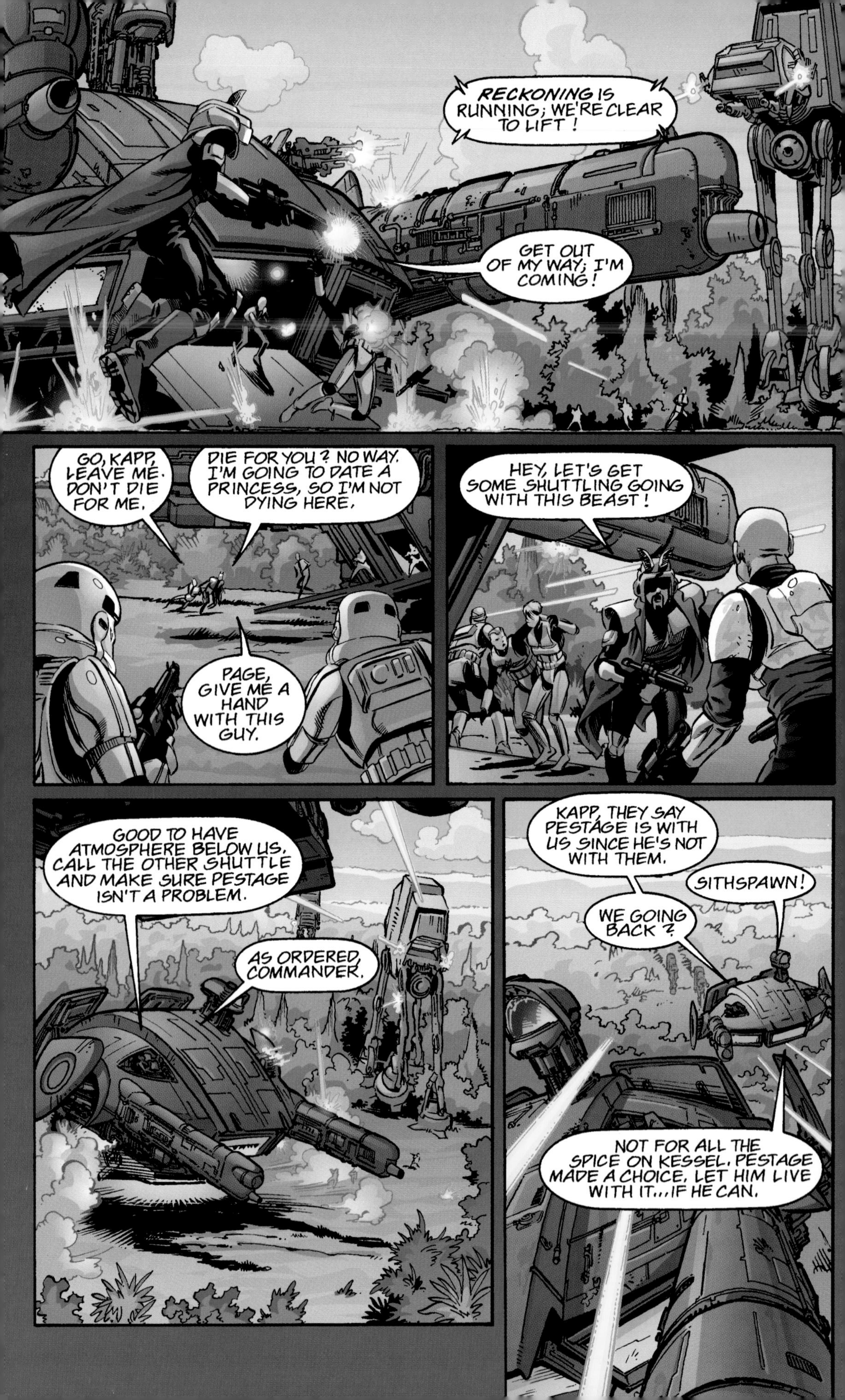
RECKONING IS RUNNING; WE'RE CLEAR TO LIFT!
GET OUT OF MY WAY; I'M COMING!
GO, KAPP, LEAVE ME. DON'T DIE FOR ME.
DIE FOR YOU? NO WAY. I'M GOING TO DATE A PRINCESS, SO I'M NOT DYING HERE.
PAGE, GIVE ME A HAND WITH THIS GUY.
HEY, LET'S GET SOME SHUTTLING GOING WITH THIS BEAST!
GOOD TO HAVE ATMOSPHERE BELOW US. CALL THE OTHER SHUTTLE AND MAKE SURE PESTAGE ISN'T A PROBLEM.
AS ORDERED, COMMANDER.
KAPP, THEY SAY PESTAGE IS WITH US SINCE HE'S NOT WITH THEM.
SITHSPAWN!
WE GOING BACK?
NOT FOR ALL THE SPICE ON KESSEL. PESTAGE MADE A CHOICE. LET HIM LIVE WITH IT... IF HE CAN.

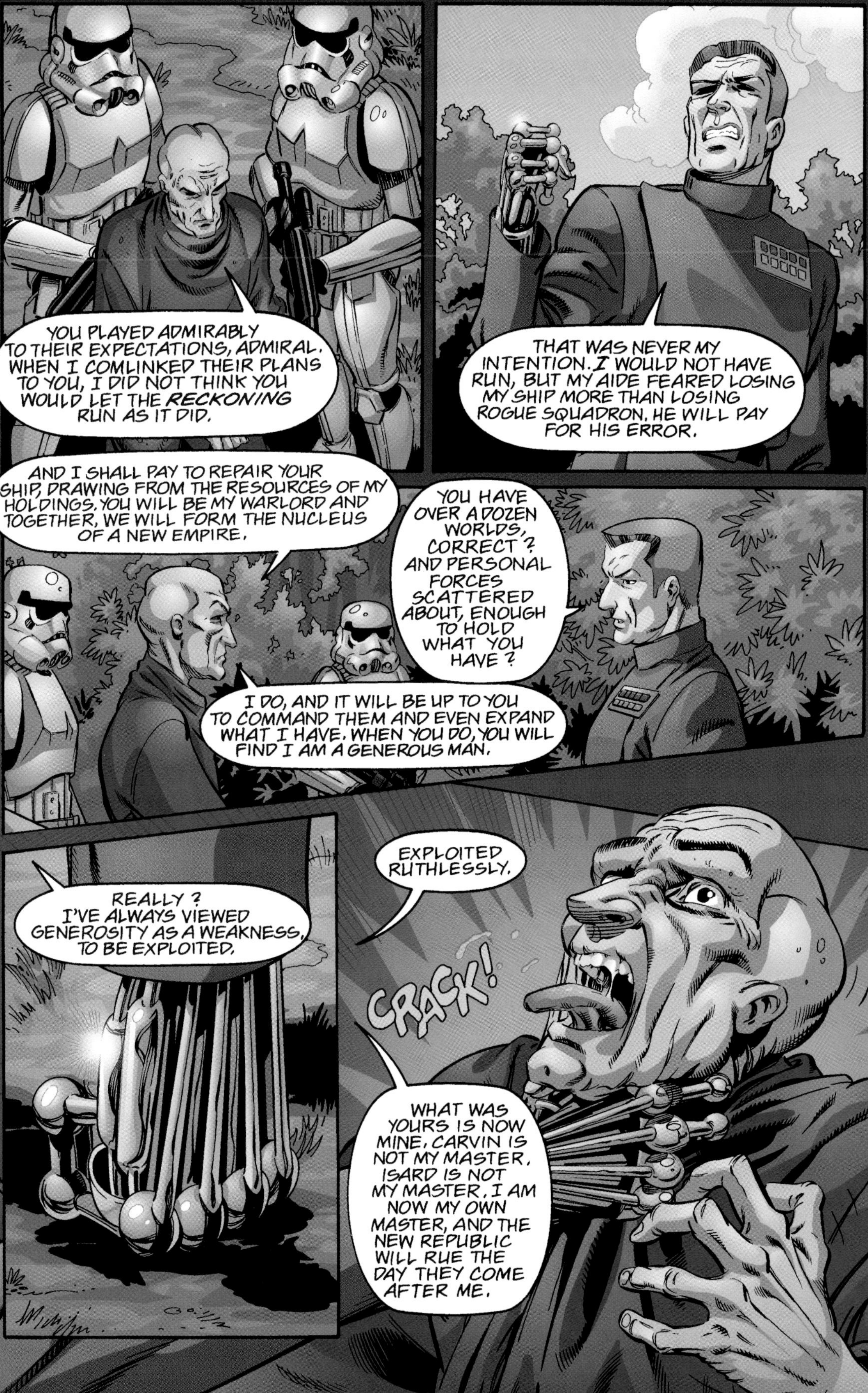
YOU PLAYED ADMIRABLY TO THEIR EXPECTATIONS, ADMIRAL. WHEN I COMLINKED THEIR PLANS TO YOU, I DID NOT THINK YOU WOULD LET THE *RECKONING* RUN AS IT DID.
THAT WAS NEVER MY INTENTION. *I* WOULD NOT HAVE RUN, BUT MY AIDE FEARED LOSING MY SHIP MORE THAN LOSING ROGUE SQUADRON. HE WILL PAY FOR HIS ERROR.
AND I SHALL PAY TO REPAIR YOUR SHIP, DRAWING FROM THE RESOURCES OF MY HOLDINGS. YOU WILL BE MY WARLORD AND TOGETHER, WE WILL FORM THE NUCLEUS OF A NEW EMPIRE.
YOU HAVE OVER A DOZEN WORLDS, CORRECT ? AND PERSONAL FORCES SCATTERED ABOUT, ENOUGH TO HOLD WHAT YOU HAVE ?
I DO, AND IT WILL BE UP TO YOU TO COMMAND THEM AND EVEN EXPAND WHAT I HAVE. WHEN YOU DO, YOU WILL FIND I AM A GENEROUS MAN.
REALLY ? I'VE ALWAYS VIEWED GENEROSITY AS A WEAKNESS, TO BE EXPLOITED.
EXPLOITED RUTHLESSLY.
CRACK!
WHAT WAS YOURS IS NOW MINE. CARVIN IS NOT MY MASTER. ISARD IS NOT MY MASTER. I AM NOW MY OWN MASTER, AND THE NEW REPUBLIC WILL RUE THE DAY THEY COME AFTER ME.

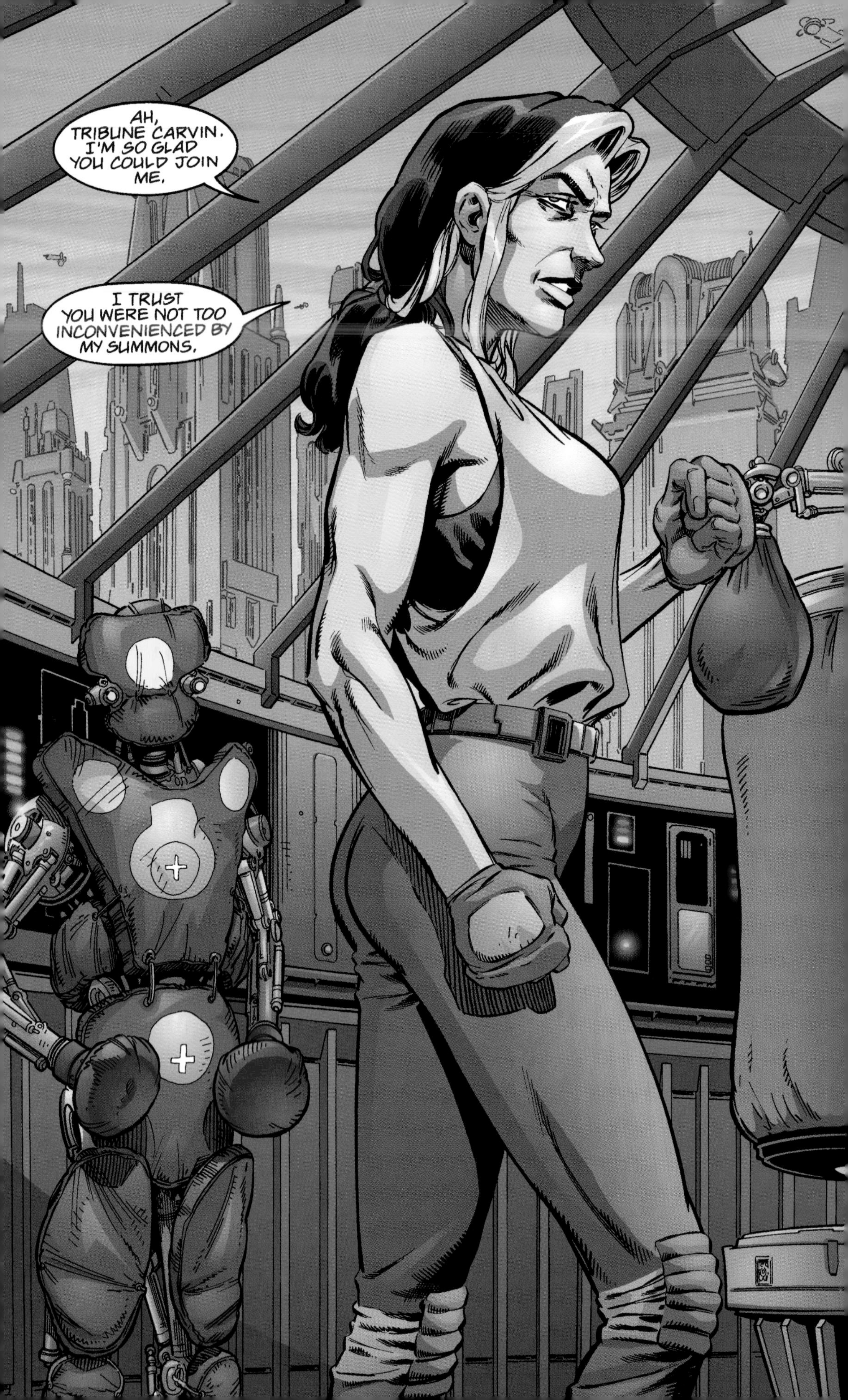
AH, TRIBUNE CARVIN. I'M SO GLAD YOU COULD JOIN ME.
I TRUST YOU WERE NOT TOO INCONVENIENCED BY MY SUMMONS.

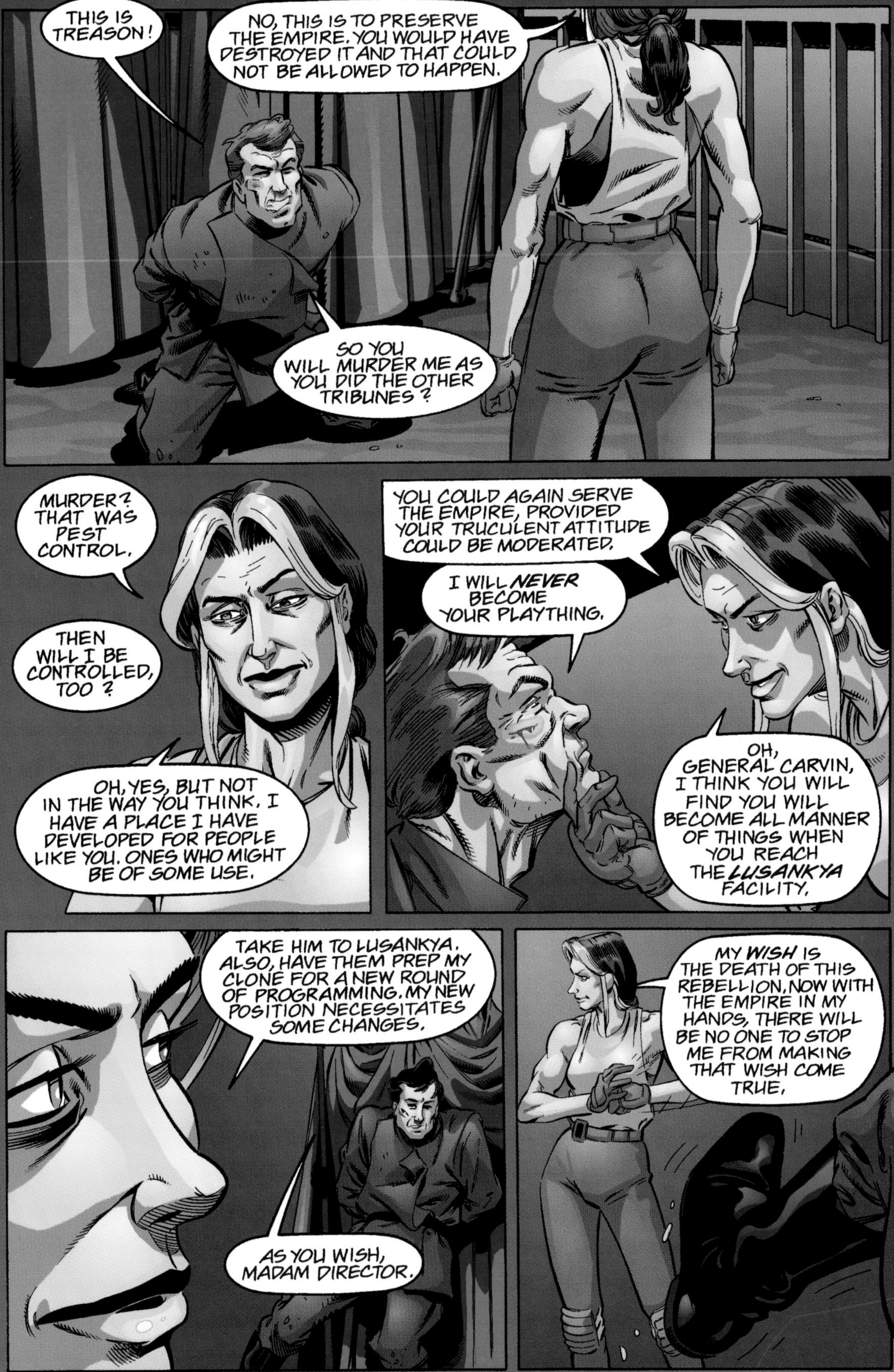
THIS IS TREASON!
NO, THIS IS TO PRESERVE THE EMPIRE. YOU WOULD HAVE DESTROYED IT AND THAT COULD NOT BE ALLOWED TO HAPPEN.
SO YOU WILL MURDER ME AS YOU DID THE OTHER TRIBUNES?
MURDER? THAT WAS PEST CONTROL.
THEN WILL I BE CONTROLLED, TOO?
OH, YES, BUT NOT IN THE WAY YOU THINK. I HAVE A PLACE I HAVE DEVELOPED FOR PEOPLE LIKE YOU. ONES WHO MIGHT BE OF SOME USE.
YOU COULD AGAIN SERVE THE EMPIRE, PROVIDED YOUR TRUCULENT ATTITUDE COULD BE MODERATED.
I WILL NEVER BECOME YOUR PLAYTHING.
OH, GENERAL CARVIN, I THINK YOU WILL FIND YOU WILL BECOME ALL MANNER OF THINGS WHEN YOU REACH THE LUSANKYA FACILITY.
TAKE HIM TO LUSANKYA. ALSO, HAVE THEM PREP MY CLONE FOR A NEW ROUND OF PROGRAMMING. MY NEW POSITION NECESSITATES SOME CHANGES.
AS YOU WISH, MADAM DIRECTOR.
MY WISH IS THE DEATH OF THIS REBELLION, NOW WITH THE EMPIRE IN MY HANDS, THERE WILL BE NO ONE TO STOP ME FROM MAKING THAT WISH COME TRUE.

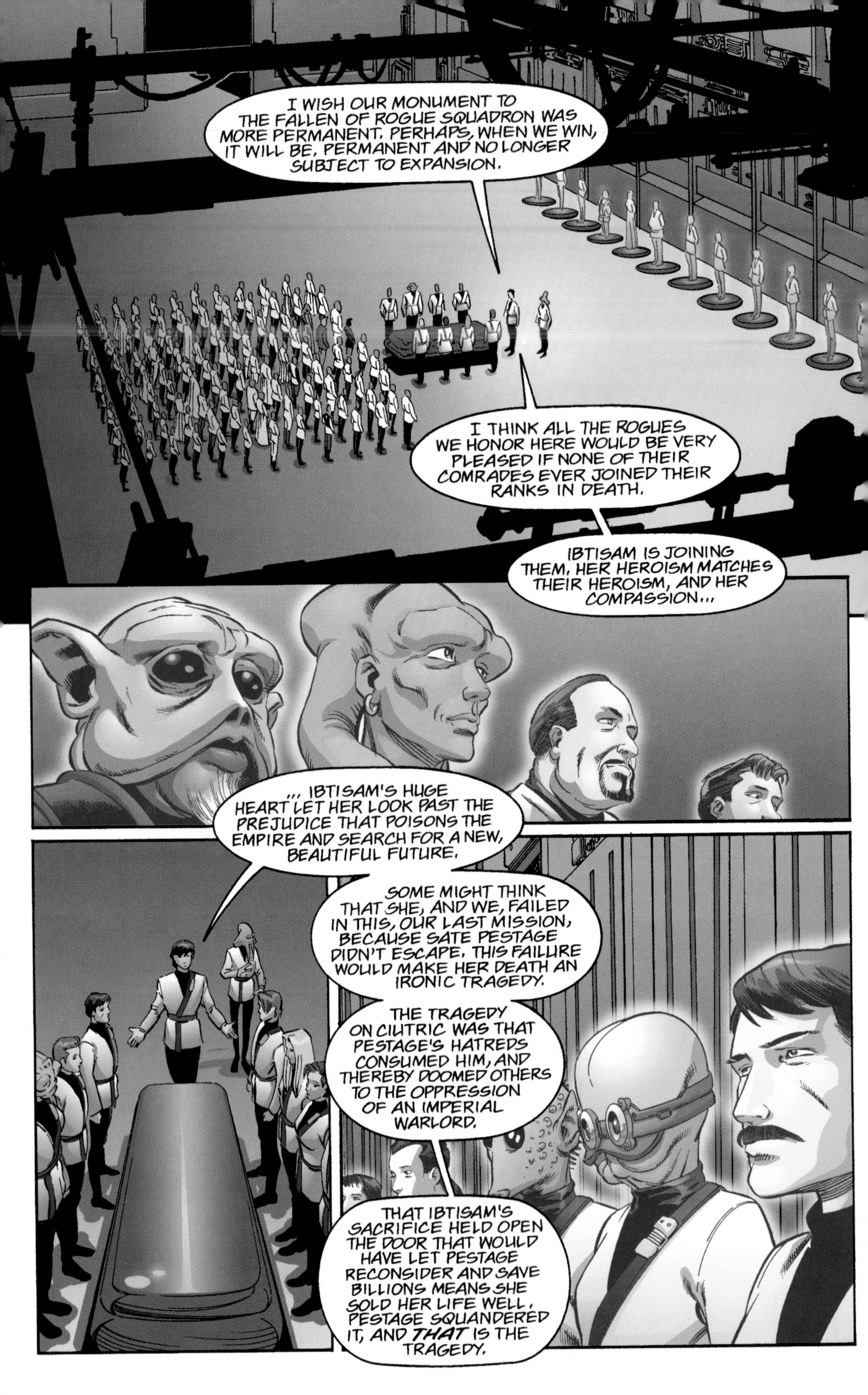
I WISH OUR MONUMENT TO THE FALLEN OF ROGUE SQUADRON WAS MORE PERMANENT. PERHAPS, WHEN WE WIN, IT WILL BE, PERMANENT AND NO LONGER SUBJECT TO EXPANSION.
I THINK ALL THE ROGUES WE HONOR HERE WOULD BE VERY PLEASED IF NONE OF THEIR COMRADES EVER JOINED THEIR RANKS IN DEATH.
IBTISAM IS JOINING THEM. HER HEROISM MATCHES THEIR HEROISM, AND HER COMPASSION...
... IBTISAM'S HUGE HEART LET HER LOOK PAST THE PREJUDICE THAT POISONS THE EMPIRE AND SEARCH FOR A NEW, BEAUTIFUL FUTURE.
SOME MIGHT THINK THAT SHE, AND WE, FAILED IN THIS, OUR LAST MISSION, BECAUSE SATE PESTAGE DIDN'T ESCAPE. THIS FAILURE WOULD MAKE HER DEATH AN IRONIC TRAGEDY.
THE TRAGEDY ON CIUTRIC WAS THAT PESTAGE'S HATREDS CONSUMED HIM, AND THEREBY DOOMED OTHERS TO THE OPPRESSION OF AN IMPERIAL WARLORD.
THAT IBTISAM'S SACRIFICE HELD OPEN THE DOOR THAT WOULD HAVE LET PESTAGE RECONSIDER AND SAVE BILLIONS MEANS SHE SOLD HER LIFE WELL. PESTAGE SQUANDERED IT, AND *THAT* IS THE TRAGEDY.

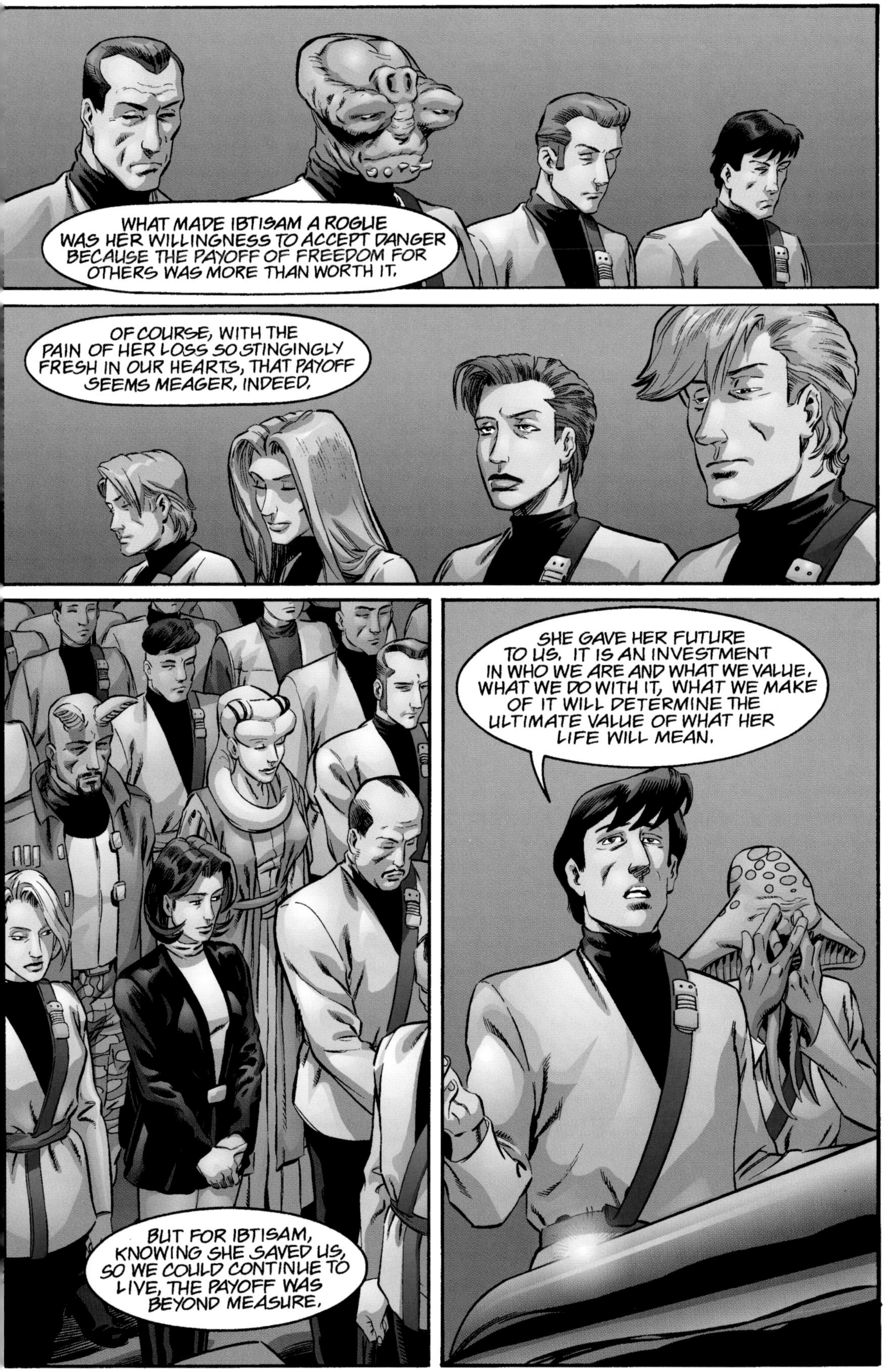
WHAT MADE IBTISAM A ROGUE WAS HER WILLINGNESS TO ACCEPT DANGER BECAUSE THE PAYOFF OF FREEDOM FOR OTHERS WAS MORE THAN WORTH IT.
OF COURSE, WITH THE PAIN OF HER LOSS SO STINGINGLY FRESH IN OUR HEARTS, THAT PAYOFF SEEMS MEAGER, INDEED.
BUT FOR IBTISAM, KNOWING SHE SAVED US, SO WE COULD CONTINUE TO LIVE, THE PAYOFF WAS BEYOND MEASURE.
SHE GAVE HER FUTURE TO US. IT IS AN INVESTMENT IN WHO WE ARE AND WHAT WE VALUE. WHAT WE DO WITH IT, WHAT WE MAKE OF IT WILL DETERMINE THE ULTIMATE VALUE OF WHAT HER LIFE WILL MEAN.

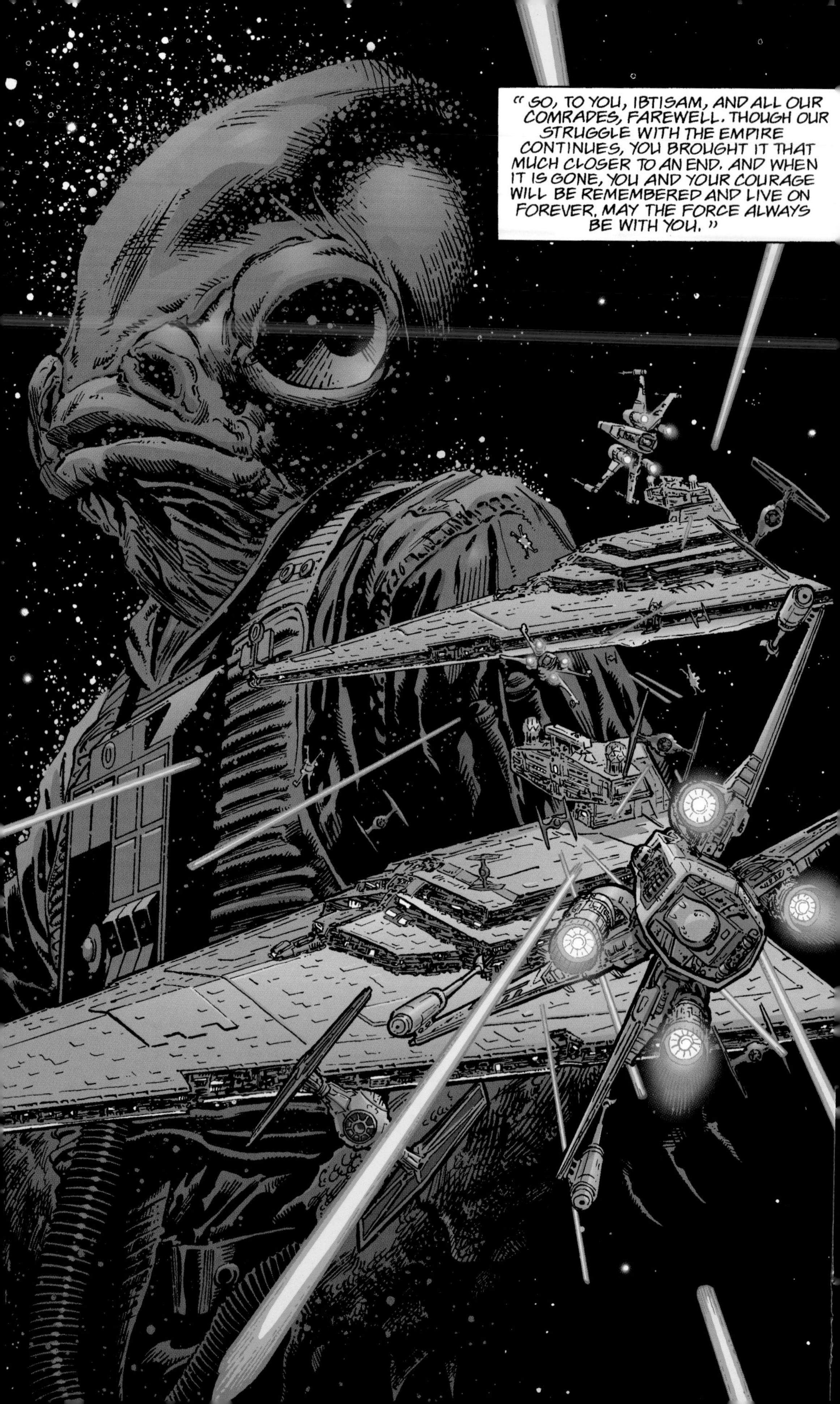
"SO, TO YOU, IBTISAM, AND ALL OUR COMRADES, FAREWELL. THOUGH OUR STRUGGLE WITH THE EMPIRE CONTINUES, YOU BROUGHT IT THAT MUCH CLOSER TO AN END. AND WHEN IT IS GONE, YOU AND YOUR COURAGE WILL BE REMEMBERED AND LIVE ON FOREVER. MAY THE FORCE ALWAYS BE WITH YOU."

In the studio with
TERESE NIELSEN

An in-depth look into the creative process that produced the cover illustration for *Star Wars: X-Wing Rogue Squadron — Mandatory Retirement*

Everything started with a phone call from Chris Warner, the Editor in Chief, at Dark Horse Comics. When I said I was available to do a cover for their *Star Wars* trade paperbacks, he sent me a fat packet of information, including four issues of *Mandatory Retirement*. He had tagged several pages that he thought were significant and might provide me with cover ideas. Also, he let me know that *Mandatory Retirement* needed to include several elements: a strong space battle, and floating heads of some of the major players.

Terese in her studio

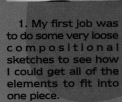

1

1. My first job was to do some very loose compositional sketches to see how I could get all of the elements to fit into one piece.

2

2. Next, I went on a hunt to gather as much photo reference as I could. On average, I spend at least one-third of my time locating reference material. From all that I collected, I narrowed it down to the images that had the right lighting and the right design, based on my overall composition.

3

3. Then it was time to tighten up my idea enough to get approval from Dark Horse. Chris had a few comments on positioning, but for the most part liked what I had done. I enlarged the sketch with my copy machine, and laid tracing paper over the top of it to do the final tight sketch version. At this stage I ironed out all of the size relationships, and fine tuned the positioning of each element.

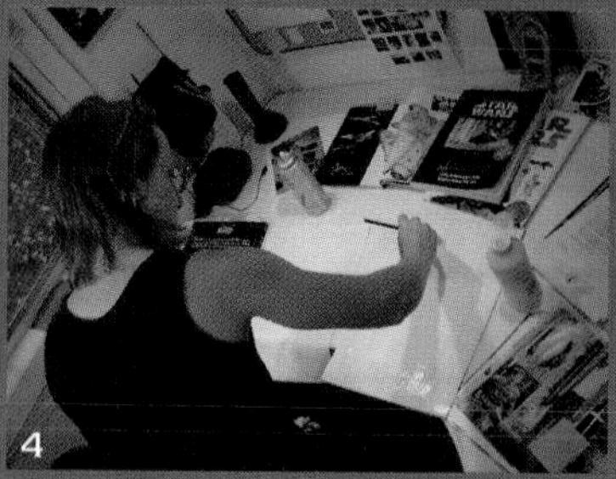
4

4. After the final sketch was completed and approved, I xeroxed it onto one-ply Strathmore paper and sealed it with Crystal Clear. I cut a piece of heavy-weight illustration board and covered it with a thick layer of matte medium using a wide brush. Next I took the Strathmore paper, which had the final sketch xeroxed on it, over to the sink. I let water run over the front and back of it for about one minute, until it was totally wet.

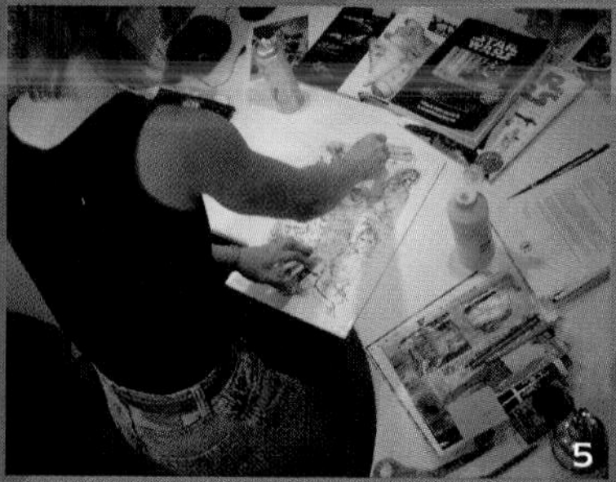
5

5. I took the xerox back to where my illustration board was waiting with freshly applied matte medium, and positioned the sketch where I wanted it. I used a brayer to push the bubbles and excess medium out from under the xerox. A plain old paper towel worked to wipe it clean.

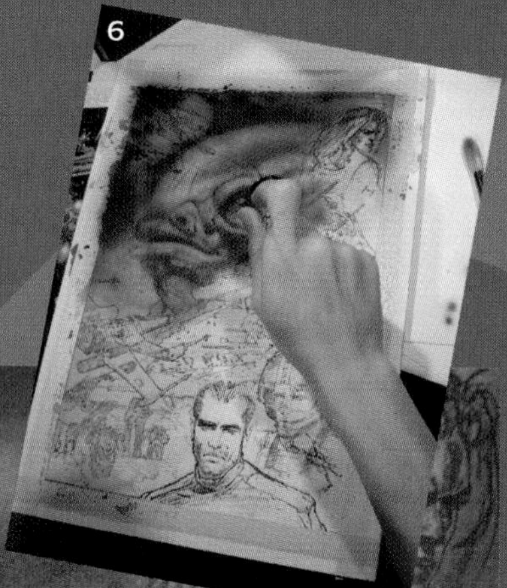
6

6. At this point, I was ready to paint. I usually try and cover the whiteness of the board as quickly as possible. In this case, I used gouache to wash in some deep blues, which gave me a middle value to work with. From there I darkened the shadow areas with glazes of transparent airbrush using a combination of indigo and black.

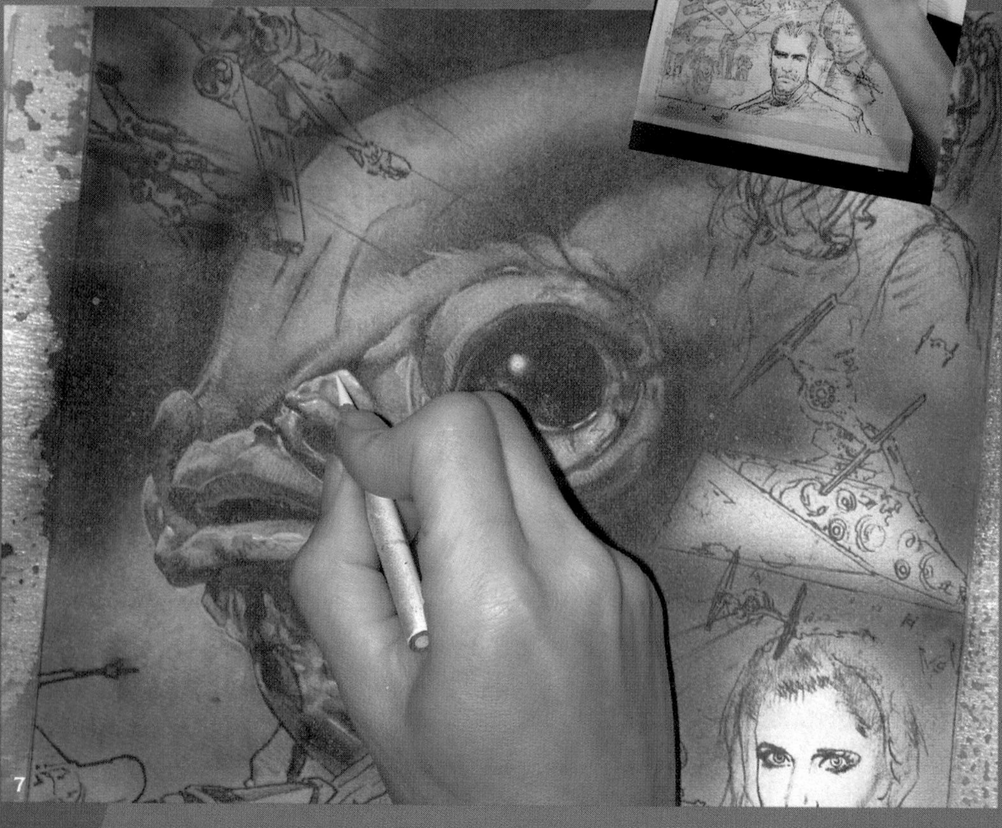
7

7. Next I started lifting out some of the lighter areas with a white Prismacolor pencil. I was careful not to get too carried away with the detail of this one area yet, though. I wanted to bring the whole painting up at the same time.

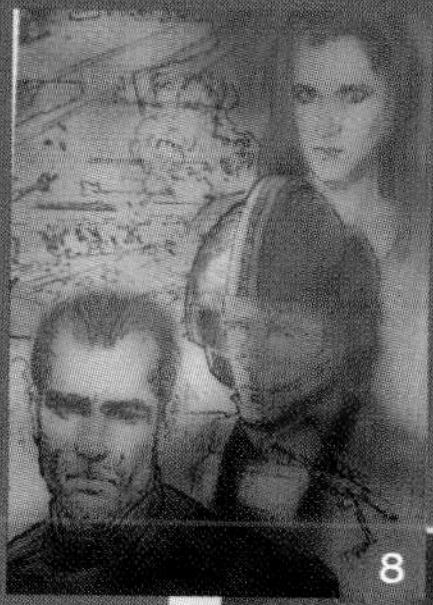

8. I tackled the three faces on the right by using the airbrush to glaze in warm colors, punching in a few darks here and there. This gave me a nice base to paint on top of.

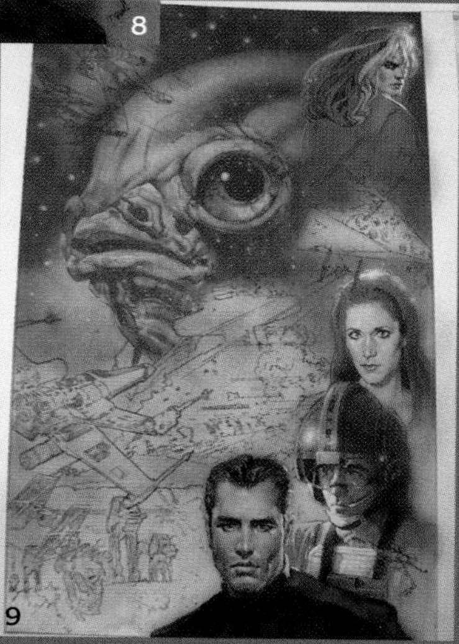

9. I rendered out the heads using Prismacolor pencil for some of the line work, and oils for the softer, blended areas.

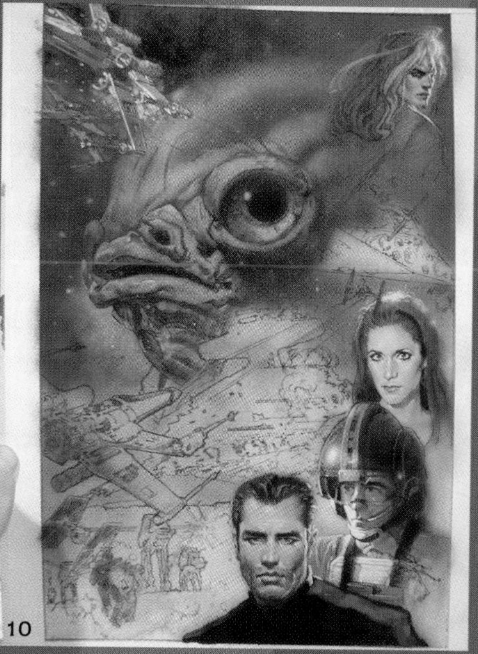

10. After those areas (the fun parts) were almost done, I took a deep breath and turned my attention to the space ships and explosions.

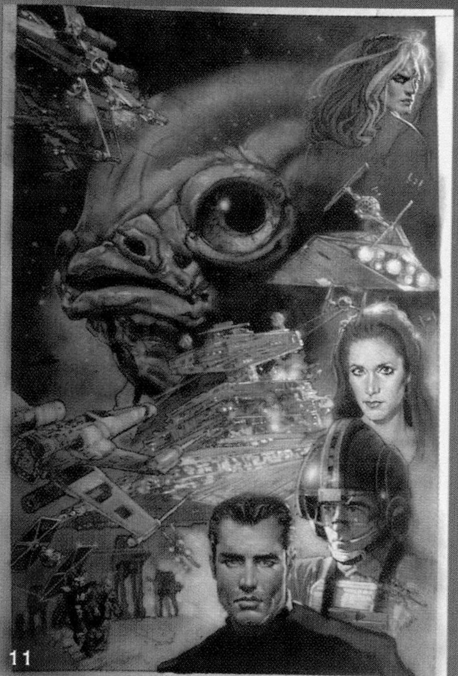

11. When I felt that the piece was about 90% done, I spent most of my time just looking at it to see which areas needed more detail or subtle value enhancements.

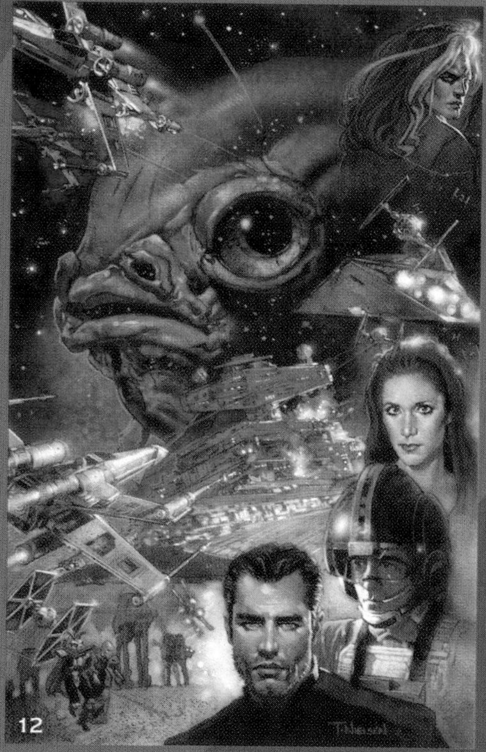

12. To finish it off, I added more colored pencil texture around the closest X-wing and some speckled texture on the ground area, which I achieved by pulling the needle almost out of the airbrush so it spattered the paint. I was tired of looking at it by this time, so I sent it in.

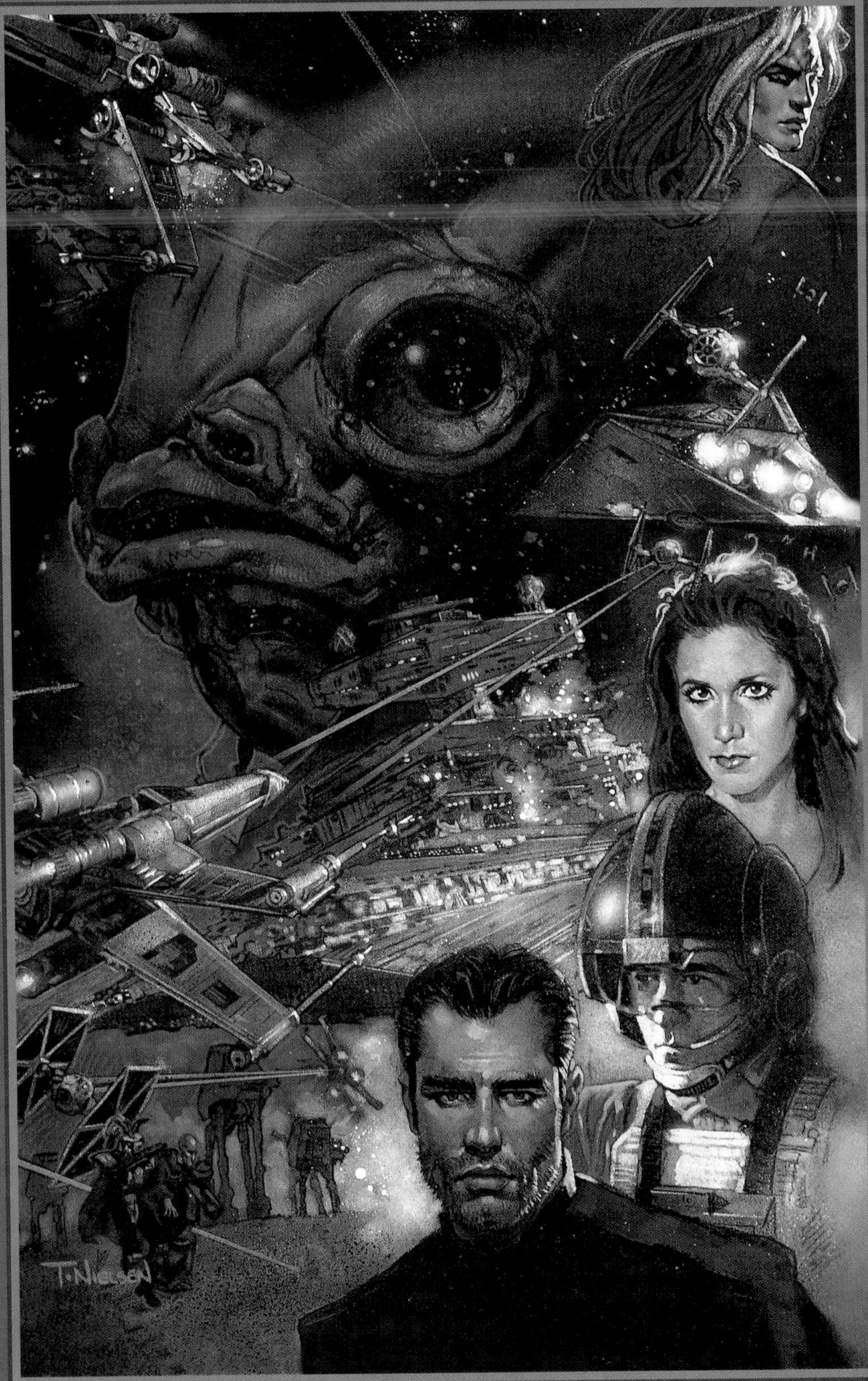
T.NIELSON

13. Lucas Licensing had a few minor revisions, and Dark Horse returned the original. I changed the laser fire to green, rounded out Princess Leia's face, and made Fel's eyes brown.